Wineries & Vineyards
of New Zealand 2006

Wineries & Vineyards
of New Zealand 2006

Compiled by Barbara Dyer

Hodder Moa

A catalogue record for this book is available from the National Library of New Zealand

ISBN 1-86971-020-7

A Hodder Moa Book
Published in 2005 by Hachette Livre NZ Ltd
4 Whetu Place, Mairangi Bay
Auckland, New Zealand

Text © Hachette Livre NZ Ltd 2005
Design and format © Hachette Livre NZ Ltd 2005

All rights reserved. No part of this publication may be reproduced or transmitted in any form or by any means, electronic or mechanical, including photocopying, recording, or any information storage and retrieval system, without permission in writing from the publisher.

Designed and produced by Hachette Livre NZ Ltd
Printed by Everbest Printing Co. Ltd, China

Contents

Acknowledgements	6
Introduction	7
Wine Regions of New Zealand	8
Wine Varietals	9

North Island

Northland	10
Auckland	18
Waikato & Bay of Plenty	30
Gisborne	40
Hawke's Bay	50
Wairarapa	72

South Island

Nelson	84
Marlborough	94
Canterbury	122
Central Otago	132

Index of Wineries & Vineyards	147
Index of Place Names	149
Tasting Notes	150

This year we invited wineries throughout the country to take part in this project and we're very happy that over 100 wineries agreed to do so. So a special thanks goes to the people from these wineries who made this book possible. Thank you to all those who provided support and encouragement, and thank you to Hachette Livre NZ for giving me the opportunity to put this book together and especially to the editorial and production team who have made the manuscript into a reality.

In the process of creating *Wineries & Vineyards of New Zealand* I have been privileged to travel to all the wine regions throughout New Zealand and have been reminded of what a fabulous country New Zealand really is with its magnificent landscape and friendly people.

Barbara Dyer
September 2005

Introduction

New Zealand has long been famed for its stunning, unspoiled landscape. Equal to the international acclaim for its beauty is that for its fine wines. Climate, geography and human skill have combined to produce highly distinctive, premium-quality wines, which are 'the riches of a clean, green land'.

INTERNATIONAL ACCLAIM
New Zealand Sauvignon Blanc is rated throughout the world as the definitive benchmark style for this varietal. The growing recognition for New Zealand Chardonnay, Pinot Noir, Méthode Traditionnelle sparkling wines, Riesling, Cabernet Sauvignon and Merlot blends is helping to further cement New Zealand's position as a producer of world-class wines.

DIVERSE STYLES
New Zealand is a country of contrasts with dense native forest, snow-capped mountains and spectacular coastline. With wine-growing regions spanning the latitudes of 36 to 45 degrees and covering the length of 1000 miles (1600 km), grapes are grown in a vast range of climates and soil types, producing a diverse array of styles. The northern hemisphere equivalent would run from Bordeaux (between the latitudes of 44 and 46 degrees) down to southern Spain.

TEMPERATE MARITIME CLIMATE
New Zealand's temperate maritime climate has a strong influence on the country's predominantly coastal vineyards. The vines are warmed by strong, clear sunlight during the day and cooled at night by sea breezes. The long, slow ripening period helps to retain the vibrant varietal flavours that make New Zealand wine so distinctive.

FOOD-FRIENDLY WINES
New Zealand cuisine draws inspiration from the traditional kitchens of France and Italy, as well as the exotic dishes of Asia and the Pacific Rim. Wine styles have evolved to complement this extensive menu. There are bright and zesty wines such as Sauvignon Blanc and Riesling for fresh and subtly spiced dishes, while complex, mellow Chardonnay, Cabernet Sauvignon/Merlot blends and Pinot Noir offer a timeless marriage with the classical dishes of Europe.

ENSURING THE FUTURE
New Zealand's small population, distant location and agricultural economy have earned the country a 'clean, green' image. Visitors often describe it as 'an unspoiled paradise'. New Zealand's winemakers are determined to keep it this way. Innovative practices in the vineyard and winery, which deliver quality in a sustainable and environmental manner, ensure that New Zealand meets a growing world demand for wines that have been produced in a 'clean and green' fashion.

For further information on the NZ wine industry,
go to www.nzwine.com the industry body's official website.

Wine Regions of New Zealand

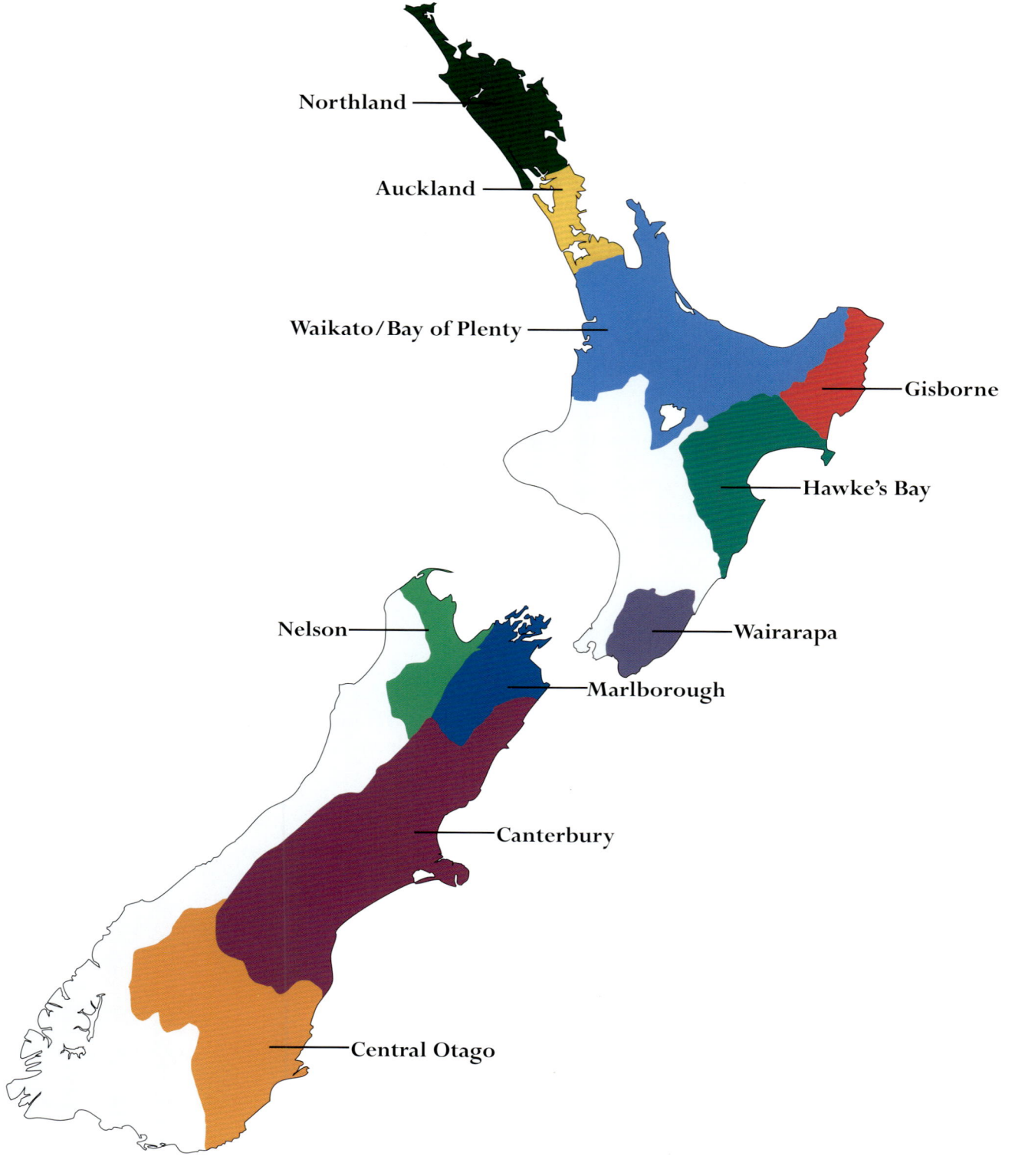

Wine Varietals

New Zealand offers a vast portfolio of wines. Over 25 different grape varieties are planted in commercial quantity in New Zealand, although the classic varieties of Chardonnay, Sauvignon Blanc, Pinot Noir, Cabernet Sauvignon, Merlot and Riesling account for the lion's share.

Varieties that respond to warmer growing conditions, such as Cabernet Sauvignon and Merlot, are more popular in the North Island. Varieties which favour cooler conditions such as Sauvignon Blanc, Riesling and Pinot Noir are more widely planted in the cooler South Island regions and in some North Island sites such as Martinborough.

SAUVIGNON BLANC

New Zealand Sauvignon Blanc is acclaimed throughout the world as the definitive benchmark style for the varietal. Its exuberant, pungent flavours have dazzled wine critics everywhere.

Sauvignon Blanc can produce lush, fleshy wine with nectarine and peach flavours in Hawke's Bay or more pungent and zestier wine with gooseberry, passionfruit and capsicum flavours when it is made from Marlborough-grown grapes.

CHARDONNAY

New Zealand Chardonnay is all about quality and diversity. The varied regional conditions combined with a winemaker's skill and innovation mean that Chardonnay in New Zealand comprises a myriad of ever evolving styles, capable of appealing to a wider range of palates.

Gisborne Chardonnay is often soft and beguiling with pineapple and peach flavours, while Chardonnay grown in Canterbury is more likely to be crisper with strong citrus/grapefruit and white peach characters.

AROMATICS

With a climate ideal for the production of Aromatic wines, praise is now resounding for the increasing number of vibrant, world-class and regionally distinctive examples of New Zealand Riesling, Gewürztraminer and Pinot Gris.

SPARKLING WINE

A temperate climate, combined with the planting of the classical Champagne varieties Chardonnay, Pinot Noir and Pinot Meunier, plus the use of the latest winemaking technology have enabled New Zealand to produce outstanding sparkling wine, now acclaimed throughout the world. Local winemakers have adapted traditional winemaking methods, but they produce wine styles unique to New Zealand with subtle fruit flavours that express the character of an array of vineyard sites.

PINOT NOIR

New Zealand is now acknowledged as one of the few countries to have successfully come to grips with this fickle, but supremely aristocratic, grape variety. The temperate climate and long sunshine hours have combined with winemaker passion and skill to produce world-class highly sought after Pinot Noir.

Martinborough Pinot Noir is typically intense and rich with ripe plum flavours while Central Otago Pinot Noir tends to be finer and more aromatic, with the distinctive flavour of black cherries.

CABERNET SAUVIGNON AND MERLOT

The aristocratic stablemates, Cabernet Sauvignon and Merlot are star performers, particularly in New Zealand's warmer northern region. New Zealand Cabernet Sauvignon boasts structure and elegance, whilst a richness and warmth exude from New Zealand Merlot. In partnership, Cabernet Sauvignon and Merlot can be vibrant or richly mellow, powerful or subtly elegant.

Northland

Gareth Eyres

Northland is New Zealand's smallest wine region producing around 0.1 per cent of the national crop. However, the region is expanding rapidly with a small number of vineyards and wineries producing award-winning wines. Grape-growing is spread over a large geographical area, from Kaitaia on the west coast in the Far North, to around the Bay of Islands on the east coast, and near Whangarei in the south-east of the region. While all experience the country's warmest ripening conditions, the terrain, soils and climatic conditions vary widely between these districts.

This highly popular tourist region is renowned for its beautiful beaches and water-based activities, as well as for its magnificent kauri forests, spectacular scenery and historic significance along with arts & crafts and fine regional cuisine. All wineries are easily located on the tourist route and welcome visitors for tasting and cellar door sales.

For more information on Northland visit:
www.northland.org.nz or contact

Bay of Islands i-SITE Visitor Centre
The Wharf, Marsden Rd, Paihia
Tel: 09 409 7345
Email: visitorinfo@fndc.govt.nz

Whangarei i-SITE Visitor Centre
92 Otaika Rd, Whangarie
Tel: (09) 438 1079
Email: whangarei@clear.net.nz

Karikari Estate Vineyard & Winery

HISTORY

Northland has the distinction of being the birthplace of New Zealand grape-growing and winemaking. This is largely due to Northland being the first area settled by Europeans, and being the centre of early administration. The Anglican missionary the Reverend Samuel Marsden first planted vines in Kerikeri in 1819. The first wine was made in Waitangi in the 1930s by James Busby, the British Government representative, who planted a vineyard near the historic Treaty House.

Later, Dalmatian immigrants who came to dig kauri gum in the North, brought with them their European wine making and wine drinking culture. Their emphasis was on fortified wines though as demand for this style of wine declined, winemaking almost died out in the region by 1990.

The last decade has seen a resurgence of interest in vineyards and winemaking in the north driven by the nationwide growth in the industry and vineyard development in the other northern sub-region of Matakana just north of Auckland. This has in turn led to the search for new, suitable terroir. Expansion is still continuing, but Northland remains the smallest wine region in the country.

SOILS

With no major rivers, Northland does not have the large well-draining, sandy, fertile alluvial plains of Hawke's Bay and Marlborough. The land here is generally more rugged. Soils in the north are predominantly clay and tend to waterlogging and poor drainage. However, there are wide variations in the area and vineyards tend to be developed where the soil is more suitable on easy slopes and alluvial flats with a range of soils from shallow clay over sand clay subsoils to free-draining fertile volcanic loams around Kerikeri.

CLIMATE

Known in New Zealand as the winterless north, the climate in the region is subtropical, the temperatures being consistently among the highest in the nation and frosts being extremely rare. Humidity is generally high due to high rainfall and proximity to the sea. The climate provides some of the earliest ripening fruit in New Zealand. Conditions during the fruit-ripening season can vary greatly. The southern oscillation El Niño/La Niña phenomenon brings a range from drier prevailing south westerlies to moist easterlies. While typically the ripening season is hot and dry there can be very difficult moist years.

GRAPE VARIETIES AND WINE STYLES

The long growing season and temperatures are best suited to the slower ripening Cabernet Sauvignon, Merlot, Shiraz and Chardonnay, the region's three predominant grape varieties. You will also find Sémillon, Pinot Gris and other red varieties such as Pinotage and Malbec.

Karikari Estate Vineyard & Winery (Gareth Eyres)

Okahu Estate Ltd

Karikari Estate Vineyard & Winery (Gareth Eyres)

Karikari Estate Vineyard & Winery (Gareth Eyres)

Events

- **Taste Bay of Islands.** A celebration of the tastes of the Bay of Islands with local wineries, speciality food producers and live music. Held at the Copthorne Hotel grounds, Waitangi in September.

- **'Savouring the Source'** at the Bay of Islands Show. New Zealand's oldest show, featuring Northland boutique wines and food producers. Held at the Waimate North Showgrounds in November. www.bayofislands.co.nz/show

For more information on Northland visit: www.northland.org.nz or contact

Marsden Estate

Wineries featured in this book
Other 'open to visit' wineries

NORTHLAND

Maitai Bay Rd
Karikari Peninsula
Northland
Tel: (09) 408 7222
Fax: (09) 408 7414
Email: info@karikariestate.co.nz
Website: www.karikariestate.co.nz

DIRECTIONS
From Kerikeri take SH10 to Mangonui (approx. 40 mins). Then 13km from Mangonui turn right onto the Karikari Peninsula. Travel 18km along Inland Rd, turning left into Maitai Bay Rd, entrance on right.

OPENING HOURS
Labour Weekend–end April: Mon–Sun, 11am–4pm
May–Labour Weekend: phone for opening hours

WINERY SALES
Cellar door, retail, mail order and Internet

PRICE RANGE
From $19.50

TASTING & TOURS
Tastings range from $3. Tours by appointment (includes tour of barrel room and tasting), $15 per person.

CAFÉ
Vineyard Tasting Platters featuring local produce are available from the cellar door along with a limited menu featuring produce from Carrington Farms and espressos.

ACCOMMODATION
Neighbouring Carrington Resort, with luxury lodge rooms or fully self-contained 2-bedroom villas.
Tel: 64 9 408 7222.

OTHER FACILITIES
The winery is available for private group functions.

OWNER
Paul Kelly

WINEMAKER
Ben Dugdale

DATE ESTABLISHED
1998, first vintage: 2003

Karikari Estate Vineyard & Winery

Karikari Estate is New Zealand's northernmost vineyard and winery set in the historical home of New Zealand's now burgeoning and internationally recognised wine industry.

Nestled on Northland's stunning Karikari Peninsula, with vineyards covering more than 100 acres of the rolling coastal land of Carrington Farms, Karikari Estate is at once a wine lover or leisure seeker's paradise. The unique meso climate and clay soils of the Karikari Peninsula combine to produce full-bodied, distinctive and stylish wines. Karikari Estate is planted out in Chardonnay, Viognier, Sémillon, Syrah, Cabernet Sauvignon, Merlot, Malbec, Cabernet Franc, Pinotage and Montepulciano.

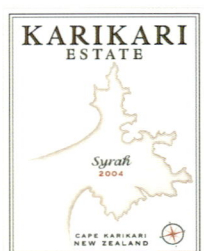

For those that want to spend a bit longer enjoying this unique location, accommodation is available on the neighbouring Carrington Resort, with luxury lodge rooms or fully self-contained two-bedroom villas. Guests can use the resort's Club Carts to travel to Karikari Estate via the purpose-built tracks.

Whether it's a tasting, a vineyard tour, or a weekend experience, Karikari Estate Vineyard and Winery is a whole new experience to savour.

WINES
Karikari Estate Chardonnay, Silver Bay (Chardonnay/Sémillon/Viognier), Viognier Sémillon, Sauvignon Blanc, Merlot/Malbec/Cabernet Sauvignon, Syrah, Pinotage, Cabernet Merlot, Rosé

RECENT AWARDS
Karikari Estate Merlot/Malbec/Cabernet 03 – Silver: Air New Zealand Wine Awards 2005; Karikari Estate Pinotage 03 – Silver: Air New Zealand Wine Awards 2005; Karikari Estate Chardonnay 03 – Silver: Liquorland Top 100

NORTHLAND

Marsden Estate

Lying to the sun amidst the citrus-covered slopes of Northland is Marsden Estate, Kerikeri's award-winning winery. It is named after Samuel Marsden who introduced the grapevine to New Zealand with 100 plantings at Kerikeri in 1819.

The plantings at Marsden Estate are a little more recent, but both the wine and the estate building have a timeless quality. A favourite for visitors and locals, this is a great place to eat and experience the flavours of Northland. Original cuisine complemented by estate-grown wines can be enjoyed in a relaxed courtyard atmosphere overlooking the lake and vines. Wine sales, tasting and tours are also available.

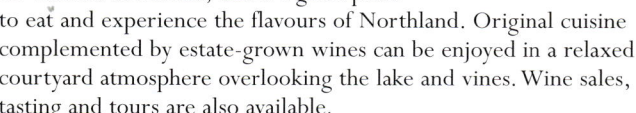

WINES
Marsden Estate Pinot Gris, Chardonnay, Sauvignon Blanc, Cabernet/Malbec/Merlot, Pinotage, Port, Chambourcin

RECENT AWARDS
NZ Pinot Gris 2004 – 4 stars: *Cuisine* Top Five; Black Rocks Chardonnay 2000 – Gold: Liquorland Top 100 2002

Wiroa Rd, Kerikeri
Tel: (09) 407 9398
Fax: (09) 407 9398
Email: marsdenestate@xtra.co.nz
Website: www.marsdenestate.co.nz

DIRECTIONS
Located on Wiroa Rd heading towards the airport, 300m on the right from SH10 turn-off.

OPENING HOURS
Sept–June: 7 days, 10am–5pm
July–Aug: 6 days, 10am–4pm, closed Monday

WINERY SALES
Retail, cellar door, mail order, Internet

PRICE RANGE
$17.50–$30

TASTING & TOURS
Tasting is free of charge. Tours by appointment only.

RESTAURANT
Open 7 days, 10am–5pm (except Jun & Jul), closed Mondays. Evenings by appointment. Reservations: (09) 407 9398

OWNERS
Cindy & Rod MacIvor

WINEMAKER
Rod MacIvor

DATE ESTABLISHED 1993

NORTHLAND

Okahu Estate Ltd

Okahu Estate is a family owned and operated business situated near the small township of Kaitaia. Since the first trial plantings in 1984, owner Monty Knight has coaxed the best wine possible from the soils and sub-tropical climate of the Far North, his aim being to produce the highest-quality wine with distinctive regional and varietal style. Now specialising in premium Chardonnays and Rhône-style reds, all wines are named after local places or people associated with the estate. Over the years they have earned a reputation for consistent quality, winning numerous awards and shining accolades. Today Okahu Estate crush around 100 tonnes annually and plan to double that in the next few years.

WINES
Labels: Shipwreck Bay, Ninety Mile, Clifton, Okahu, Kaz
Wine styles: blended reds, Chardonnays, Rosé, Sauvignon and a premium selection of reserve reds featuring Merlot/Cabernet Franc, Chambourcin, Pinotage and Syrah

Cnr Okahu & Pukepoto Rds
Kaitaia, Northland
Tel: (09) 408 2066 or Freephone 0800 806 806
Fax: (09) 408 2686 or Freefax 0800 253 253
Email: okahuestate@xtra.co.nz
Website: www.okahuestate.co.nz

DIRECTIONS
3.5km from Kaitaia on the road to Ahipara, which is at the southern end of Ninety Mile Beach.

OPENING HOURS
Dec–Feb: 7 days, 10am–5pm
March–Nov: Mon–Fri, 10am–5pm

WINERY SALES
Cellar door, mail order, retail, Internet

PRICE RANGE
$12.95–$49.95

TASTING & TOURS
Tasting is free of charge. Tours for groups of 4 or more by arrangement, $10 pp (excl. vintage when wine is being made on the premises).

ACCOMMODATION
Okahu vineyard accommodation consists of a modern 3-bedroom cottage on-site.

Nestled amongst the Syrah vines this is a unique weekend getaway – or perfect holiday base from which to discover the Far North.

OWNERS
Monty Knight, Managing Director
Paula Knight, Marketing & Sales

WINEMAKER
Chief Winemaker: Jen Bound
Winemaker: Alan Colinson

DATE ESTABLISHED 1984

Auckland

AUCKLAND, in the north of the North Island, is New Zealand's seventh largest wine region, producing around one per cent of the national crop. In this warm, humid region the vineyards are scattered over a large area and produce chiefly warm, ripe reds and ripe, rounded Chardonnays. Auckland's soils are mainly shallow clays over hard silty clay subsoils or sandy loams. Many of New Zealand's largest wine companies have their headquarters and production facilities in **Auckland**, processing grapes grown around the country. West of Auckland is the Henderson Valley, the region's traditional winemaking area, while newer vineyards are clustered in the north-west around the townships of **Kumeu**, **Huapai** and **Waimauku**. Outlying sub-regions include Matakana and Mahurangi, north of Auckland around the townships of **Warkworth** and **Matakana**, which has an enviable reputation for Cabernet Sauvignon and has undergone a very rapid expansion in both red and white wine production. The Hauraki Gulf island of Waiheke is known for high-quality red wines based on Cabernet Sauvignon, Merlot and Cabernet Franc. There are also vineyards in South Auckland and more recently in rolling farmland further south around **Clevedon**.

For more information on Auckland visit:
www.aucklandnz.com, www.matakanawine.com,
www.waihekewine.co.nz or contact

Auckland Visitor Information Centre
Sky City Atrium
Cnr Federal & Victoria Streets, Auckland
Email: info@aucklandnz.com
Tel: (09) 979 2333

Takatu Vineyard & Lodge

HISTORY

Auckland has held a key place in New Zealand's wine history, with many well-known families in the wine industry, especially those of Croatian (Dalmatian), Yugoslav and Lebanese descent, having pioneered winemaking in West Auckland in the late 19th century and early 1900s. The product of Lebanese immigrant Assid Corban's winery at Henderson became the first nationally distributed local brand. Winemakers produced mainly substitute ports and sherries until table wines became more popular in the 1960s. From this time, however, as the grape-growing industry moved to cheaper, drier regions further south in New Zealand, the region's importance began to decline. In recent years, the successes of Auckland-grown wines have helped inject new vigour into the region.

SOILS

Around Auckland soils are mainly free-draining shallow clays over silty clay subsoils or sandy loams. Drainage can be a problem with heavier clay soils. Waiheke Island's soils generally comprise free-draining weathered sedimentary rock.

CLIMATE

Auckland's climate is challenging, with plentiful rain and high humidity creating problems with fungal diseases. Vineyard management and exposure to breezes, such as on Waiheke, help combat this problem. Winters are mild and the region's warmth and sunshine favours red-wine production.

GRAPE VARIETIES AND WINE STYLES

Major varieties include Chardonnay, Merlot and Cabernet Sauvignon with lesser amounts of Cabernet Franc, Pinot Gris, Pinotage and Syrah. Ripe, rounded, tropical fruit-flavoured Chardonnays are a key style. Reds include soft, plummy Merlots and Cabernet Sauvignons with concentrated fruit flavours. Cabernet Franc is generally blended. Pinot Gris is made with either ripe stone-fruit characters or in dry, quince-flavoured wines. The region's rich, soft Pinotage is well respected as are its full-flavoured Syrahs.

SUB-REGIONS

Matakana and Mahurangi, north of Auckland, produce ripe, robust Cabernet Sauvignon, Merlot and excellent, intensely flavoured Chardonnays on free-draining soils.

Kumeu/Huapai/Waimauku, in the north-west, produces excellent wines across a range of varieties and styles from locally grown grapes as well as those from further afield.

West Auckland, in the Henderson Valley, produces little from locally grown fruit but a lot from outside of the region.

South Auckland and Clevedon are newer areas, with north-facing hillsides in Clevedon being home to specialist vineyards producing chiefly red wines, including Merlot, Cabernet Sauvignon, Malbec and Syrah.

Waiheke, in the Hauraki Gulf, has since the 1980s produced intensely concentrated Cabernet Sauvignon wines, ripely flavoured Merlots and rich, full-bodied Chardonnays.

Ransom Wines

Takatu Vineyard

Twilight Vineyards

Babich Wines

Villa Maria Auckland

Kumeu River Wines

Events

- **Devonport Wine & Food Festival.** The region's largest annual wine and food festival with wines from around New Zealand. Held in Devonport, Auckland in February. www.devonportwinefestival.co.nz
- **Waiheke Island Wine & Food Festival.** A celebration of the island's vinous offerings. Held in February. www.waihekewine.co.nz
- **Kumeu Wine & Food Festival.** Showcases West Auckland wineries and local food. Held in February.
- **Clevedon Wine & Food Festival.** Showcases the area's wine and food industry. Held at the Tipapa Events Centre in October. www.clevedonwineandfood.com

For more information on events visit: www.aucklandnz.com

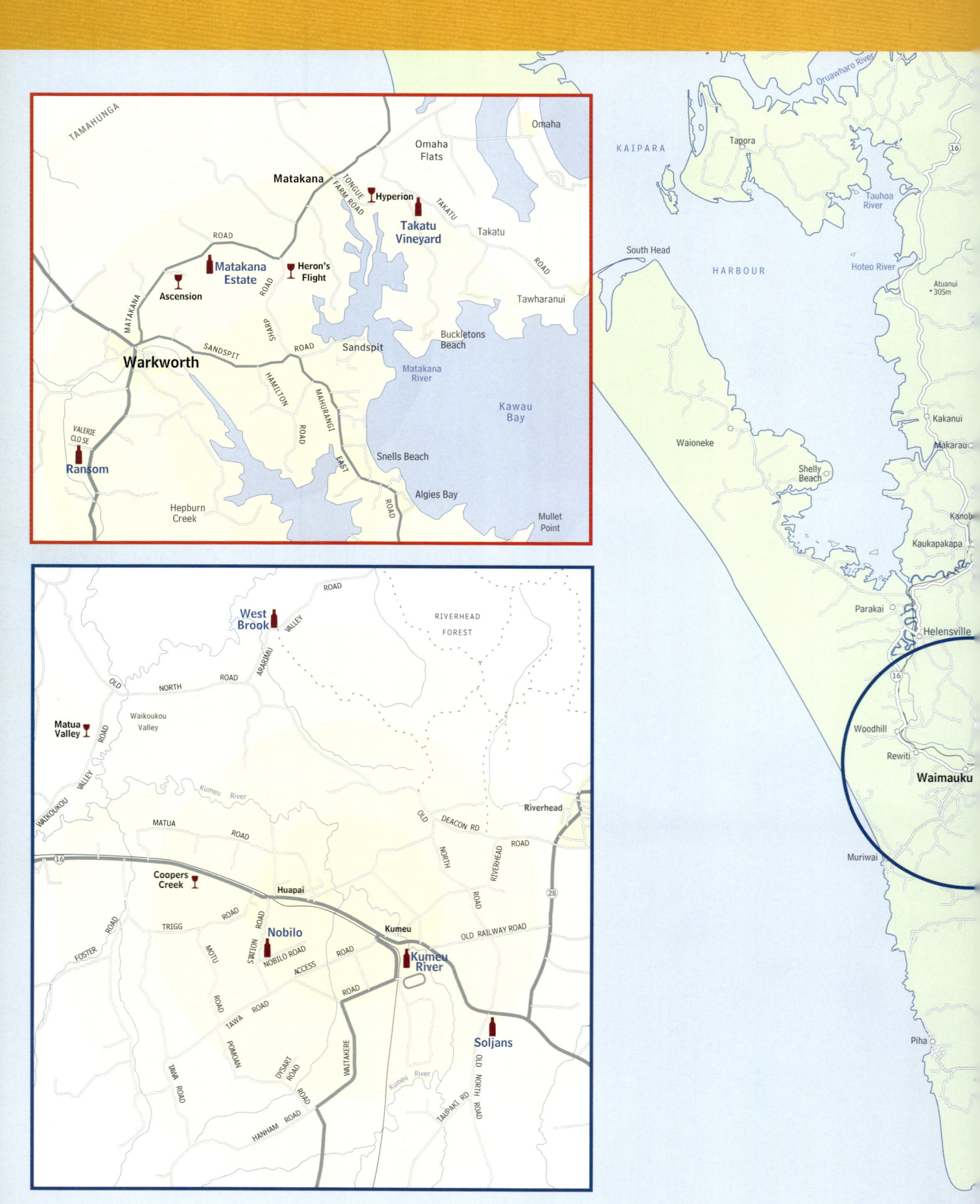

AUCKLAND
Matakana

Matakana Estate

MATAKANA ESTATE

Matakana Estate was established for the sole purpose of crafting distinctly individual, high-quality wines — wines that capture the natural characteristics of each grape variety and reflect the unique Matakana terroir. Visiting Matakana Estate is an intriguing experience for anyone with an appreciation for fine wine. Here, you can enjoy a wine-tasting experience that allows you to discover Matakana Estate wines and the winemaking approach in a relaxing and reflective environment. Visitors are encouraged to sit back and relax with a tray of tasting samples and a booklet of tasting notes whilst overlooking the stunning vista of vines stretching out into the valley in neatly ordered rows below them.

WINES
Sémillon, Pinot Gris, Chardonnay, Cabernet Merlot Malbec Franc, Syrah

RECENT AWARDS
Matakana Estate Pinot Gris was listed in *The Wine List 2004: The Top 250 Wines of the Year* (UK's No. 1 wine guide)

Matakana Rd, Matakana
Tel: (09) 425 0494
Fax: (09) 425 0595
Email: cellar@matakana-estate.co.nz

DIRECTIONS
Turn off SH1 at the traffic lights just north of Warkworth. Turn left and follow Matakana Rd for 3km. Entrance is at the far end of the vineyard.

OPENING HOURS
Mon–Sun, 10am–5pm

WINERY SALES Cellar door, mail order, restaurants, selected fine wine stores

PRICE RANGE $22–$35

TASTING
Tasting fee: $5, refundable on purchase.

OWNERS
Kevin Fitzgerald & Pat Vegar-Fitzgerald, Peter & Jean Vegar, Paul Vegar, Maree Vegar

WINEMAKER
James Graham

DATE ESTABLISHED 1996

AUCKLAND
Matakana

Ransom Wines

From Auckland, Ransom Wines is the first vineyard you reach on the Matakana wine trail. Family owned and operated, their 8-hectare vineyard is planted in Pinot Gris, Chardonnay, Cabernet Sauvignon, Merlot, Cabernet Franc and Malbec vines. The very stylish winery building is an impressive example of contemporary New Zealand architecture. Designed so that visitors can view the winemaking process, the airy glass and timber gallery opens out onto a courtyard with expansive views over the vineyards to the bush-clad Mahurangi hills. At the wine bar visitors can taste the full flight of available wines accompanied by delicious platters of local speciality foods.

WINES
Clos de Valerie Pinot Gris, Gumfield Chardonnay, Barrique Chardonnay, Vin Gris (a cabernets-based Rosé), **Mahurangi** Cabernet, Franc, Merlot; **Dark Summit** Cabernet, Franc, Merlot, Grand Mère Noble Chardonnay

46 Valerie Close, Warkworth
Tel: (09) 425 8862
Fax: (09) 425 8864
Email: info@ransomwines.co.nz
Website: www.ransomwines.co.nz

DIRECTIONS
Turn off SH1 just 3km south of Warkworth. The winery is 500m off the main road.

OPENING HOURS
Summer: 7 days, 10am–5pm
Winter: Tues–Sun, 10am–5pm

WINERY SALES
Cellar door, retail, selected restaurants, mail order, Internet

PRICE RANGE $17–$35

TASTING & TOURS
Tasting trays are available. Tours by arrangement.

FOOD OPTIONS
Lunch platters; wine & cheese matching a speciality.

OTHER FACILITIES
Available for private functions.

OWNERS
Marion & Robin Ransom

WINEMAKER
Robin Ransom

DATE ESTABLISHED 1993

AUCKLAND
West

Babich Wines

Family owned and operated Babich Wines was founded over 80 years ago by Josip Babich and today is one of New Zealand's leading wineries. The company has vineyards in the prime grape-growing regions of Marlborough, Hawke's Bay and Henderson, which is the original vineyard and home to the winery. Surrounded by rolling countryside, the Babich winery has one of the loveliest vineyard views in Auckland. Visitors are welcome to relax and enjoy the views from the outdoor deck or enjoy a game of pétanque in the picnic area. The cellar shop stocks all the present vintage wines as well as speciality wines only available from the shop.

WINES
All wines produced are marketed under the Babich brand. This incorporates the Babich Value Varietals, Babich Premium Varietals, 'Winemakers Reserve', 'Irongate', and 'The Patriarch' ranges. Varieties include: Chardonnay, Sauvignon Blanc, Pinot Gris, Riesling, Viognier, Gewürztraminer, Merlot, Syrah, Pinotage, Cabernet Sauvignon, Pinot Noir and blends.

RECENT AWARDS
Babich wines have always been well awarded and highly acclaimed both internationally and in New Zealand.

Babich Rd, Henderson
Tel: (09) 833 7859
Fax: (09) 833 9929
Email: info@babichwines.co.nz
Website: www.babichwines.co.nz

DIRECTIONS
Take the Lincoln Rd turn-off from the Northwestern Motorway. Turn right into Universal Drive, left into Swanson Rd, right into Metcalf Rd, left into Simpson Rd and then left into Babich Rd.

OPENING HOURS 7 days: Mon–Fri, 9am–5pm; Sat, 10am–5pm; Sun, 11am–5pm

WINERY SALES Cellar door, retail, mail/phone/fax orders

PRICE RANGE $10–$70

WINE TASTING
Tasting is free of charge. Large groups by appointment (tasting fee may apply).

FOOD OPTIONS
Cheeseboards, deli and snack foods are available to accompany tasting and for picnics.

PICNIC AREA
Located in the gardens with tables and a pétanque court.

OTHER PRODUCTS Wine accessories, clothing, wine gift packs, wine books and magazines

OWNERS Joe & Peter Babich

WINEMAKER
Adam Hazeldine

DATE ESTABLISHED 1916

AUCKLAND
Kumeu

Kumeu River Wines

Kumeu River Wines was established in 1944 when Mick and Katé Brajkovich and their son Mate settled in Kumeu. Mate died in 1992 and Kumeu River is now run by his wife Melba and their four children. Michael is the winemaker and has the distinction of being New Zealand's first Master of Wine; Milan, an engineer, is in charge of the vines; Marijana is the part-time accountant and Paul is marketing & export manager. Melba is managing director and is also often seen running the cellar-door shop. All of Kumeu River's grapes (except for a Marlborough Sauvignon) come from its surrounding vineyards where they have access to 39 hectares of vines and produce a range of wines that have built a huge reputation worldwide.

WINES
Kumeu River (premium range): Mate's Vineyard Chardonnay, Chardonnay, Pinot Gris, Melba (red blend), Merlot, Pinot Noir
KR Village: Chardonnay, Pinot Noir, Merlot, Rosé

RECENT AWARDS
The Chardonnays from Kumeu River are particularly renowned internationally. Kumeu River Chardonnay — placed in *Wine Spectator*'s Top 100 wines of the world on six occasions. Kumeu River Chardonnay & Mate's Vineyard Chardonnay — rated as Super Classics by Michael Cooper, *Buyer's Guide to NZ Wines 2005*

550 SH16, Kumeu
Tel: (09) 412 8415
Fax: (09) 412 7122
Email: enquiries@kumeuriver.co.nz
Website: www.kumeuriver.co.nz

DIRECTIONS On SH16, just before Kumeu village.

OPENING HOURS Mon–Fri, 9am–5.30pm; Sat, 11am–5pm

WINERY SALES Cellar door, retail, mail order, Internet

PRICE RANGE $12.50–$47

TASTING & TOURS Tasting is free of charge, but a fee applies for groups of $10 pp which includes a tutored tasting and a tour. Tours need to be booked in advance and normally require a minimum of 10 people.

OWNER
The Brajkovich family

WINEMAKER
Michael Brajkovich MW

DATE ESTABLISHED 1944

AUCKLAND
Kumeu

Nobilo Wine Group Huapai Winery

Rich in history, and with friendly and accommodating staff, Nobilo offers a comprehensive range of high-quality local and international wines — notably the award-winning Nobilo, Selaks and Drylands portfolios. The history of the company in New Zealand stretches back to the early 1940s when the Croatian Nobilo family landed in New Zealand. They settled in Huapai and started planting vines in 1943. The company has since established and built up a thriving and respected wine business, and is now the second largest wine company in New Zealand. Nobilo strives to 'over-deliver' on quality — an objective which was acknowledged at the prestigious 2003 International Wine & Spirit Competition in London when Nobilo Wine Group was awarded New Zealand Wine Producer of the Year.

WINES
Labels: White Cloud, Fernleaf, Fall Harvest, Station Road, House of Nobilo, Nobilo Icon, Selaks Premium Selection, Selaks Founders Reserve, Drylands, Castle Cliffs
Wine styles: Sauvignon Blanc, Chardonnay, Riesling, Pinot Gris, Pinot Noir, Syrah, Merlot, Cabernet Sauvignon, Sparkling, Dessert Wines

RECENT AWARDS
Highest Awarded Winery Trophy: IWSC Chardonnay Challenge 2003; Nobilo Icon Chardonnay 2001 – Chardonnay of the Year Trophy: *Winestate* magazine Wine of the Year Awards 2003; House of Nobilo Poverty Bay Chardonnay 2002 – Best Buy of the Year: *Michael Cooper's Buyer's Guide to New Zealand Wines 2004*

---

45 Station Rd, Huapai
Tel: (09) 412 6666
Fax: (09) 412 7224
Email: nobilo@nobilo.co.nz
Website: www.nobilo.co.nz

DIRECTIONS Follow the Helensville signs from Auckland City then turn left into Station Rd just past Kumeu village.

OPENING HOURS 7 days: Mon–Fri, 9am–5pm; weekends & holidays, 10am–5pm

WINERY SALES Cellar door and mail order

PRICE RANGE $8–$100

TASTING Tasting is free of charge.

OTHER PRODUCTS Comprehensive range of imported wines from Australia, as well as South Africa and Italy

OWNER Constellation Brands Inc.

WINEMAKER Chief Winemaker: Darryl Woolley

DATE ESTABLISHED 1943

AUCKLAND
Kumeu

West Brook Winery

Located in the beautiful Ararimu Valley, the West Brook vineyard and winery complex includes a winery, cellar door and superb visitor facilities. These include a designated tasting gallery overlooking the inner winery, the vineyards and rolling country vistas. Outside, landscaped terraced seating areas, shaded by trees, lead down to a brook to provide a tranquil setting for picnics. Wines are made from grapes sourced from their eight-hectare Waimauku estate and from vineyards in Hawke's Bay and Marlborough regions. Produced under two labels: the West Brook Selection is true to varietal character and for early drinking; and the Blue Ridge Selection; the Vintage Reserve range is made only in small quantities when conditions are ideal.

WINES
The West Brook Selection Marlborough Sauvignon Blanc, Marlborough Riesling, Barrique Fermented Chardonnay, Pinot Noir and Merlot/Malbec/Cabernet; **Blue Ridge Selection** Marlborough Sauvignon Blanc, Chardonnay, Late Harvest Riesling, Cabernet, Merlot, Merlot/Cabernet and Pinot Noir.

AWARDS
West Brook has amassed Gold, Silver and Bronze medals in competitions worldwide. They have also won trophies for their Chardonnay and Riesling.

---

215 Ararimu Valley Rd
Waimauku
Tel: (09) 411 9924
Fax: (09) 411 9925
Email: info@westbrook.co.nz
Website: www.westbrook.co.nz

DIRECTIONS From SH16 (towards Kumeu) turn right into Old North Rd and drive 7km, turn right into Ararimu Valley Rd. West Brook is 2km on the left.

OPENING HOURS All year: Mon–Sat, 10am–5pm; Sun, 11am–5pm

WINERY SALES Cellar door, retail, mail order

PRICE RANGE $17.95–$30.95

TASTING Tasting is free of charge for groups of less than 8; otherwise a tasting fee applies (bookings required).

FOOD OPTIONS A range of snacks is available for picnics.

PICNIC AREA In the landscaped terraced seating areas, shaded by trees, or by the brook; tables provided.

EVENTS & ACTIVITIES Food, wine and music festival held on Labour Weekend Sunday and Monday.

OWNERS Anthony & Sue Ivicevich

WINEMAKERS Anthony Ivicevich & James Rowan

DATE ESTABLISHED 1935

Soljans Estate

Bartul Soljan planted the first Soljan vineyard in New Zealand in 1932, leaving a legacy that has been carried on by his son Frank and then grandson and current owner, Tony Soljan. Today, Soljans represents three generations of winemaking with over 70 years' experience. In 2002, Tony put his own stamp on the family winemaking heritage resulting in a new winery complex located in Kumeu.

Situated at the gateway to Kumeu Classic Wine Country, the new complex offers a complete winery experience. The four-hectare vineyard is planted with Pinotage, Merlot and Cabernet Franc but like most Auckland wineries, Soljans draws the majority of its grapes from New Zealand's major wine-growing regions. At the Cellar Door the visitor can participate in winery tours and tasting while browsing the vast selection of wine and wine-related products.

The restaurant has an extensive menu that pairs each dish with one of Soljans' award-winning wines. This emphasis on wine and food matching has helped craft winemaking style towards food-friendly wines creating the ultimate wine and food experience.

WINES
Soljans Estate Marlborough Sauvignon Blanc, Riesling, Gewürztraminer, Chardonnay, Rosé, Merlot Cabernet, Pinotage, Dessert Gewürztraminer; **Soljans Reserve** Chardonnay, Merlot, Founders Port; **Premium Reserve** Tribute (Merlot/Malbec); **Soljans Sparking** Legacy Méthode Traditionnelle, Fusion Sparkling Muscat

RECENT AWARDS
Soljans' cache of 8 medals was awarded over the 2 most recent wine shows, the NZ Royal Easter Wine Show and the Air NZ Wine Awards. 'Fusion' received a gold medal and trophy at the 2004 Winewise Small Vigneron Awards held in Australia.

AUCKLAND
Kumeu

366 SH16, Kumeu
Tel: (09) 412 5858
Fax: (09) 412 5859
Email: cellar@soljans.co.nz
Website: www.soljans.co.nz

DIRECTIONS
At the end of the Northwestern Motorway, turn left onto SH16: Soljans is 6km on the left.

OPENING HOURS
Cellar door: 7 days, 9am–5.30pm
Café: Oct–Apr, Mon–Fri, 10am–4pm; Sat & Sun, 9am–4pm;
May–Sep, Mon–Fri, 11am–3.30pm; Sat & Sun, 9am–4pm

WINERY SALES Cellar door, retail, mail order, Internet

PRICE RANGE $13.50–$35

TASTING & TOURS
Tasting is free of charge for groups of 10 and under; otherwise $5 pp. Tours for groups of 10 or more by appointment. Fee: $12 pp including souvenir wine glass.

CAFÉ
Open 7 days for breakfast and lunch. Reservations: (09) 412 2680.

OTHER PRODUCTS
The cellar stocks a full range of wine-related souvenirs, giftware and gourmet food products.

OTHER FACILITIES
Pétanque courts, children's playhouse and playground. Available for weddings, private and corporate functions.

EVENTS & ACTIVITIES
Soljans' Annual Harvest Celebration, Berba, is held each year over Easter and the Budburst Festival is held each year over Labour Weekend. Soljans' Annual Winter Fair is held the first week of July.

OWNERS
Tony & Colleen Soljan

WINEMAKER
Mark Compton

DATE ESTABLISHED 1937

AUCKLAND
Central & South

118 Montgomerie Rd
Mangere
Phone: (09) 255 0666
Email: enquiries@villamaria.co.nz
Website: www.villamaria.co.nz

DIRECTIONS
Access is off George Bolt Dr (extension of the Southwestern Motorway) leading directly to Auckland Airport. Turn onto Montgomerie Rd (just 2km north of the airport).

OPENING HOURS
Mon–Fri, 9am–6pm, Sat & Sun, 9am–5pm

WINERY SALES
Cellar door, retail and mail order

PRICE RANGE Over $10

TASTING & TOURS
Wine tasting is offered across the range with a 4-tiered pricing programme for Premium, Super Premium, Ultra Premium and Vertical (refundable on purchase). Tours are charged at $5 pp.

OWNER
George Fistonich

WINEMAKERS
Group Winemaker: Alastair Mailing
Senior Winemaker: Corey Ryan

DATE ESTABLISHED 1961

Villa Maria Auckland

Founded in 1961, Villa Maria Estate is New Zealand's largest privately owned winery. Owner and Managing Director, George Fistonich, has led the company to achieve an extraordinary record of success in over 40 years of winemaking. Villa Maria produces New Zealand's most awarded wines and has received acclaim, both nationally and internationally, since the early 1980s. This outstanding achievement is due to an uncompromising commitment and dedication to quality at all stages of the grape-growing and winemaking processes.

The latest addition to Villa Maria's impressive track record is the architectural award-winning Winery and Vineyard Park recently opened in Auckland as the head office for all things Villa Maria. This beautiful park-like 40-hectare vineyard development is situated inside the crater of a 20,000-year-old extinct volcano on the Ihumatao peninsula at the gateway to Auckland City.

The Cellar Door is open 7 days for sales and tastings and regular tours of the winery are scheduled throughout the day. A strong wine tourism focus has influenced the development with a purpose-built catwalk within the winery designed to showcase the impressive facility and the company's boutique approach to large-scale winemaking. The stunning setting and convenient location only minutes from Auckland Airport makes it the perfect location for entertaining visitors from both New Zealand and abroad.

WINES
Villa Maria produces four distinctive ranges.
Labels: **Private Bin** — a popular selection of varietal wines, which are well structured, and display true varietal characteristics; **Cellar Selection** — an emphasis on fruit quality and minimal handling results in intensely flavoured, elegant, food-friendly wines; **Reserve** — only produced from the best vineyards in New Zealand's top wine-growing areas to ensure they exhibit the finest regional characteristics possible. Wines must be of exceptional quality to justify the 'Reserve' marque; **Single Vineyard** — these wines are created from vineyards of exceptional quality and only when vintage conditions allow these sites to fully express their individual characteristics.
Wines Styles: Chardonnay, Sauvignon Blanc, Riesling, Pinot Gris, Gewürztraminer, Late Harvest Riesling, Late Harvest Gewürztraminer, Noble Riesling, Pinot Noir, Merlot, Merlot/Cabernet Sauvignon

RECENT AWARDS
Four Trophies, 10 gold and 11 silver medals: Royal Easter Show Wine Awards 2005; Eight trophies, 14 gold and 11 silver medals: Air New Zealand Wine Awards 2004; Villa Maria Reserve Pinot Noir 2003 received Champion Wine of the Show twice, and the Best Pinot Noir Trophy at three international shows in 2004 including the Royal Hobart Wine Show; Owner George Fistonich was short-listed for three consecutive years as one of 50 prominent figures in the wine industry by UK *Wine International* magazine 2003–05, was named New Zealander of the Year by *National Business Review* in 2004, was named a 'top ten New Zealander' by the *New Zealand Herald* in 2004, and was awarded with a Distinguished Companion of the New Zealand Order of Merit in 2005.

AUCKLAND
Central & South

Twilight Vineyards

Bruce and Joy Peart own and operate their boutique Twilight Vineyard in the picturesque Clevedon Valley, south of Auckland City. Even though the vineyard is located in Twilight Rd the name was chosen to mean 'The first light of day, promising much, and the last light of evening (the afterglow of the sun) — a great time to reflect on the day, enjoy good company and drink fine wine'.

The first plantings were made in 1995 and now Twilight Vineyards consist of an eight-hectare Clevedon property and six and a half hectares in Gisborne's Ormond Valley. The Cellar Door is on the vineyard at Clevedon — follow the Rosé-lined driveway through the vines and take time to enjoy the extensive range of fine wines and beautiful views over the Clevedon Valley. Visitors are also welcome to picnic in the beauty of the rural surroundings.

WINES
Twilight Pinot Gris, Chardonnay, Chenin Blanc, Diamond and Pearls (Sparkling Muscat), Merlot/Cabernet Sauvignon

RECENT AWARDS
2002 Reserve Chardonnay – Bronze: Air NZ Wine Awards 2003, Bronze: NZ Wine Society Royal Easter Wine Show 2004; 2002 Twilight Chardonnay & Twilight Diamonds and Pearls – Best Buy Nov 03: *Tizwine*

105 Twilight Rd, Clevedon
Tel: (09) 292 9502
Fax: (09) 292 9502
Email: info@twilightvineyards.com
Website: www.twilightvineyards.com

DIRECTIONS Twilight Rd branches from the main road in Clevedon Village. The vineyard is 1km along on the left.

OPENING HOURS
Summer: Thurs–Sun & public holidays, 11am–4pm; Jan: 7 days, 11am–4pm. Winter: weekends only. By appointment throughout the year.

WINERY SALES Cellar door, retail, mail order, Internet

PRICE RANGE $14.95–$24.95

TASTING & TOURS
Tasting: a small fee applies. Tours and groups by appointment.

PICNIC AREA By the cellar door with extensive rural views over the Clevedon valley.

OTHER PRODUCTS Local artwork, preserves, sunhats, monogrammed tasting glasses and flutes

OWNER Bruce Peart

WINEMAKER Made under contract in Hawke's Bay.

DATE ESTABLISHED 1996

AUCKLAND

Open By Appointment

Takatu Vineyard & Lodge

Takatu Vineyard is sited on a warm north-facing hillside above Matakana village. Each of the hand-tended, densely planted vines help create a truly distinctive wine. Low yields, open canopies and no irrigation give balanced ripe fruit with wonderful aromas and flavour intensity. Sustainable viticultural practices are adhered to and all major jobs, including harvesting, are done by hand. Hence their dictum 'fruit of the vine, work of human hands'.

Situated amongst the vines is Takatu Lodge. It is architectural and contemporary in design, where whole walls of glass capture stunning views of the surrounding vineyard, mountain ranges and sea beyond. It is a unique experience for guests to stay on a working vineyard and enjoy the highest standards of elegance and comfort.

Wines: Takatu Pinot Gris, Merlot/Franc/Malbec
Winery sales: Cellar door (by appointment), mail order, retail, Internet
Price range: From $29

Contact:
518 Whitmore Rd, Matakana
Tel/Fax: (09) 423 0299
Email: info@takatuwine.co.nz
Website: www.takatuwine.co.nz, www.takatulodge.co.nz
Owners: John & Heather Forsman

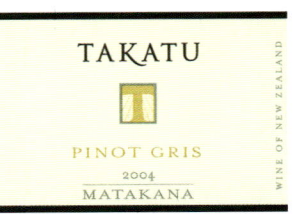

Takatu Vineyard & Lodge

Waikato & Bay of Plenty

WAIKATO/BAY OF PLENTY, south of Auckland in the North Island, is one of the country's smallest wine regions, producing just 0.3 per cent of the national crop. Its vineyard plantings occupy scattered pockets amid the rolling dairying and horticultural belt of the Waikato and Bay of Plenty. The larger wineries, based here generally for proximity to markets, obtain most or all of their grapes from other regions. Most Waikato vineyards are north of the city of **Hamilton** around the rural towns of **Te Kauwhata** and **Mangatawhiri**, and some lie south of the city near **Te Awamutu**. Bay of Plenty vineyards are predominantly around the coastal city of **Tauranga**, with others near the seas not far from the city of **Whakatane**, and inland near the town of **Murupara**. Soft, mouth-filling wines with ripe fruit flavours are the hallmark of the region, including tropical fruit-flavoured Chardonnays and Sauvignon Blancs. Full-bodied Cabernet Sauvignons and botrytised dessert wines are also successfully produced.

Hamilton, with its river and gardens, is the centre of the Waikato region. Tauranga is a thriving city and gateway to the Bay of Plenty's beaches and horticultural areas.

For more information visit:
www.waikatonz.com, www.hamiltonevents.co.nz, www.bayofplentynz.com, www.tauranga.govt.nz or contact

Hamilton i-SITE Visitor Information Centre
Transport Centre, Cnr Bryce & Anglesea Sts, Hamilton
Tel: (07) 839 3580, Email: hamiltoninfo@wave.co.nz

Tauranga i-SITE Visitor Information Centre
95 Willow St, Tauranga
Tel (07) 578 8103, Email: trgvin@tauranga.govt.nz

Mills Reef Winery

HISTORY

The government's Viticultural Research Station was established at Te Kauwhata in 1897 (now the site of Rongopai Wines), giving an impetus to grape-growing in the region. In the 1960s, Montana established vineyards at Mangatangi in the northern Waikato and Cooks planted vineyards and developed a winery at Te Kauwhata. By the 1980s the region was producing close to six per cent of the national crop. However, since then there has been a steady decline in its importance as grape-growing has moved to drier regions in the south.

SOILS

Heavy loams over clay subsoils are common in the Waikato, their fertility demanding good management to control vine vigour. The Bay of Plenty vines grow chiefly in volcanic loams.

CLIMATE

Both Waikato and Bay of Plenty enjoy a moderately warm, mild climate and high sunshine hours. Humidity and rainfall are high, but most of the rain tends to fall after harvest in autumn. Inland Bay of Plenty sites near Murupara experience hot days and cold nights.

GRAPE VARIETIES AND WINE STYLES

The major varieties are Chardonnay, Cabernet Sauvignon and Sauvignon Blanc. Chardonnays produced feature tropical-fruit flavours and most undergo malolactic fermentation to soften their acidity. Cabernet Sauvignon and Sauvignon Blanc are made in full-bodied styles with ripe flavours. The region's relatively humid climate helps in the production of sweet botrytised dessert wines. Pinot Noir wines in berry fruit-flavoured styles are also showing promise in the region.

SUB-REGIONS

Waikato, on heavy loams among fertile farmlands, principally north of the city of Hamilton around Te Kauwhata and Mangatawhiri, as well as south of the city near Te Awamutu.

Bay of Plenty, on volcanic loams, includes vineyards around Tauranga and Whakatane, and inland at Galatea near Murupara.

Colefield Vineyard, Morton Estate

Firstland Vineyards

Events

- **Brightstone Blues, Brews & BBQ's.** An afternoon and evening of live music, boutique beer and food. Held annually on the second Thursday in January each year in Tauranga.
- **Katikati Wine & Food Funfest.** A celebration of summer, fine cuisine and wine.
- **Tauranga Food & Wine Festival.** Annual celebration of fine wine, food and entertainment held in the Wharepai Domain in February.
- **The International Food & Wine Festival.** An international celebration of food and wine that includes a German Beer Fest and a Wine Expo. Held annually in May at the Waikato Events Centre, Hamilton. www.ifwf.co.nz

For more information on events visit:
www.waikatonz.com or www.bayofplentynz.com

WAIKATO

Cook's Landing

Halfway between Auckland and Hamilton and nestled in a picturesque valley with panoramic views overlooking the vineyards of Te Kauwhata is the Cook's Landing Restaurant, Café and Wine Bar. A large deck overlooks the seven-hectare home vineyard that produces a range of award-winning wines under the 'Old Vines' label, named because the vines were planted more than 25 years ago. These can be sampled and purchased at the Wine Bar and to complement your tasting the restaurant serves a wide range of fabulous food from light snacks to lunches. This is a popular venue for Sunday brunch with live music from top NZ artists.

WINES
Old Vines Chardonnay, Sauvignon Blanc, Cabernet Sauvignon; Quarry Road Chardonnay, Sauvignon Blanc, Merlot, Cabernet Sauvignon, Dessert wines

26 Paddy Rd, Te Kauwhata
Tel: (07) 826 0004
Fax: (07) 826 3611
Email: www.cookslanding@xtra.co.nz
Website: www.cookslanding.co.nz

DIRECTIONS
45 minutes' drive south of Auckland on SH1. Turn off at the top of the Te Kauwhata Hill, Paddy Rd is on the left travelling south.

OPENING HOURS
7 days, 10am–4pm. Open any evening year round for group bookings of 15 or more.

WINERY SALES
Retail through Cook's Landing Café and Cellar Door

PRICE RANGE
$14.95–$25.95

TASTING
Tasting fee: $3, refundable on purchase.

RESTAURANT
Indoor and outdoor dining with an excellent range of snacks, lunches and coffee. Reservations: (07) 826 0004.

OTHER FACILITIES
Available for weddings, corporate and private functions.

OWNERS
Shaftspry Ltd T/A Cook's Landing Ltd

WINEMAKERS
Toby Cooper

WAIKATO

Firstland Vineyards

Firstland Vineyards is based at Hotel du Vin in the picturesque Mangatawhiri Valley, 45 minutes south of Auckland. With 100 per cent of the company's wines being produced from Marlborough fruit, the original winery on the premises has been decommissioned and is now a luxury day spa — Spa du Vin. Firstland's grape supply comes from the company's Lauren Vineyard and from contract growers in Marlborough's Wairau Valley.

Firstland Vineyards is primarily an export company with more than 90 per cent of the wines being sold in the USA, Hong Kong, Australia and Korea. In keeping with its export focus, the production of Sauvignon Blanc has been increased.

WINES
Firstland Marlborough Sauvignon Blanc, Riesling, Chardonnay, Pinot Noir; Hawke's Bay Cabernet blends

500 Lyons Rd, Mangatawhiri
Tel: (09) 233 6314
Fax: (09) 233 6215
Email: info@firstland.co.nz
Website: www.firstland.co.nz

DIRECTIONS
45 minutes' drive south of Auckland on SH2. Turn left into Lyons Rd. Firstlands is at the end of Lyons Rd.

OPENING HOURS
Cellar Door: 7 days, 9.30am–5pm
Restaurant: 7 days for lunch and dinner

WINERY SALES
Cellar door, retail, mail order, Internet

PRICE RANGE $15–$20

TASTING
Tasting is free of charge; group tastings on application.

RESTAURANT
The Vineyard Restaurant offers superb dining in an elegant setting. Diners also have the option of the private Vintage and De Redcliffe Rooms and the outside terrace areas.

ACCOMMODATION
Hotel du Vin has 48 well-appointed, spacious chalets set in lush gardens surrounding the original winery and reception building.

ACTIVITIES
Spa du Vin offers personalised spa treatments. In the finest Balinese-style décor.

A wide range of leisure activities is also available at Hotel du Vin for day visitors.

OWNERS
Ed & Barbara Aster

WINEMAKER
Craig Murphy

DATE ESTABLISHED 1976

WAIKATO

Rongopai Wines

In the heart of the Waikato, above beautiful Lake Waikare, lies the small town of Te Kauwhata and the home of Rongopai Wines. A short half-hour drive south of Auckland and set in the picturesque research station built by Italian viticulturist Romeo Bragato in 1902, Rongopai is the birthplace of New Zealand winemaking research and one of our leading producers of botrytised wine.

With established vineyards in three key wine-growing regions — Hawke's Bay, Gisborne and Marlborough — Rongopai is both a familiar and reliable source of great wines. Numerous medals and awards have shown New Zealand and the world the quality and strength of their selection.

The evident beauty of the winery itself makes Rongopai Wines a popular place to visit. If you like truly great wines and beautiful, historic settings then you'll love Rongopai. Visitors are welcome to drop in, sample wines at the cellar door and relax in the park-like surroundings — or by telephoning in advance arrange a tour of the highest-classed historic winery in New Zealand.

WINES
Labels: Seasonal Series, Reserve Range, ULTIMO Collection (premium range)
Wine Styles: Sauvignon Blanc, Chardonnay, Viognier, Merlot; Sweet wines varieties include Chardonnay, Riesling and Würzer

RECENT AWARDS
ULTIMO Noble Late Harvest 2002 – Gold: Royal Easter Wine Show 2004, Gold: Challenge International du Vin 2004; ULTIMO Chardonnay 2002 – Silver: Royal Easter Wine Show 2004, Silver: Challenge International du Vin 2004; Reserve Merlot 2002 – Silver: New World Wine Awards 2003; Reserve Gisborne Chardonnay 2002 – Silver: Liquorland Top 100 2003

---

55 Te Kauwhata Rd, Te Kauwhata
Tel: (07) 826 3891
Fax: (07) 826 3462
Email: shop@rongopaiwines.co.nz
Website: www.rongopaiwines.co.nz

DIRECTIONS
45 minutes' drive south of Auckland on SH1. Turn off at Te Kauwhata and follow the signs.

OPENING HOURS
Mon–Fri, 9am–5pm
Weekends, 10am–4pm

WINERY SALES
Cellar door retail, mail order, Internet

PRICE RANGE $12.95–$75

TASTING & TOURS
Tasting fee: $2 pp to taste the Seasonal and Reserve Range; refundable on purchase. Tours by appointment only. Tour fee: $5 (includes free tasting).

PICNIC AREA
Beautiful park-like area with picnic tables.

OWNERS
D & J Reid, R Burney & E Bolliger

WINEMAKER
Emmanuel Bolliger

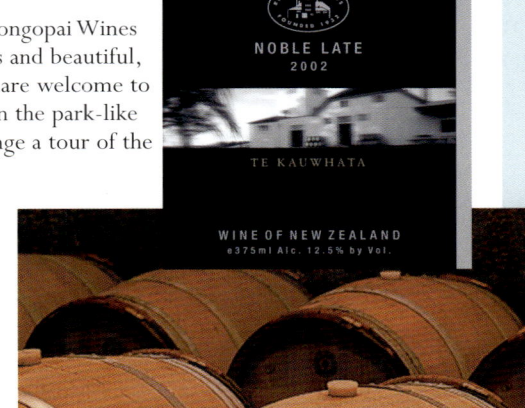

DATE ESTABLISHED 1932

WAIKATO

Vilagrad Wines

Vilagrad Wines is the region's oldest winery, established over 80 years ago by Dalmatians, the Milicich family. Still family owned and operated, Vilagrad now encompasses 4 generations of winemaking. Vilagrad captures the spirit of a traditional European lifestyle. Sunday lunches in an enclosed, cobbled courtyard under a canopy of vines are a relaxing affair where you can enjoy succulent meat off the spit, Mediterranean vegetables, salads and mouth-watering desserts accompanied by their award-winning wines. You can teach your taste buds and educate your palate on the tasting tour of the vineyard and cellar where traditional methods of winemaking are still faithfully practised to produce their excellent range of medal-winning wines.

WINES
Vilagrad Mt Pirongia Chardonnay, Mt Pirongia Cabernet Merlot, Chardonnay/Traminer, Reserve Chardonnay, Reserve Cabernet/Merlot/Malbec, Méthode Traditionnelle

RECENT AWARDS
Vilgrad's wines, all grown and produced in the Waikato, have won 42 awards over the last six seasons.

702 Rukuhia Rd
RD 2, Ohaupo
Tel: (07) 825 2893
Fax: (07) 825 2093
Email: wines@vilagrad.co.nz
Website: www.vilagradwines.co.nz

DIRECTIONS
10 minutes south of Hamilton on SH3. Turn off at Rukuhia Rd and follow for 7km — Vilagrad is on the right.

OPENING HOURS
Cellar Door: 7 days, 9am–4pm
Restaurant: Sun, 12pm–4pm

WINERY SALES
Cellar door, retail, mail order, Internet

PRICE RANGE
$16–$34

TASTING & TOURS
Tasting is free of charge; 1-hour educational tasting and tour by appointment: $10 pp. Tour, educational tasting & nibbles platter: $15 pp.

RESTAURANT
Vilagrad Restaurant: open for Sunday lunches. Available for conferences, private functions and weddings.

EVENTS & ACTIVITIES
Harvest Festival held in April.

OTHER PRODUCTS
Personalised wine labels: personalise your own bottle(s) of wine for a special gift or event.

OWNERS
Pieter & Nelda Nooyen

WINEMAKER
Jacob Nooyen

CHEF
Kristian Nooyen

DATE ESTABLISHED 1922

WAIKATO

Wishart Estate

The owners of Wishart Estate are from one of the oldest winemaking families in Hawke's Bay. Their grandfather Robert Bird established the winery known today as Esk Valley Estate (now owned by Villa Maria) in 1933 when there were only four wineries in Hawke's Bay. Wishart Estate's winery and vineyards are still located in the Esk Valley and have a reputation for producing high-quality Merlot, Syrah and Chardonnay. In 2001 Wishart identified the potential in Taupo to grow Pinot Noir and took the opportunity to plant a vineyard, Huka Winery, at Huka Village that produced its first commercial crop of Pinot Noir in 2005. The Cellar Door is located here and is the first in the Taupo region.

WINES
Premium Wines Alexis (blended red), Orion's Belt Pinot Noir, Alluvion Syrah, Muritai Chardonnay, **Te Puriri** Sauvignon Blanc, Barrique Fermented Chardonnay, Unoaked Chardonnay, Merlot, Cabernet Franc/Merlot, Merlot Rosé, Muscat, Dessert Merlot, Late Harvest Chardonnay

RECENT AWARDS
Alexis (was the Reserve Merlot 2001) – 4½ stars: *Winestate* magazine, Best of Best NZ Reds: *Food & Beverage* magazine; Muritai Chardonnay 2002 & 2003 – 4 stars: *Winestate* magazine

Huka Village,
Huka Falls Rd, Taupo
Tel: (07) 378 5426
Fax: (07) 376 9438
Email: sales@wishartwinery.co.nz
Website: www.wishartwinery.co.nz

DIRECTIONS
On the Huka Falls Rd 500 metres from the SH1 turn-off as you enter Taupo from the north.

OPENING HOURS
Cellar Door: 7 days, 10am–6pm (summer); 10am–5pm (winter)
Restaurant: lunch & dinner, 7 days

WINERY SALES
Cellar door, mail order, retail

PRICE RANGE $17–$45

TASTING & TOURS
Tasting is free of charge. Visitors can inspect the vineyard and historical church.

RESTAURANT
Huka Vineyard Restaurant caters for lunches, dinners and special events. Tel: (07) 377 2326.

PICNIC AREA
There is a large picnic area in front of the winery and restaurant.

ACCOMMODATION
Huka Village, next to the winery. Tel: 0800 485 28

EVENTS
Evening wine appreciation courses (July/Aug/Sept); Harvest Festival (Mar)

OWNER
Wishart Estate Winery Limited

WINEMAKER
Evert Nijzink

DATE ESTABLISHED 1999

BAY OF PLENTY

Mills Reef Winery

Mills Reef Winery and Restaurant has established itself as a major Tauranga landmark — though the vineyards are situated in Hawke's Bay. With its Art Deco architectural style it has been acclaimed as one of the most stylish and attractive winery buildings in New Zealand. Set on expansive grounds, the winery is purpose-built for wine production and wine appreciation and has been recognised as a world-class facility. The complex has full winemaking and bottling capacity, a 500-barrel cellar, an aged wine cellar and spacious wine-tasting areas. An award-winning restaurant completes the picture with a relaxed outdoor dining area, pétanque courts and beautifully landscaped grounds.

WINES
Labels: Mills Reef, Reserve and Elspeth
Wine Styles: Chardonnay, Riesling, Sauvignon Blanc, Gewürztraminer, Syrah, Merlot, Cabernet Merlot, Cabernet Franc, Malbec and Mills Reef's Icon Blend 'Elspeth One'

RECENT AWARDS
Over 250 medals, 11 Champion Wine trophies, NZ Winemaker Of The Year 2004: *Winestate* magazine

143 Moffat Rd, Bethlehem
Tauranga
Tel: (07) 576 8800
Fax: (07) 576 8824
Email: info@millsreef.co.nz
Website: www.millsreef.co.nz

DIRECTIONS
From the north and Tauranga, take SH2 to Bethlehem, turn onto Moffat Rd; Mills Reef is 500m on the right.

OPENING HOURS
Tasting room: 7 days, 10am–5pm
Restaurant: lunch 7 days, 10am–5pm, dinner by arrangement

WINERY SALES
Cellar door, retail, Internet

PRICE RANGE $15–$50

TASTING
Tasting is free of charge.

RESTAURANT
Relaxed indoor and outdoor dining in a rural setting. Pacific Rim-style cuisine and gourmet pizzas. Reservations: (07) 576 8800.

EVENTS & ACTIVITIES
Winemakers dinners, Annual Mills Reef Concert on the lawn (in January, Auckland Anniversary Weekend)

OTHER FACILITIES
Available for weddings and functions.

OWNER
The Preston family

WINEMAKERS
Paddy & Tim Preston

DATE ESTABLISHED 1989

BAY OF PLENTY

Morton Estate

With estates in the prime wine-growing regions of Hawke's Bay and Marlborough, Morton Estate has built a reputation for consistently producing some of New Zealand's most exceptional wines, confirmed by numerous accolades in the most rigorous international wine competitions. Famous for its Chardonnays, Morton Estate is now making a name for itself with its Sauvignon Blancs and reds. Located on the main highway in Katikati, the distinctive Cape Dutch-style winery is a popular spot to spend a day, with cellar-door wine sales and tasting, and memorable dining at Morton Restaurant. The menu features delectable game dishes, and after a leisurely lunch and sampling wines you can then visit the cellar door to make your purchases.

WINES
Labels: Coniglio, Morton Estate Black Label, Reserve Range, Individual Vineyard Series, Méthode Traditionnelle, White Label, Mill Road
Wine styles: Chardonnay, Sauvignon Blanc, Riesling, Sémillon/Chardonnay, Syrah, Merlot, Merlot/Cabernet, Sparkling, Pinot Gris, Pinot Noir

RECENT AWARDS
Coniglio 2000 – Regional NZ Chardonnay Trophy: *Decanter* World Wine Awards 2005; Non Vintage Brut – Champion Sparkling Trophy: Air NZ Awards 2003; Stone Creek Marlborough Sauvignon Blanc 2002 – Best Sauvignon Trophy: London International Wine Challenge 2003

SH2, Katikati
Tel: (07) 552 0795
Fax: (07) 552 0651
Email: auckland@mortonestatewines.co.nz
Website: www.mortonestate.co.nz

DIRECTIONS
In Katikati, 15 minutes north of Tauranga on SH2.

OPENING HOURS
Cellar door: 7 days, 9.30am–5pm (closed Christmas Day)
Restaurant: lunch: 6 days, 11.30am–3pm, closed Mon; dinner: Thurs–Sat from 6pm

WINERY SALES
Cellar door, retail, mail order, Internet

PRICE RANGE $10–$80

TASTING & TOURS
Tasting is free of charge. Tours available on request.

RESTAURANT
Morton Restaurant. French provincial cuisine.
Reservations: (07) 552 0620.

OTHER FACILITIES
State-of-the-art Méthode Traditionnelle Centre. Available for functions.

OWNER John Coney

WINEMAKERS
Evan Ward & Chris Archer

DATE ESTABLISHED 1978

Gisborne

GISBORNE, on the eastern tip of the North Island, with the first vines in the world to see the sun each day, is New Zealand's third largest wine region, comprising 15.6 per cent of the national crop. Spreading out behind the coastal city of Gisborne, the Gisborne Plains form a sheltered triangle of land bordered by mountain ranges and the sea in Poverty Bay. Most plantings occur in the Ormond Valley in the northern apex of the triangle, and along plains bordering the Waipaoa River that runs the length of the region. Some vineyards are creeping into hillside areas. Chardonnay is the key grape, comprising over half of all plantings, produced with the soft, lush, tropical-fruit flavours that characterise most of Gisborne's white wines, including Gewürztraminer, Sémillon and Chenin Blanc. Warm, soft, fruity Merlots are also made, and Pinot Noir finds its way into Méthode Traditionnelle wines. The region is one of the country's sunniest and warmest, with grapes ripening relatively early.

Gisborne is the gateway to the unspoilt East Coast region and the city offers popular surf beaches, wine trails, restaurants and historical sites.

For more information visit:
www.gisborne.co.nz, www.gisbornewine.co.nz or contact

Gisborne Visitor Information Centre
209 Grey Street, Gisborne
Tel: (06) 868 6139
Email: info@gisbornenz.com

The Millton Vineyards

HISTORY

The first wines in Gisborne were planted by Marist priests in the 1850s. German winemaker Friedrich Wohnsiedler pioneered commercial winemaking in the region, establishing vines at Waihirere and releasing his first wine in 1921. (Wohnsiedler's winery was eventually purchased by Montana in 1973.) The modern era of grape-growing began in the late 1960s when Corbans and Montana began contracting local farmers to raise grapes for processing at their Auckland wineries. Vineyards spread rapidly and bulk wine production dominated the region in the 1970s and 1980s. This was followed by some downsizing and shifting of varietal focus. Montana has invested heavily in the region's vineyards and its hugely popular Montana Gisborne Chardonnay, first made in 1973, is one of its biggest-volume wines.

SOILS

Gisborne's soils are chiefly alluvial clay loams of moderate to high fertility, requiring vine vigour to be kept in check. Soils do not vary greatly across the region, so different rootstocks and clones are used to produce fruit with a range of flavours. Newer hillside sites outside of the plains areas have lower-fertility soils.

CLIMATE

Gisborne is very sunny, and warm temperatures lead to early grape harvest. The region is relatively sheltered from strong winds, and coastal areas are cooled by sea breezes, helping grapes retain their crispness. Frequent autumn rainfall can cause strong risk of fungal disease.

GRAPE VARIETIES AND WINE STYLES

Chardonnay occupies around half of Gisborne's vineyards and white varieties make up most of the balance. Chardonnay is produced in soft, fruit-forward styles. Müller-Thurgau, often used in blends, shows floral, citrus characters. Most Muscat produced is used in Montana's popular sparkling wine, Bernadino. Gisborne is also one of the best regions in the country for crisp Sémillons and Gewürztraminers that range from elegant, floral wines to rich, spicy complex examples. Soft, plummy and fruity Merlot is the key red while Pinot Noir is used mainly for sparkling wine production.

SUB-REGIONS

Patutahi, in the west, has around a third of the region's vines, mainly Chardonnay along with Gewürztraminer, and produces premium, richly flavoured wines.

Ormond, in the northern end of the plains, has produced superb Chardonnays since the 1980s.

Manutuke, the oldest sub-region, closer to the coast south of the Waipaoa River, produces mainly Chardonnay, Chenin Blanc, Malbec, varietal Muscat and Pinot Noir.

Hexton, on the north-eastern edge of the plains, is known for its Chardonnay, along with Gewürztraminer, Merlot, Malbec and Viognier.

Matawhero, alongside the Waipaoa River nearer the coast, produces mostly Chardonnay and Gewürztraminer.

Waihirere, in the north of the plains, is home to the first commercial vineyard and to Montana Gisborne Chardonnay, produced from the sub-region's key variety.

Makauri/Bushmere, in the centre of the plains, produces mainly Chardonnay, Merlot, Sémillon, Muscat and Müller-Thurgau.

Waipaoa Valley, at the northern end of the plains, on free-draining soils close to the Waipaoa River, is a newer sub-region planted mainly in Chardonnay, Sémillon and Pinot Noir.

Kirkpatrick Estate Winery

Gisborne countryside near Patutahi

The Millton Vineyards

Montana Gisborne Winery

The Millton Vineyards

Events

- **Gisborne Wine Week**. A festival of wine-related activities, incorporating The Gisborne Wine & Food Festival and the International Chardonnay Challenge. Held annually to include Labour Weekend in October.
- **Taste Gisborne**. Wine, art, food music. Six hours of non-stop entertainment at the historic Waiohika Estate vineyard. Held annually at the end of January.

For more information on events visit: www.gisbornewine.co.nz

Montana Gisborne Winery & Lindaur Cellars

Kirkpatrick Estate Winery

Ormond
Waipaoa
River
Waihirere
Waituhi
TW
2
WAIMATA VALLEY ROAD
BACK ORMOND ROAD
Hexton
TUCKER ROAD
BUSHMERE ROAD
Patutahi
Kirkpatrick
Estate Winery
WHAREKOPAE ROAD
Pouparae
Park
36
Waipaoa River
Taruheru River
Makaraka
RIVERPOINT RD
Matawhero
Matawhero
AWAPUNI ROAD
2
Montana Giborne
Winery
GISBORNE
The Millton
Vineyard
PAPATU ROAD
36
Gisborne Wine Co.
Manutuke
Turanganui
River
Te Arai River
TE ARAI ROAD
POVERTY
BAY
Waipaoa
River

Waiomoko River

Waimata River

36

Amor-Bendall
Wainui

▌ **Wineries featured in this book**
▼ **Other 'open to visit' wineries**

GISBORNE

Gisborne Wine Company

The Gisborne Wine Company is located in a former freezing works, built in 1906 and once the largest brick façade in the Southern Hemisphere. The building's former design lends itself well to its new life as The Works Café and Winery with the rear providing perfect cellaring conditions. Winemaker John Thorpe processes over 200 tonnes of grapes each year producing a variety of premium Gisborne wines for a range of local vineyards including his own award-winning Longbush Wines and exclusive Works Café Wines. John Thorpe is also a trained chef and inspires a seasonal Works Café menu that focuses on Taste Tairawhiti, offering Waimata cheeses, truffles, and a huge range of local seafood and hill meat.

WINES
Longbush Reserve Chardonnay, Unoaked Chardonnay, Chardonnay, Gewürztraminer, Chenin Blanc, Reserve Merlot, Merlot, Brut Méthode Traditionnelle (12 years old);
Works Chardonnay, Sauvignon Blanc, Muscat, Rosé, Cabernet Franc, Merlot

The Esplanade, Gisborne
Tel: (06) 863 1285 or 0800 gizwine
Fax: (06) 863 0973
info@gisbornewinecompany.co.nz
www.gisbornewinecompany.co.nz

DIRECTIONS On Gisborne's inner harbour, The Esplanade is off the main road heading north.

OPENING HOURS
Sales and tastings during café hours: 7 days, 10am–late and at The House of Wine, 10am–5pm

WINERY SALES Cellar door, retail, mail order, Internet

PRICE RANGE $12–$40

TASTING & TOURS
Tasting fee: $10, includes a platter of Waimata cheeses; $5 at The House of Wine, refunded on purchase. Local vineyard tours: $60 pp, minimum of 2 people, twice daily, 10am & 2pm. Bookings essential. Picnic hampers, $10 pp.

CAFÉ
The Works Café: (06) 863 0973

OTHER FACILITIES
The Works Café is available for group functions. The House of Wine retail gallery, 66 Customhouse St, Gisborne.

OWNER
John Thorpe

WINEMAKER
John Thorpe

DATE ESTABLISHED 1999

GISBORNE

Kirkpatrick Estate Winery

Kirkpatrick Estate Winery (KEW) is Gisborne's newest winery located on the fine wine-producing Patutahi Plateau near Gisborne. The eight-hectare vineyard is planted on a terraced hill near where the Kirkpatrick family has farmed for 150 years. The owners Simon and Karen Kirkpatrick are passionate about food and wine with Karen running her own catering business Fintray — the perfect complement to owning a winery and vineyard. Visitors are warmly welcomed at the Cellar Door to taste some of their excellent wine, which can be accompanied by delicious gourmet burgers and KEW platters. Children are catered for with special 'Buds' platters.

WINES
KEW Wild Rosé, Unwooded Chardonnay, Barrel Fermented Reserve Chardonnay, Estate Merlot, Top Flat Reserve Merlot, Malbec

RECENT AWARDS
Wild Rosé 2004 – Bronze medal: Romeo Bragato Awards, Air NZ Wine Awards, Top 5 Rosés in NZ: Cuisine magazine

OTHER PRODUCTS
Fouette ice cream, Fintray spreads

569 Wharekopae Rd, RD2, Gisborne
Tel: (06) 862 7722
Fax: (06) 862 7750
Email: info@kew.co.nz
Website: www.kew.co.nz

DIRECTIONS
Head south from Gisborne over Waipaoa Bridge, turn right at the roundabout, follow Wharekopae Rd and look for the terraced vineyard on your left and the KEW sign.

OPENING HOURS
Summer (Labour Weekend–Easter): 7 days, 10am–6pm; Spring & Autumn: Fri–Mon, 11am–4pm; Winter: Sat–Sun, noon–4pm.

WINERY SALES
Cellar door, retail, mail order, Internet

PRICE RANGE
$18–$30

TASTING & TOURS
Tasting fee: $5, refundable on purchase. Winery tours by appointment.

FOOD OPTIONS
Platters of local produce and freshly baked breads, gourmet burgers, breads & dukkah, 'Buds' platters for children available.

OTHER FACILITIES
Fintray cater for special parties and weddings.

OWNERS
Simon & Karen Kirkpatrick

WINEMAKER
Anita Ewart-Croy

DATE ESTABLISHED 2004

GISBORNE

Solander St, Gisborne
Phone: (06) 868 2757
Fax: (06) 867 9817
Email: GisborneCellarDoor@adwnz.co.nz
Website: www.adwnz.com

DIRECTIONS
Situated on Solander Street in the heart of Gisborne.

OPENING HOURS
7 days, 10am–5pm

WINERY SALES
Cellar door, retail

PRICE RANGE $14–$80

TASTING & TOURS
Tasting is free of charge. Museum tours daily at 10.30am & 2pm.

CAFÉ
7 days, lunch from 11.30am. Cheeseboards available all day.

OTHER FACILITIES
There is a shade sail, pétanque court and grass area to enjoy. The Lindauer Cellars can cater for private functions for up to 80 people.

OTHER PRODUCTS
Premium wines, quality gifts and accessories.

OWNER
Allied Domecq Wines (NZ) Ltd

WINEMAKERS
Steve Voysey & Brent Laidlaw

DATE ESTABLISHED 2002

Montana Gisborne Winery & Lindauer Cellars

The former Corbans Winery in Gisborne has been transformed into a striking, modern cellar door, complete with an extensive wine shop, a private tasting room, a shady courtyard and a winery museum. Visitors walk through an imposing colonnade with a pétanque court and grassy area to their left, a large outdoor fire directly ahead of them and the extensive cellar door to their right. With its exposed wooden beams and pebble stone flooring, the cellar door opens onto the courtyard. An extensive selection of Montana wines are available to taste, purchase, or enjoy in the sheltered courtyard. Lunches are also available in the winery café.

A feature of the tastings is a winery tour and the opportunity to venture into the winery museum that highlights the production of Méthode Traditionnelle wines such as Lindauer and the history of winemaking in the region. Housed in a former cuve room, the museum is dark and cavernous with lots of uplighting to try and replicate the feeling of being underground in the Champagne caves of France.

WINES
Lindauer, Fraise, Lindauer Special Reserve, Lindauer Blanc de Blancs, Montana Gisborne Chardonnay, Ormond Estate Chardonnay, Patutahi Gewürztraminer, Corbans Chardonnay

RECENT AWARDS
Grandeur – Silver: Air New Zealand Wine Awards 2004, Silver: Japan International Wine Challenge 2004; Lindauer Special Reserve – Silver: London International Wine Challenge 2004, Silver: Japan International Wine Challenge 2004, Silver: Japan International Wine Challenge 2003; Lindauer Special Reserve Blanc de Blancs – Silver & Recommended Top Six: International Chardonnay Challenge (Gisborne) 2004

GISBORNE

The Millton Vineyard

In 1984 James and Annie Millton established their winery on the banks of the Te Arai River where the early settlers first planted grapevines in 1871. The Millton Vineyards is New Zealand's first fully certified commercial organic vineyard and winery. Following the indications given by Dr Rudolf Steiner, bio-dynamic techniques are used in all areas of production. Their philosophy is to produce specialised wines expressive of the natural flavours of the grapes harvested from their Gisborne vineyards. At the cellar door, visitors can taste and discuss the wine styles while enjoying a tranquil traditional garden setting.

WINES
The Growers Series
Gewürztraminer McIldowie Vineyard, Viognier Briant Vineyard; **Millton** Chardonnay Opou Vineyard, Riesling Opou Vineyard, Chenin Blanc Te Arai Vineyard, Merlot Te Arai Vineyard, Gisborne Chardonnay Vineyard; **Clos de Ste Anne** Chardonnay, Pinot Noir and Viognier

RECENT AWARDS
Recognition has been achieved by winning numerous gold and silver medals, and trophies at national and international wine competitions.

119 Papatu Rd, Manutuke
Tel: (06) 862 8680
Fax: (06) 862 8869
Email: info@millton.co.nz
Website: www.millton.co.nz

DIRECTIONS
From Gisborne, follow SH2 to Napier for 10 minutes. Papatu Rd is just before Manutuke. Turn up Papatu Rd for 1.5km.

OPENING HOURS
Summer: Mon–Sat, 10am–5pm
Winter: by appointment

WINERY SALES
Cellar door, mail order, Internet

PRICE RANGE $18–$45

TASTING & TOURS
Tasting is free of charge. Tours by appointment.

PICNIC AREA
In summer months only.

OWNERS
James & Annie Millton

WINEMAKER
James Millton

DATE ESTABLISHED 1984

GISBORNE

Open By Appointment

TW Wines
Award-winning wines from the owner's vineyards on the Golden Slope. For vineyard tours, cellar sales, and tastings, please phone Geordie 027 450 2339 or Paul 021 864 818.
Back Ormond Rd
Gisborne
Email: info@twwines.co.nz, Website: www.twwines.co.nz

Kirkpatrick Estate Winery

Kirkpatrick Estate Winery

TW Wines

New plantings, Ormond Valley

The Millton Vineyards

Hawke's Bay

HAWKE'S BAY, on the sheltered east coast of the North Island, is the country's second largest wine region, producing 18.8 per cent of the national crop. Grape-growing takes place from Mahia Peninsula in the north to Cape Kidnappers in the south of Hawke's Bay. There is a diversity of sites within the region, with vineyards spread from high-country foothills in the west, down warmer inland flats and along the cooler coastal plains around the cities of **Hastings** and **Napier**. With a range of soils and climatic influences, there are almost a dozen sub-regions, from **Esk Valley** in the north, inland in the west to **Crownthorpe**, and south to **Central Hawke's Bay**. These produce a wide diversity of varieties and styles, although Hawke's Bay has made its name with soft, fruit-flavoured Sauvignon Blancs, well-rounded Chardonnays and robust reds, including Merlot and Cabernet Sauvignon.

The warm, sunny Hawke's Bay, with the Art Deco city of Napier at its centre, draws visitors to its seaside boulevards and beaches, historical cities, wine trails and restaurants.

For more information visit:
www.hawkesbaynz.com or contact

Napier i-SITE Visitor Centre
100 Marine Parade, Napier
Tel: (06) 834 9611
Email: info@napiervic.co.nz

Hastings i-SITE Visitor Centre
Cnr Heretaunga & Russell Sts
Hastings
Tel: (06) 873 5526
Email: vic@hastingstourism.co.nz

Mike Hollman

HISTORY

Hawke's Bay has a 150-year heritage in wine. Marist missionaries planted the first vines at Pakowhai south of Napier in 1851, and by the 1890s the Mission was selling wines, as were several wealthy landowners. Spanish-born Anthony Vidal was the first commercial winemaker to begin operation, in 1905. The industry languished through the Depression and world wars but several pioneers were producing fortified wines. McWilliam's, established in 1947, was the major winery for many years, producing well-known white and red wines. In the 1960s contract grape-growing helped Hawke's Bay onto the wine map but it was not until the 1990s that the area under vines mushroomed, and careful selection of sites and varieties saw superior wines being produced.

SOILS

There is a diverse range of soil types, from fertile, silty loams with a high water table to free-draining shingle. There are 22 categories of soil types on the Heretaunga Plains alone, from stones to hard pans to heavy silts. Most districts have alluvial flood-plain soils of moderate fertility. Three meandering rivers in the region have laid down deposits over a long period of time. Generally, soils become more fertile the further they are from old riverbeds.

CLIMATE

Hawke's Bay enjoys high sunshine hours, with warm summer temperatures and dryish autumns, but it is frost-prone in cooler months. Shelter from the western mountains means the Bay is less windy than many other regions. Its east coast location also means rainfall is moderate.

GRAPE VARIETIES AND WINE STYLES

Major varieties are Chardonnay, Merlot, Cabernet Sauvignon, Sauvignon Blanc, Pinot Noir and Cabernet Franc. Sweet dessert wines and sparkling wines are also produced. The Chardonnays display rich flavours of stone-fruit and citrus, while Merlot and Cabernet Sauvignon produce wines with rich fruit flavours, among them some of the country's finest reds. The Bay's soft Sauvignon Blancs with melon and stone-fruit flavours are becoming well known. Pinot Noir does not generally ripen well enough in the region's warmth to make premium stand-alone wines, although they do produce good sparkling wine.

SUB-REGIONS

Esk Valley, near the coast north of Napier, cooled by sea breezes.

Dartmoor Valley, based around the Tutaekuri River, often experiences high temperatures, known for both reds and whites.

Crownthorpe (Matapiro), a new sub-region in the west, thought to suit early-ripening varieties.

Mangatahi, in the western foothills, higher than the plains, produces excellent Chardonnay.

Korokipo and Fernhill, including warm sites around the Tutaekuri River that produce excellent Chardonnay. Fertile plains land produces mainly Sauvignon Blanc.

Gimblett Gravels, an area of free-draining alluvial gravels on the inland edge of the Heretaunga Plains, known especially for its late-ripening reds and Chardonnay.

The Red Metal Triangle, also on the edge of the Heretaunga Plains, named for its red metal subsoils that suit earlier-ripening red varieties like Merlot.

Havelock Hills and Te Mata, around the town of Havelock North, has some of the sunniest sites in the region, producing great reds and whites.

Te Awanga, on the southern coastal edge of the Bay, cooled by sea breezes, is producing excellent Chardonnay and early-ripening reds.

Central Hawke's Bay, around the towns of Waipukurau and Waipawa, are new grape-growing areas, higher and cooler than the plains, with free-draining soils.

Church Road Winery

Kim Crawford Wines

Crab Farm

Te Awa Winery

Events

- **Harvest Hawke's Bay.** Annual celebration of wine, food, art and entertainment. Held early February at various vineyards. www.harvesthawkesbay.co.nz
- **WETA Wine & Food Festival.** Wine, food and music at Waipukurau in February. (06) 858 64
- **Matariki Festival.** Celebrations held in June to mark the beginning of the Maori or lunar New Year www.matarikifestival.co.nz. The festival includes The Matariki Wine Dinner, www.matarikiwines.co.nz and Hawke's Bay Vintners' Charity Wine Auction. www.hawkesbaywineauction.co.nz
- **A Month of Wine & Roses.** A festival of Hawke's Bay wine, gardens, art and music, held in November. www.hawkesbaynz.com
- **Wine & Food Safari.** For wine and food lovers a weekend of wine, food, art and jazz. www.wineandfoodsafari.co.nz

For more information on events visit:
www.hawkesbaynz.com

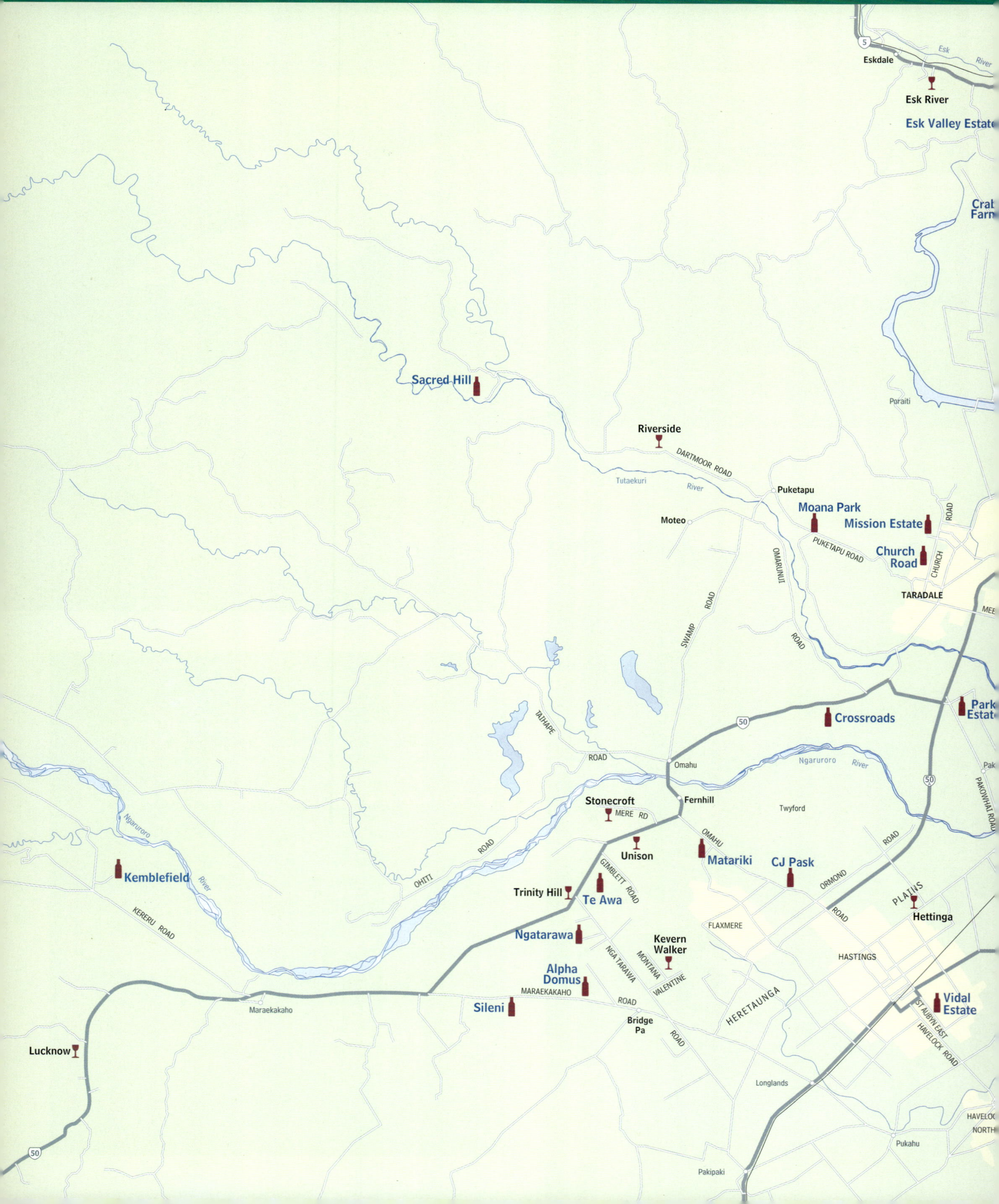
Eskdale
Esk River
Esk Valley Estate
Crab Farm
Sacred Hill
Poraiti
Riverside
DARTMOOR ROAD
Tutaekuri River
Puketapu
Moana Park
Mission Estate
Moteo
PUKETAPU ROAD
Church Road
OMARUNUI ROAD
CHURCH ROAD
TARADALE
SWAMP ROAD
Park Estate
Crossroads
TAIHAPE ROAD
Omahu
Ngaruroro River
Fernhill
Stonecroft
MERE RD
Twyford
PAKOWHAI ROAD
OMAHU ROAD
Unison
Matariki
CJ Pask
Kemblefield
OHITI ROAD
GIMBLETT ROAD
Trinity Hill
Te Awa
ORMOND ROAD
PLAINS
Hettinga
KERERU ROAD
Ngatarawa
FLAXMERE
Kevern Walker
HASTINGS
NGA TARAWA
MONTANA
VALENTINE
Alpha Domus
MARAEKAKAHO ROAD
Sileni
Maraekakaho
Bridge Pa
HERETAUNGA ROAD
Vidal Estate
ST AUBYN EAST
HAVELOCK ROAD
Lucknow
Longlands
Pukahu
Pakipaki

Map labels:

- y View
- Westshore
- Bluff Hill
- NAPIER
- WILLOWBANK
- Meeanee
- **Brookfields**
- Clive
- Whakatu
- Tukituki River
- Haumoana
- Mangateretere
- TE MATA
- **Askerne**
- Te Awanga
- **Clearview Estate**
- **Kim Crawford**
- Clifton
- MANGATERETERE ROAD
- Tukituki River
- Maraetotara River
- **Te Mata** **Akarangi**
- TE MATA RD
- **Black Barn**
- **Craggy Range**

Legend:
- Wineries featured in this book
- Other 'open to visit' wineries

HAWKE'S BAY

Alpha Domus

Situated in the heart of the renowned viticultural district of the Heretaunga Plains, Alpha Domus is dedicated to the production of premium wines. In 2004 Alpha Domus '2000 The Aviator' was judged Best New World Red Wine and selected New Zealand's best Bordeaux-style Red by *Decanter* magazine. The wines are produced exclusively from the well-established vineyards surrounding the winery and are matured in on-site cellars. The friendly, knowledgeable cellar-door team will be glad to take you through an exciting selection of estate wines that include Viognier, Sémillon, Chardonnay, Bordeaux varietal blends and dessert wines. If you are passionate about wine, a visit to Alpha Domus is a must.

WINES
Labels: The Pilot, Alpha Domus including The Navigator, AD including The Aviator.
Wine Styles: Sauvignon Blanc, Chardonnay, Viognier, Sémillon, Rosé, Pinot Noir, Merlot, Merlot/Cabernet, Bordeaux varietal blends of Cabernet Sauvignon/Merlot/Cabernet Franc/Malbec, Late Harvest Sémillon, Noble Sémillon

---

1829 Maraekakaho Rd, Hastings
Tel: (06) 879 6752
Fax: (06) 879 6952
Email: wine@alphadomus.co.nz
Website: www.alphadomus.co.nz

DIRECTIONS Driving south out of Hastings on Maraekakaho Rd from Stortford Lodge, turn right at the roundabout, where Maraekakaho Rd continues. Drive through Bridge Pa and Alpha Domus is 1km on the right.

OPENING HOURS
Summer: 7 days, 10am–5pm
Winter: Fri–Mon, 10am–4pm

WINE SALES
Cellar door, retail, mail order

PRICE RANGE $15–$50

TASTING & TOURS
Tasting is free of charge. Tours by appointment.

OTHER FACILITIES
Shaded area with tables.

OWNER
The Ham family

WINEMAKER
Kate Galloway

DATE ESTABLISHED 1991

HAWKE'S BAY

CJ Pask Winery

CJ Pask has an impressive record of award-winning wines from some of New Zealand's oldest vines. They are the founder of the Gimblett Road appellation where they own 100 hectares of vineyards and are well known internationally for the production of Merlot, Chardonnay, Syrah and Bordeaux blends. The original production of one barrel of Cabernet Sauvignon has now increased to over 45,000 cases and the 2004 vintage has been one of the best, harvesting around 550 tonnes. At the Mediterranean-style winery they produce three tiers of wine in the Roy's Hill, Gimblett Road and Reserve ranges. Each offers a different style, from the fruit-driven, easy-drinking style of Roy's Hill, to the concentrated, full-bodied Reserve wines.

WINES
Roy's Hill Sauvignon Blanc, Chardonnay, Merlot and Cabernet Merlot; **Gimblett Road** Chardonnay, Syrah, Merlot, Cabernet Merlot; **Reserve** Chardonnay, Syrah, Merlot, Declaration (Bordeaux blend)

RECENT AWARDS
Reserve Merlot 1998 – Bordeaux & Cabernet Trophy: International Wine Challenge, London 2000, Champion Wine of Show: Air New Zealand Wine Awards 2000; Kate Radburnd – Hawke's Bay Winemaker of the Year 2001

1133 Omahu Rd, Hastings
Tel: (06) 879 7906
Fax: (06) 879 6428
Email: info@cjpaskwinery.co.nz
Website: www.cjpaskwinery.co.nz

DIRECTIONS On the Fernhill side of the Napier–Hastings Expressway/Omahu Rd intersection, approx. 10 mins from Hastings City centre. Omahu Rd is a key arterial road running from Hastings.

OPENING HOURS
All year: Mon–Fri, 9am–5pm; Sat & public holidays, 10am–5pm; Sun, 11am–4pm

WINERY SALES Cellar door, retail, mail order, Internet

PRICE RANGE $14.50–$45

TASTING & TOURS Tasting is free of charge. Tours by appointment only.

OWNERS
Chris Pask, Kate Radburnd & John Benton

WINEMAKERS
Kate Radburnd & Russell Wiggins

DATE ESTABLISHED 1985

Black Barn Vineyards

Black Barn is a small vineyard focusing on premium Bordeaux-style red varieties such as Merlot, Cabernet Sauvignon and Cabernet Franc; their award-winning whites include Chardonnay and Sauvignon Blanc. All wines are estate-grown and the fruit is hand-picked. With just over 20 acres of vines many of the wines are only available through the cellar door.

Its spectacular location on the warm north-facing slopes of the Te Mata foothills is not only an excellent location for grape-growing, it also provides stunning views across Hawke's Bay to the ocean and mountains, a warm sheltered microclimate and a perfect situation for visitors to spend a few hours, a night, or even a week or two. You can taste wines, have lunch in the Bistro, spend a summer Saturday morning at the Village Growers Market, visit the Art Gallery, watch an evening concert in the amphitheatre, or enjoy all of the above by staying in one of their luxuriously appointed properties.

WINES
Black Barn Sauvignon Blanc, Rosé, Unoaked Chardonnay, Barrel Fermented Chardonnay, Merlot Cabernet Franc (estate blend), Reserve Merlot

RECENT AWARDS
Black Barn Vineyards 2004 Barrel Fermented Chardonnay & 2002 Reserve Merlot both won Gold medals at the Royal Easter Wine Show 2005.

OTHER ACTIVITIES
Village Growers Market: Sat mornings from Labour Weekend during summer. Black Barn Gallery: features smaller works by leading New Zealand artists. Large purpose-built terraced amphitheatre for summer concerts.

HAWKE'S BAY

Black Barn Rd, Havelock North
Tel: (06) 877 7985
Fax: (06) 877 7816
Email: info@blackbarn.com
Website: www.blackbarn.com

DIRECTIONS
Follow Te Mata Rd out of the Havelock North village. Soon after you reach the 70kph zone you will find Black Barn on the right.

OPENING HOURS
Cellar door: 7 days, 10am–5pm. Bistro: Wed–Sun, 12pm–3pm for lunch. Functions by arrangement.

WINERY SALES
Cellar door, retail, Internet

PRICE RANGE
$20–$60

TASTING & TOURS
Tasting fee: $2, refundable on purchase. Tours by appointment.

CAFÉ
Black Barn Bistro: Open airy restaurant with beautiful views, a sheltered vine-covered courtyard for outdoor dining and innovative seasonal menu. Reservations: (06) 877 7985.

OTHER FACILITIES
Private functions and dinners can be held in the Bistro, Art Gallery, Underground Cellars and the Growers Market.

PICNIC AREA
The vineyard has walkways and park-like grounds to explore and find your own picnic spot.

ACCOMMODATION
The Black Barn private retreats are Hawke's Bay's most sought after accommodation. In spectacular locations and luxuriously appointed, they sleep from 1–6 couples. Two of the six properties are on the vineyard; the others are at a nearby beach, a river and Cape Kidnappers. View at www.blackbarn.com.

OWNERS
Andy Coltart & Kim Thorp

WINEMAKER
Dave McKee

DATE ESTABLISHED 2003

HAWKE'S BAY

150 Church Rd, Taradale
Napier
Tel: (06) 844 2053
Fax: (06) 844 3378
Email: thecellardoor@churchroad.co.nz
Website: www.churchroad.co.nz

DIRECTIONS
The Church Rd Winery is on Church Rd in Taradale, just 15 minutes from the Napier and Hastings town centres.

OPENING HOURS
7 days, 9am–5pm

WINERY SALES
Cellar door, retail, mail order (through the winery newsletter Church Rd Cellar Notes)

PRICE RANGE $15–$135

TASTING
Sample the wines that have been specially selected (no charge for these samples) or buy a Cellarmaster's Tasting Tray.

TOURS
Daily at 10am, 11am, 2pm and 3pm: small charge applicable; bookings for groups essential.

RESTAURANT
Church Rd Restaurant. Lunch from 11.30am daily. Bookings advisable. Reservations: (06) 845 9140.

OTHER PRODUCTS
Older vintage Church Rd wines and the limited-edition Church Rd Cuve Series, other premium wines and quality gifts and accessories.

OTHER FACILITIES
The historic Church Rd Winery offers superb function and conference facilities, and is an ideal venue for business meetings, weddings, social events or special private celebrations.

OWNER
Allied Domecq Wines (NZ) Ltd

WINEMAKER
Chris Scott

DATE ESTABLISHED 1897

Church Road Winery

Founded in 1897, the historic Church Road Winery offers a uniquely New Zealand wine tourism experience. Trace a fascinating journey through winemaking history with a tour of the country's first wine museum and visit the magnificent Tom McDonald Cellar, created in memory of the father of quality red-winemaking in New Zealand. The museum, opened in 1998, celebrates the history of wine. Housed underground in wine tanks once used by Tom McDonald, some of the exhibits on display date back to Roman times. Others are among the oldest winemaking relics in the country, while local sculptor Owen Yeomans' lifelike mannequins bring the scene alive. The Tom McDonald Cellar contains hundreds of oak barrels used for the maturation of premium wines.

Sample the wines that have been specially selected or buy a Cellarmaster's Tasting Tray. For those who just want to relax in an elegant rustic setting, modern European-style food can be enjoyed indoors in the charming Tiffen Room or served alfresco in the picturesque garden.

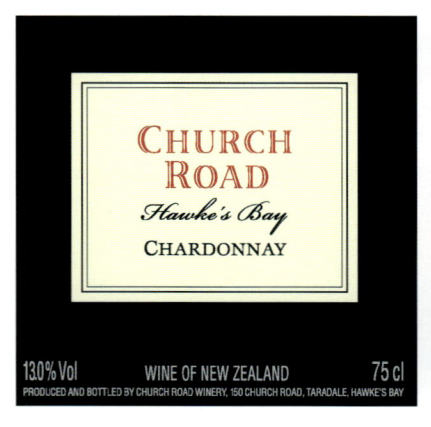

WINES
Tom, Virtu, Cuve Series Chardonnay, Sauvignon Blanc, Viognier, Malbec; **Church Road Reserve** Merlot Cabernet, Chardonnay, Noble Sémillon; **Church Road** Chardonnay, Sauvignon Blanc, Merlot Cabernet

RECENT AWARDS
Church Road Merlot Cabernet 2002 – Five stars: Michael Cooper, *Sunday Star-Times*, May 04; Church Road Chardonnay 2002 – Silver: NZ Wine Society Royal Easter Wine Show 2003; Four stars: Best Wines of 2003, *Winestate Annual* 04; Four stars: *Cuisine* magazine Jul 05; Church Road Reserve Chardonnay 2002 – Silver: Liquorland Top 100 2004; Virtu 2000 – Gold: Liquorland Top 100 2004, Top 100 & Blue-Gold: Sydney International Wine Challenge 2004

HAWKE'S BAY

Clearview Estate Winery & Restaurant

Clearview Estate is a small, established boutique winery and vineyard on the coast of Hawke's Bay, with stunning views to Cape Kidnappers. Hand-crafted, award-winning wines are produced from intensively managed vines, which enjoy the long ripening season of the coastal microclimate. All grapes are estate-grown and hand-picked. The Clearview restaurant has received the Beef & Lamb award 5 times since 1998 and was recently voted as being among the top six winery restaurants of New Zealand by the *Dominion Post*. The Cellar Door has been voted as being one of the top 13 in Australasia by *Gourmet Traveller Wine*, Autumn 2005.

WINES
Clearview Sauvignon Blanc, Unwooded Chardonnay, Beachhead Chardonnay, Sémillon, Gewürztraminer, Merlot, Reserve Sauvignon Blanc, Reserve Chardonnay, Old Olive Block (Bordeaux blend), Enigma (Bordeaux blend) Noble Harvest Chardonnay

RECENT AWARDS
Noble 51 Dessert Wine – Trophy: International Chardonnay Competition 2003; Tim Turvey – Champion Wine Maker, Reserve Chardonnay 2000 – Champion of Champions Wine: Hawke's Bay A&P Mercedes-Benz Show 2001

194 Clifton Rd, RD2, Hastings
Tel: (06) 875 0150
Fax: (06) 875 1258
sales@clearviewestate.co.nz
Website: www.clearviewestate.co.nz

DIRECTIONS
Situated just before the township of Te Awanga, 20 minutes' drive from Napier or Hastings along the coastline towards Cape Kidnappers.

OPENING HOURS
Cellar door & restaurant:
Summer: 7 days, 10am–5pm
Winter: Fri–Tues, 10am–5pm

WINERY SALES
Cellar door, mail order, retail, trade

PRICE RANGE $16–$200

TASTING & TOURS
Full range available and tasting is free of charge. Group tastings by appointment only. Vineyard & winery tours: 11am & 3pm.

RESTAURANT
Cosy indoor and outdoor dining, in a sheltered courtyard or amongst the vines. The seasonal menu uses the best of local produce. Tel: (06) 875 0150

EVENTS & ACTIVITIES
Winemaker workshops, monthly dinners, seafood safaris, weddings

OWNERS
Tim Turvey & Helma van den Berg

WINEMAKERS
Tim Turvey

DATE ESTABLISHED 1989

HAWKE'S BAY

Crab Farm Winery & Kitchen

When winemaker Hamish Jardine's great-grandfather first acquired land at Bay View he was alarmed to find it covered with tidal water, rushes and hundreds of crabs — the family jokingly called it 'Crab Farm'. In 1931 the great Hawke's Bay earthquake lifted the land above sea level creating the site of the present-day 12-hectare vineyard and rustic winery. Hamish Jardine produces wine with solid memorable character at extremely good value from this coastal Hawke's Bay vineyard.

Renovations over the winter months will take the cellar door and cuisine experience to a new innovative style. It's a dare-to-be-different approach with genius.

WINES
Crab Farm Gewürztraminer, Sauvignon Blanc, Chardonnay, Cabernet Sauvignon, Cabernet Franc, Cabernet Merlot, Merlot, Pinot Noir, Hamish Jardine Pukera Terraces Malbec Merlot.

RECENT AWARDS
Crab Farm wines regularly receive awards and star rating in NZ and overseas.

511 Main North Rd
Bay View, Napier
Tel: (06) 836 6678
Fax: (06) 836 7379
Email: info@crabfarmwinery.co.nz
Website: www.crabfarmwinery.co.nz

DIRECTIONS
Situated just north of Napier and Hawke's Bay Airport. Only 5 minutes from city centre.

OPENING HOURS
Summer: 7 days, 10am–4pm
Winter: 6 days (closed on Tues), 10.30am–3.30pm

WINERY SALES
Cellar door, retail, mail order

PRICE RANGE
$14.95–$30

RESTAURANT
Kitchen open for lunch, summer and winter. Reservations essential: (06) 836 6678

OWNER
James Jardine

WINEMAKERS
Hamish Jardine

DATE ESTABLISHED 1978

HAWKE'S BAY

253 Waimarama Rd, Havelock North
Tel: (06) 873 7126
Fax: (06) 873 7141
Email: info@craggyrange.com
Website: www.craggyrange.com

DIRECTIONS
Head out of Havelock North village on Te Mata Rd, turn right at the T intersection of Te Mata Rd and Waimarama Rd and go up and over the hill to Craggy Range which is on your left.

OPENING HOURS
7 days, from 10am

WINERY SALES
Cellar door, retail, mail order

PRICE RANGE
$20–$60

TASTING & TOURS
Tasting fee $5, refundable on purchase. Winery tours through the Bordeaux fermentation hall and underground cellar. Weekends, 11am (reservations recommended), $20 pp, duration 90 minutes.

RESTAURANT
Winery restaurant Terrôir at Craggy Range. Reservations: (06) 873 0143

PICNIC AREA
Picnics made to order by Terrôir at Craggy Range.

ACCOMMODATION
Cellar Master's Cottage sleeps 4, Te Hau Lodge sleeps 6. Reservations and rates: (06) 873 7126

EVENTS & ACTIVITES
Refer website: www.craggyrange.com

OWNERS
The Peabody & Smith families

WINEMAKERS
Adrian Baker & Rod Easthope

DATE ESTABLISHED 1999

Craggy Range Vineyards

Nestled in the Tukituki Valley is the home of Craggy Range. With one of New Zealand's most beautiful trout fishing rivers to the east and the massive symbolic escarpment of Te Mata Peak to the west, the Craggy Range Giants Winery is a very special place.

Terrôir, the restaurant of Craggy Range, prides itself on providing the best of New Zealand food, with a French country theme. It specialises in rotisserie and wood-fired oven cooking while showcasing the single vineyard wines from Craggy Range.

In the heart of the Giants Winery complex is the Craggy Range Cellar Door. Experienced and passionate about wine, the cellar-door staff will take you through the Craggy Range wines from their vineyards in Hawke's Bay, Marlborough, Martinborough and the Waitaki Valley.

Amongst the Chardonnay vines is the Cellar Master's Cottage. This self-contained luxury accommodation has two double rooms, both with en suites and views of Te Mata Peak and the Tukituki River Valley.

WINES
Labels: Craggy Range Varietal Collection and Prestige Collection
Wine styles: Chardonnay, Sauvignon Blanc, Pinot Noir, Pinot Gris, Syrah, Merlot

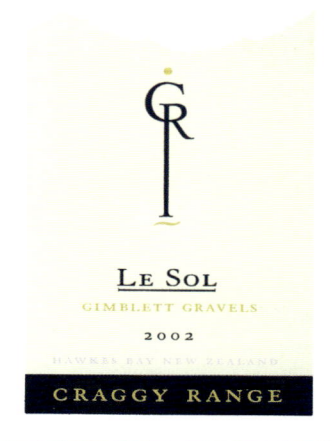

Crossroads Winery

Crossroads Winery and Vineyard sits in the wine-growing district of Fernhill. A boutique winery founded in 1990 it has rapidly gained a reputation for producing elegant wines of high quality and consistency. The company selects premium fruit from its vineyards in Hawke's Bay located on the north-facing terraces of the beautiful Ngauroro River and in the Gimblett Gravels, and Marlborough where the stony, free-draining soils and sunny climate result in full fruit-style wines. At Crossroads the quality of its wines, the ambience of the winery and vineyards and the warmth of the welcome from the cellar-door team make it a very attractive place to visit.

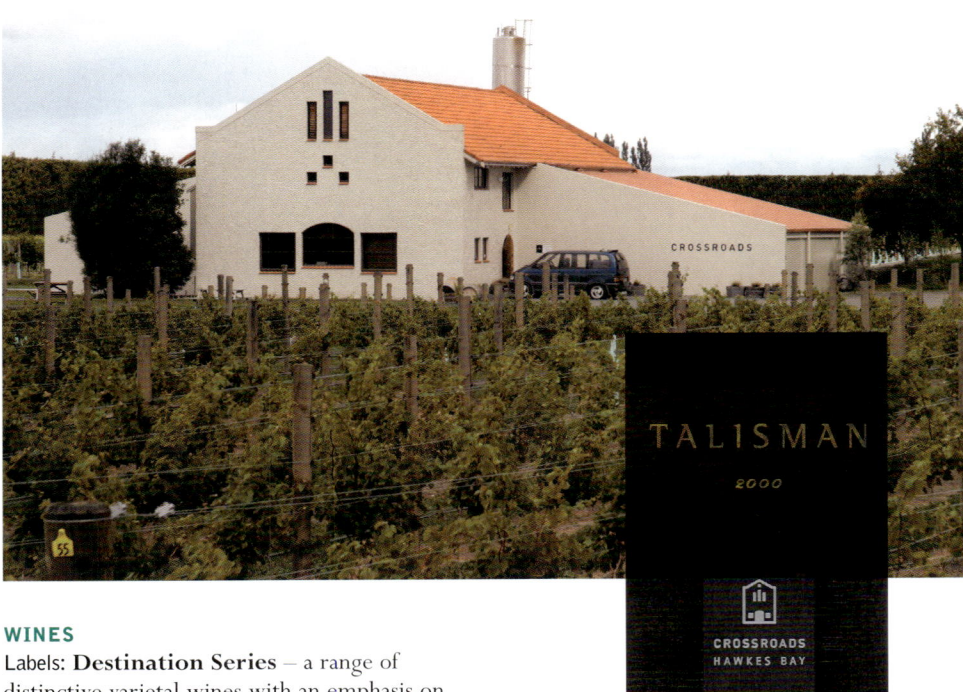

WINES

Labels: Destination Series – a range of distinctive varietal wines with an emphasis on obvious fruit character, regional typicity and superior drinkability. **Collectors Edition** – a limited range of wine, made only in years where the exceptional fruit quality dictates extra-special attention in the vineyard and winery. These wines tend to be richer, more complex and benefit from careful cellaring. **Talisman** – Crossroads' flagship brand, Talisman is a full-bodied dry red made from a mystery blend of six grape varieties.
Wine Styles: Riesling, Gewürztraminer, Sauvignon Blanc, Chardonnay, Pinot Noir, Merlot/Cabernet Sauvignon, Cabernet/Merlot, Syrah

RECENT AWARDS

Crossroads Destination Series Marlborough Sauvignon Blanc 2004 – Gold: Starwine Award, Pennsylvania USA; Crossroads Destination Series Hawke's Bay Merlot Cabernet 2001 – Silver: Starwine Award, Pennsylvania USA; Crossroads Talisman 2000 – Top 50 Wines from 2000: *Wine Magazine* UK

HAWKE'S BAY

1747 Korokipo Rd
SH50, Fernhill
Tel: (06) 879 9737
Fax: (06) 879 6068

DIRECTIONS
5 minutes from Taradale on SH50 and 10 minutes from Hastings travelling along Omahu Rd to Fernhill.

OPENING HOURS
Summer (Labour Weekend–Easter Weekend): 7 days, 10am–5pm
Winter (Easter Weekend–Labour Weekend): 7 days, 11am–4pm

WINERY SALES
Cellar door, retail, mail order, Internet, winery newsletter

PRICE RANGE
$9.95–$38

TASTING & TOURS
Tasting is free of charge for groups of 8 or less. Large groups by appointment.

PICNIC AREA
Visitors are welcome to picnic on the lawn and stroll through the vineyard. Picnic tables and umbrellas are available.

OWNER
Ager Sectus Company Ltd

WINEMAKERS
Matthew Mitchell & Miles Dinneen

DATE ESTABLISHED 1989

HAWKE'S BAY

Esk Valley Estate

Esk Valley Estate is one of Hawke's Bay's leading boutique wineries specialising in creating exceptional hand-crafted wines. Winemaker Gordon Russell places emphasis on quality rather than quantity and his quirky yet fun character helps give Esk Valley wines their uniqueness.

A trip to Esk Valley is an opportunity to taste and buy wines, including limited-quantity wines sold only through the cellar door. One of the most attractive vineyard sites in New Zealand, winery, cellar shop and famed Terraced Vineyard are nestled in a small picturesque valley with stunning views over the Hawke's Bay coastline and Pacific Ocean.

WINES
Black Label Chardonnay, Sauvignon Blanc, Merlot and Merlot/Cabernet Sauvignon, Viognier, Riesling, Pinot Gris, Chenin Blanc, Rosé; **Reserve** Chardonnay and a Merlot/Malbec/Cabernet blend; **Terraces** (only available *en primeur*)

RECENT AWARDS
Four of the last five vintages of Esk Valley's Reserve Red have received 5 Stars from *Cuisine* magazine. Two of the last five vintages have been trophy winners in prestigious competitions.

Main Rd, Bay View
Napier
Tel: (06) 836 6411
Fax (06) 836 6413
Email: enquiries@eskvalley.co.nz
Website: www.eskvalley.co.nz

DIRECTIONS
12km north of Napier on SH2. Ten mins from Napier Airport.

OPENING HOURS
7 days, 10am–5pm

WINERY SALES
Cellar door, retail, mail order and Internet

PRICE RANGE From $18.95

TASTING & TOURS
Tasting is free of charge. Tours by appointment only ($5 pp).

OTHER FACILITIES
Picnic area with tables.

OWNER
George Fistonich

WINEMAKER
Gordon Russell

DATE ESTABLISHED 1933

HAWKE'S BAY

Kemblefield Estate Winery

In the early 1990s Californians John Kemble and Kaar Field began their search for a location to establish what has become Kemblefield Estate Winery. John researched several sites in New Zealand before finally settling on Mangatahi, Hawke's Bay. He felt its unique microclimate, reminiscent of his California homeland, was the ideal place to combine his winemaking knowledge with superb Hawke's Bay grapes. From its beginning in July 1992, Kemblefield has grown and developed, turning a 200-hectare farm into the successful vineyard and winery it is today.

WINES
Winemaker's Signature Sauvignon Blanc, Chardonnay, Cabernet Sauvignon Merlot; **The Distinction** Chardonnay, Gewürztraminer, Pinot Gris, Sémillon, Merlot; **The Reserve** Malbec Merlot, Zinfandel

RECENT AWARDS
Reserve Zinfandel 2002 – Gold: International Wine Challenge London 2004; The Distinction Merlot 2002 – Gold: International Wine Challenge of Asia 2004

OTHER PRODUCTS
Kemblefield Olive Oil

Aorangi Rd, RD1, Hastings
Tel: (06) 874 9649
Fax: (06) 874 9457
Email: info@kemblefield.co.nz
Website: www.kemblefield.co.nz

DIRECTIONS
Turn into Kereru Rd at the Maraekakaho Junction. Continue for approx 5km, turn right into Aorangi Rd, and right again into Kemblefield Tce.

OPENING HOURS
Mon–Fri, 9am–4pm
Sat & Sun, 10.30am–4.30pm

WINERY SALES
Cellar door, mail order, retail, Internet

PRICE RANGE
$16–$50

TASTING & TOURS
Tasting is free of charge. For groups of more than 10, there is a charge of $2 pp. Winery tours by appointment only.

FOOD OPTIONS
A selection of picnic foods are available for purchase.

PICNIC AREA
Picnic tables and gas barbecue facilities.

OTHER FACILITIES
The Visitor & Function Centre is available for weddings, functions, and conferences.

OWNER
Kemblefield Estate Winery Ltd

WINEMAKERS
John Kemble & Richard Rhodes

DATE ESTABLISHED 1992

HAWKE'S BAY

Kim Crawford Wines

Kim Crawford Wines is located in the quiet coastal settlement of Te Awanga in Hawke's Bay. The modern tasting room has sweeping views from Mahia Peninsula across the Bay to Cape Kidnappers, taking in rural farmland and the immaculately tended Te Awanga vineyards. Visitors are welcome to try the range of award-winning wines made from grapes sourced from vineyard sites in Hawke's Bay, Marlborough and Gisborne, where Kim believes the grapes grow best. There is a widely held belief at this winery that a happy working environment is transferred to the bottle … you can almost taste it in the wine!

WINES
Kim Crawford Riesling, Pinot Gris, Sauvignon Blanc, Chardonnay, Rosé, Pinot Noir, Merlot and a range of small parcel wines from selected vineyards

RECENT AWARDS
Kim Crawford Wines received over 60 awards in 2004.

ACCOMMODATION
Above the cellar door is a self-contained, 1-bedroom apartment. Accommodation package includes ingredients for a Kiwi breakfast, antipasto platter and a bottle of wine per day. $200 per night for a 2-night stay. *Regrettably not suitable for children.*

Clifton Rd, Te Awanga
Tel: (06) 875 0553
Fax: (06) 875 1188
Email: info@kimcrawfordwines.co.nz
Website: www.kimcrawfordwines.co.nz

DIRECTIONS
Just south of Clive, turn into Mill Rd, follow the road to Haumoana and on to Clifton Rd. Kim Crawford Wines is right next to Clearview.

OPENING HOURS
Summer: 7 days, 11am–6pm
Winter: Sat–Mon, 11am–5pm

WINERY SALES
Cellar door, retail, mail order

PRICE RANGE $15–$40

TASTING
Tasting is free of charge.

OTHER FOOD OPTIONS
Picnics and tasting platters made from locally sourced ingredients.

PICNIC AREA
Visitors are welcome to picnic on the lawn, enjoy the stunning view and the peace and tranquillity of this site. Tables and picnic blankets are supplied.

OWNER
Vincor International

WINEMAKER
Kim Crawford

DATE ESTABLISHED 1996

HAWKE'S BAY

Moana Park Winery

In 1979 Ron Smith planted his first vines in Hawke's Bay's Dartmoor Valley. In 2000 (over two decades and 200,000 vines later) he began producing wines under his own label. Moana Park is now a successful privately owned boutique winery with an American-style barn for its cellar door along with a newly completed winery and barrel room. There is a friendly atmosphere and visitors are encouraged to bring a picnic and enjoy their wines in a charming rural setting. Wines are mostly single varietals that express the characteristics of the grapes sourced exclusively from their two family-owned vineyards: in Puketapu, where the winery and cellar door are situated, and nearby in the heart of the Dartmoor Valley.

WINES
Moana Park Pascoe Series (entry level) Sauvignon Blanc, Chardonnay, Rosé, Merlot Cabernet, Syrah;
Vineyard Tribute Pinot Gris, Chardonnay, Merlot, Malbec, Cabernet Franc, Syrah Symphony (top red blend)

RECENT AWARDS
Pascoe Series Sauvignon Blanc 2002 – 85/100: *Wine Spectator* (Sept 2003); Vineyard Tribute Cabernet Franc 2002 – Silver: Air New Zealand Wine Awards 2003; Pascoe Series Chardonnay 2004 – 4 stars: *Cuisine* magazine

---

530 Puketapu Rd, Napier
Tel: (06) 844 8269
Fax: (06) 844 0923
Email: sales@moanapark.co.nz
Website: www.moanapark.co.nz

DIRECTIONS
From Taradale the winery is just 5km along Puketapu Rd (5 mins from Church Rd).

OPENING HOURS
Labour Weekend–Easter: 7 days, 11am–5pm; Easter–Labour Weekend: 7 days, 1pm–4pm

WINERY SALES
Cellar door, retail, mail order

PRICE RANGE $11–$35

TASTING & TOURS
Tasting is free of charge. Tours by appointment.

FOOD OPTIONS
Cheese platters available by arrangement.

PICNIC AREA
BYO picnic. Picnic facilities: tables, pétanque.

OTHER FACILITIES
Marquee sites are available for weddings and functions.

OWNER
Ron Smith

WINEMAKER
Derek Clarke

DATE ESTABLISHED 2000

HAWKE'S BAY

52 Kirkwood Rd, RD5, Hastings
Tel: (06) 879 6226
Fax: (06) 879 6228
Email: kate@matarikiwines.co.nz
Website: www.matarikiwines.co.nz

DIRECTIONS
Kirkwood Rd is off Omahu Rd, Hastings West. Coming from Napier, take the Expressway and then make a right exit off the roundabout onto Omahu Rd. Follow Omahu Rd for approx. 5 mins. Kirkwood Rd is on the left.

OPENING HOURS
7 days: 10am–5pm

WINERY SALES
Cellar door, retail, mail order, Internet

PRICE RANGE
$17.95–$48

TASTING & TOURS
Tasting is free of charge, tours of the winery and group visits by appointment only.

EVENTS
Matariki Festival Dinner. Musical, cultural and gastronomic delights teamed with Matariki Wines. Held each year in June in the Barrel Hall.

OWNERS
John & Rosémary O'Connor

WINEMAKERS
John O'Connor & Amelia Bates

DATE ESTABLISHED 1992

John O'Connor

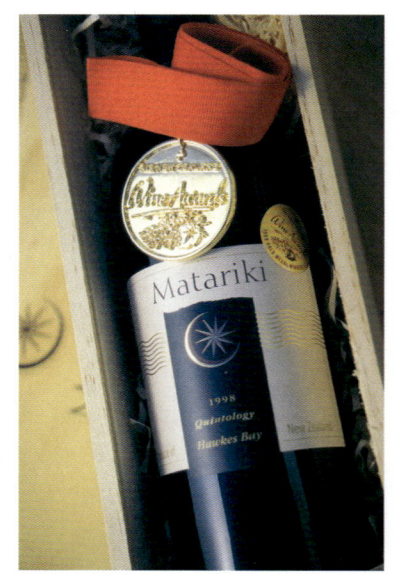

Matariki Wines

Matariki is the Maori name for the cluster of stars Pleiades whose annual journey across the sky controls the seasons and encourages the earth to provide us with her bounty. John and Rosémary established Matariki Wines in 1992 and they proudly chose the name to reflect their dedication to the land and their 100 per cent New Zealand ownership. The main vineyard lies in the heart of the prestigious Gimblett Gravels appellation where the owners carefully analysed the meandering contours of the old riverbed and matched soil types to produce their range of classic wines.

The winery and intimate cellar door is open every day and situated less than 15 minutes' drive from both Hastings and Napier city centres. Visitors are warmly welcomed to experience first-hand the internationally acclaimed wines from Matariki's exceptional vineyards. From the gold medal-winning Reserve 2003 Sauvignon Blanc and outstanding 2004 Reserve Chardonnay to the complex and elegant Bordeaux varieties of Merlot, Cabernet Sauvignon, Quintology and Matariki's well-known Syrah, you can be sure a visit to Matariki Wines will awaken your senses.

WINES
Labels: Matariki Reserve, Matariki, Matariki Aspire, Stony Bay (US only)
Wine styles: Bordeaux varieties, Syrah, Pinot Noir, Sangiovese, Sauvignon Blanc, Chardonnay, Late Harvest Riesling, Blanc de Blancs

RECENT AWARDS
Reserve Chardonnay 2004 – 5 stars: *Cuisine* magazine Jun 05; Reserve Sauvignon Blanc 2003 – Gold: New Zealand Royal Easter Show 2005; Quintology 2001 – Reserve Champion: Houston International Wine Show 2005; Quintology 1998 – Gold: International Wine Challenge London 2000; Reserve Cabernet Sauvignon 2000 – Blue-Gold: Sydney International Wine Show 2003

OTHER PRODUCTS
Matariki Olives, Olive Oil and Balsamic Vinegar

Mission Estate Winery

Established in 1851, Mission Estate is New Zealand's oldest winery – a unique historical venue. Located in Hawke's Bay, Mission Estate was established by French Catholic missionaries who originally planted vines for the production of sacramental wines. In 1875 the first recorded commercial wine sale was made.

Today Mission Estate is one of Hawke's Bay's largest wineries, with a well-respected reputation in New Zealand and overseas as a producer of consistent quality, value-for-money wines. The beautiful old seminary building has been faithfully restored and is home to the cellar door, Mission Restaurant, and Gallery at the Mission. A full range of award-winning wines are available at the Cellar Door, with historical tours being conducted twice daily. Mission Estate also includes a world-class restaurant offering both indoor and outdoor dining where visitors can enjoy magnificent vineyard and city views, delicious cuisine, discerning service and award-winning wines. The Mission Restaurant also caters for weddings, corporate functions and special occasions.

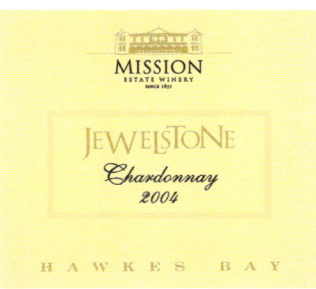

WINES
Labels: Mission Estate, Mission Vineyard Selection, Mission Reserve, Mission Jewelstone
Wine styles: Chardonnay, Sauvignon Blanc, Riesling, Gewürztraminer, Pinot Gris, Ice Wine, Sémillon, Merlot, Cabernet Merlot, Cabernet Sauvignon, Syrah

RECENT AWARDS
Mission Estate wines regularly receive awards at the major New Zealand wine shows.

OTHER ACTIVITIES
Gallery at the Mission: Stocks an extensive range of local art and craft including pottery, jewellery, woodwork, furniture, paintings, and hand-woven woollen rugs and scarves.

HAWKE'S BAY

198 Church Rd, Taradale
Napier
Tel: (06) 845 9350
Fax: (06) 844 6023
Email: missionwinery@clear.net.nz
Website: www.missionestate.co.nz

DIRECTIONS
Mission Estate is on Church Rd in Taradale, just 15 mins from Napier and Hastings town centres.

OPENING HOURS
Cellar door: Mon–Sat, 9am–5pm
Sun: 10am–4.30pm. Extended hours Labour Weekend–Easter. Restaurant: 7 days, 10am–late. The Gallery at the Mission: 7 days, 10am–5pm

WINERY SALES
Cellar door, retail, mail order, Internet

PRICE RANGE $14.95–$35

TASTING & TOURS
Groups larger than 10 persons by appointment. Winery history and underground barrel room tours: Mon–Sat, 10.30am & 2pm. Private tours & tasting by arrangement.

RESTAURANT
Reservations: (06) 845 9354

EVENTS
The annual Mission Estate concert is held in February. A unique event set outdoors in a natural amphitheatre with a line-up of memorable acts. For information: www.missionconcert.co.nz

OWNER
Marist Holdings (Greenmeadows) Ltd

WINEMAKER
Paul Mooney

DATE ESTABLISHED 1851

HAWKE'S BAY

305 Ngatarawa Rd
Bridge Pa, Hastings
Tel: (06) 879 7603
Freephone: 0508 STABLES
Fax: (06) 879 6675
Email: info@ngatarawa.co.nz
Website: www.ngatarawa.co.nz

DIRECTIONS
Driving south out of Hastings from Stortford Lodge, turn right into Maraekakaho Rd at the roundabout. Continue approx 3km and turn right into Ngatarawa Rd.

OPENING HOURS
7 days. Summer: 10am–5pm, Winter: 11am–4pm. Closed Christmas Day and Good Friday.

WINERY SALES
Cellar door, retail, mail order, Internet

PRICE RANGE
$15–$100

TASTING & TOURS
Tasting is free of charge. Groups welcome by appointment. A per person rate may apply to large tour groups. Bus and motorhome access.

FOOD OPTIONS
Platters arranged if booked in advance.

PICNIC AREA
Picturesque landscaped grounds include a large lily pond, and sweeping lawns with panoramic views over the vines. Picnic tables, gas barbecue, pétanque. Child-friendly.

OWNERS
Cousins, Alwyn & Brian Corban

WINEMAKERS
Alwyn Corban & Peter Gough

DATE ESTABLISHED 1981

Ngatarawa Wines

'In the New World of winemaking, there are few producers who have a culture of pedigree, that factor that brings generations of the *feel* of wine craft to its wines. The emergence of Ngatarawa on one of Hawke's Bay's great estates in the 1980s, its winemaking in the hands of that rarest of rarities, a fourth generation New Zealand winemaker, held the promise of a truly local expression of pedigree. Twenty years on, that promise has been realised, not just in the unique nature of the impressive Heretaunga estate on which it is located, but in the way Alwyn Corban has reflected a landed dignity in his wines . . . that they have become symbols of class to the whole community.' Keith Stewart, *NZ Management* magazine, November 2004

Ngatarawa is located on an ancient riverbed in the Bridge Pa Triangle west of Hastings. Pronounced Naa-Taa-Ra-Wa, it translates from Maori to mean 'between the ridges'. Housed in historic racing stables Ngatarawa is among the most picturesque wineries in New Zealand. Visitors to the cellar door have the opportunity to taste premium wines and enjoy their hospitality in a timeless environment.

WINES
Labels: Stables (softer, everyday), Silks (premium varietal), Glazebrook (regional reserve), Alwyn (winemakers' reserve)
Wine styles: Sauvignon Blanc, Chardonnay, Merlot and Cabernet blends, Syrah, Pinot Noir, and Riesling mainly for dessert wine

RECENT AWARDS
Alwyn Chardonnay 2002 – 5 stars: Michael Cooper, *Sunday Star-Times* Feb 04, 5 stars: *Winestate* May/Jun 04; Glazebrook Merlot 2002 – Silver: Cool Climate Wine Show 2005; Silks Chardonnay 2004 – 4 stars: *Cuisine* magazine; Stables Chardonnay 2004 – 4 stars: *Cuisine* magazine

Alwyn Corban

Peter Gough

HAWKE'S BAY

Park Estate Winery

Established on 20 hectares between the two main rivers of Hawke's Bay, Ngaruroro and Tutaekuri, family-owned Park Estate Winery has been transformed from a fruit orchard into a wine and food tourist attraction. Ideally situated halfway between Napier and Hastings, the Park Estate complex and gastronomy food store is a unique opportunity to enjoy the attributes that Hawke's Bay is famous for: a wonderful climate, friendly people, fine wines and delicious food, in-season fruits, organic beverages, and a complete taste experience in an idyllic vineyard/orchard setting. The Café/Restaurant provides a relaxing Mediterranean atmosphere ideal for alfresco summer lunches under the fruit trees or a cosy winter meal beside the open fire.

WINES
Park Estate Chardonnay, Sauvignon Blanc, Riesling, Merlot, Cabernet Franc, Cabernet Sauvignon, Pinotage, Pinot Noir, Gamay, Syrah

OTHER PRODUCTS
The Orchard Store next to the restaurant offers in-season fruits from the estate's orchard, locally made produce including organic fruit juice, vinegars (including balsamic), jams, chutneys and sauces, home-made fudge and real-fruit frozen yoghurts

2087 Pakowhai Rd, Napier
Tel: (06) 844 8137
Fax: (06) 844 6800
Email: park.est@clear.net.nz
Website: www.parkestate.co.nz

DIRECTIONS
Located halfway between Napier and Hastings. Turn into Pakowhai Rd from the Expressway (look for the Park Estate sign). Park Estate is on the left.

OPENING HOURS
Cellar door: 7 days, 10am–5.30pm. Restaurant: summer: 7 days, 11am–4pm; winter: Thurs–Mon, 11am–4pm

WINERY SALES
Cellar door, retail, mail order

PRICE RANGE $15–$28

TASTING
Tasting is free of charge.

RESTAURANT
Open for lunch with a comprehensive à la carte menu, using local fresh produce.
Reservations: (06) 844 8137

OTHER FACILITIES
Available for weddings and special events catering for up to 120 people.

OWNERS
Owen & Dianne Park

WINEMAKER
Owen Park

DATE ESTABLISHED 1995

HAWKE'S BAY

Sacred Hill Wines

Established in 1986 by the Mason family, Sacred Hill has built a reputation for producing multi award-winning hand-crafted wines from Hawke's Bay and more recently Marlborough. The winery's name is derived from the translation of Puketapu ('Sacred Hill'), a small village close to the family estate in the Dartmoor Valley. Sacred Hill has estate vineyards located in Hawke's Bay's Dartmoor and Gimblett Gravels sub-regions as well as a new vineyard which is being established in Marlborough's Waihopai Valley. The picturesque Cellar Door is situated in idyllic park-like surrounds nestled amongst mature trees within the Mason family's farm estate. Open for a limited period each year, the cellar-door staff are renowned for their friendly and informative approach to wine tasting, making Sacred Hill one of Hawke's Bay's more popular winery destinations.

WINES
Labels: Whitecliff, Reserve, Special Selection
Wine Styles: Sauvignon Blanc, Chardonnay, Riesling, Pinot Gris, Botrytis Sémillon, Rosé, White Cabernet, Merlot, Cabernet, Syrah, Pinot Noir, Bordeaux varietal blends

RECENT AWARDS
Marlborough Riesling – Trophy Champion Riesling: New Zealand Wine Society Royal Easter Show Wine Awards 2005; White Cabernet – Trophy Champion Rosé: Sydney International Wine Competition 2005; Riflemans Chardonnay – Trophy Champion Chardonnay and Champion Wine of Show: New Zealand Wine Society Royal Easter Wine Show 2004

1033 Dartmoor Rd, Puketapu
Tel: (06) 844 0138
Tel: (06) 879 8760 (admin)
Fax: (06) 879 4158 (admin)
Email: enquiries@sacredhill.com
Website: www.sacredhill.com

DIRECTIONS
10km from Puketapu on Dartmoor Rd.

OPENING HOURS
Dec–Feb: 7 days, 11am–5pm

WINERY SALES
Cellar door, retail, mail order, Internet

PRICE RANGE $15–$50

TASTING
Tasting is free of charge.

PICNIC AREA
There are plenty of beautiful picnic spots around the estate grounds with tables and a pétanque court.

OWNER
The Mason family

WINEMAKER
Tony Bish

DATE ESTABLISHED 1986

HAWKE'S BAY

2016 Maraekakaho Rd
Bridge Pa, Hastings
Tel: (06) 879 8768
Fax: (06) 879 7187
Email: info@sileni.co.nz
Website: www.sileni.co.nz

DIRECTIONS
Head south out of Hastings along Maraekakaho Rd. Follow the signs to Bridge Pa and Sileni is 3km further on.

OPENING HOURS
Cellar shop: 7 days, 10am–5pm
Restaurant: Lunch, 7 days from 11am; Dinner, Thurs–Sat from 6pm

WINERY SALES
Cellar door, retail, mail order, Internet

PRICE RANGE $19.50–$99

TASTING & TOURS
Tasting fee: $5 pp, refundable on purchase. Tours available 7 days, 11am & 2pm: $12 pp (includes wine tasting).

RESTAURANT
Open for casual lunches and evening dining. Bookings essential.
Reservations: (06) 879 4831

OTHER FACILITIES
There is a range of facilities for private functions, meetings, conferences and weddings for groups of 10–120 people. Culinary schools by appointment.

OWNER
Graeme Avery

WINEMAKER
Grant Edmonds

DATE ESTABLISHED 1998

Sileni Estates

Sileni Estates offers the visitor a total wine and food destination experience in a spectacular setting. The winery is named after the Sileni who featured in Roman mythology alongside Bacchus, the God of Wine — together they celebrated good wine, good food and good company — now the mission of Sileni Estates.

The Cellar Store, incorporating the Wine Discovery Centre, is dedicated to tasting Sileni Estates' wines and to wine education in general. You will also find an amazing gourmet food store and a comprehensive display of French winemaking antiques. Sileni Estates Restaurant showcases the best Hawke's Bay produce matched with your choice of Sileni wines, and you can choose between the newly renovated dining room or the alfresco courtyard terrace.

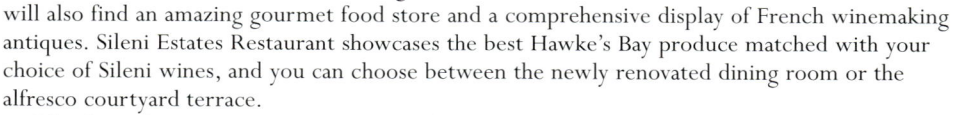

Sileni's modern new winery is committed to providing ultra-premium-quality wines that achieve world status. Crafted using traditional techniques, wines are based on classic varieties including Merlot, Cabernet Franc, Malbec and Sémillon from Bordeaux, as well as Pinot Noir and Chardonnay from Burgundy.

WINES
Labels: Sileni Estates Cellar Selection (CS), Estate Selection (ES), Exceptional Vintage (EV)
Wine Styles: Merlot/Cabernet Franc/Malbec, Pinot Noir, Sémillon, Chardonnay, Riesling, Sauvignon Blanc

RECENT AWARDS
Sileni Cellar Selection Sauvignon Blanc 2004 – NZ White Wine Trophy: London International Wine Challenge 2005, Blue-Gold Medal: Sydney International Wine Competition 2005, Gold Medal: Old Ebbitt Grill, International Wines for Oysters Competition 2004; Sileni Estate Selection Chardonnay 2004 – Gold Medal: London International Wine Challenge 2005

OTHER ACTIVITIES
The Sileni Culinary School offers a total culinary learning experience with day and evening classes for both enthusiasts interested in good food and for the professional chef.

The Gourmet Cellar Store has a controlled environment cheese larder, and stocks local and international gourmet food products along with a wide range of wine paraphernalia.

The Wine Discovery Centre has a variety of tours and tastings to accommodate a range of wine and food interests.

The Village Press Olive Oil is Hawke's Bay's largest olive oil producer. Visitors can tour the Village Press house. Olive oil is available for tasting and purchase.

HAWKE'S BAY

Te Awa Winery

Te Awa Winery is a special place. Set in the Gimblett Gravels district, one of the premium Hawke's Bay wine-growing sites, the winery's rustic charm is complimented by its tranquil garden setting, and reflects the rural New Zealand landscape. Te Awa winery is an enticing year-round destination and is open for Cellar Door tastings and sales, lunch and private evening functions seven days a week. Recently selected as one of New Zealand's Top Six Winery Restaurants, dining at Te Awa is an outstanding New Zealand wine and food experience based principally around fresh Hawke's Bay produce. A visit to Te Awa winery is truly an experience to be sought, savoured and remembered.

WINES
Te Awa Sauvignon Blanc, Chardonnay, Merlot, Syrah, Pinotage, Boundary (Merlot-dominant Bordeaux blend) and Zone 10 Cabernet Sauvignon; **Longlands** Chardonnay, Cabernet Merlot, Merlot

RESTAURANT
The winery's restaurant features dishes inspired by abundant local produce and offers a comprehensive à la carte lunch menu that pairs dishes with Te Awa's single-estate wines. Rustic outdoor tables in the tranquil garden are popular over summer, or over winter choose a table close to the glowing open fire.

2375, SH50
RD5, Hastings
Tel: (06) 879 7602
Fax: (06) 879 7756
Email: winery@teawa.com
Website: www.teawa.com

DIRECTIONS
On SH50, approx. 3km south of the Fernhill/Omahu Rd intersection; or heading north, 5km from the SH50 Maraekakaho Rd junction (almost opposite Trinity Hill winery).

OPENING HOURS
Cellar Door: 7 days, 9am–5pm
Restaurant: Summer, 7 days, 12pm–2.30pm (reservations recommended).

WINERY SALES
Cellar door, retail, mail order, Internet

PRICE RANGE
$19.95+

OTHER FACILITIES
Te Awa offers a premium venue in a unique vineyard setting. Its versatile facilities are perfect for small conference meetings through to large private dinners and celebrations.

OWNERS
Julian Robertson & Reg Oliver

WINEMAKER
Jenny Dobson

DATE ESTABLISHED 1992

Kate Radburnd at CJ Pask

Kim Crawford Wines

Black Barn Vineyards

HAWKE'S BAY

913 St Aubyn Street East, Hastings
Phone: (06) 876 8105
Fax: (06) 876 5312
Email: enquiries@vidal.co.nz
Website: www.vidal.co.nz

DIRECTIONS
From Napier Airport head south to Hastings on the Expressway. Turn left at the intersection after the Meanee Bridge on to Pakowhai Rd. Follow for approx. 5km; turn left into St Aubyn St and follow to the end.

OPENING HOURS
Cellar door: Labour Weekend–Easter Sunday, Mon–Sat, 10am–6pm; Sun, 10am–5pm; rest of year: 7 days, 10am–5pm. Restaurant: 7 days, lunch 12–3pm, dinner from 6pm. Platter menu and bar: 12pm till late.

WINERY SALES
Cellar door, retail, mail order, Internet

PRICE RANGE $16.50+

TASTING & TOURS
Tasting by appointment, a small tasting fee for groups of 10 or more, refundable on purchase. Tours by appointment.

RESTAURANT
Reservations recommended: (06) 876 8105.

OTHER FACILITIES
Two private function rooms are available for conferences, events and weddings.

OWNER George Fistonich

WINEMAKER Rod McDonald

DATE ESTABLISHED 1905

Rod McDonald

Vidal Wines

Vidal Wines in the acclaimed Hawke's Bay wine-growing region produces premium contemporary wines which truly reflect the region and vineyards from which they are sourced. A trip to Vidal Wines not only allows you to try their award-winning wines but also to dine at the renowned Vidal Restaurant, that has a reputation as one of the top spots in Hawke's Bay. Its seasonal menu utilises fresh local produce and all meals have a suggested wine match from Vidal's superb range.

Vidal Wines was established in 1905 and named after its founder — Spanish-born Anthony Joseph Vidal, who purchased a property in Hastings and converted the stables into wine cellars. This site and many of its original features remain, although they are infused with the benefits of modern technology — an approach that extends through to winemaker Rod McDonald's winemaking philosophy.

WINES

The Estate Range: A premium varietal selection for immediate enjoyment. Includes Chardonnay, Sauvignon Blanc, Riesling, Pinot Noir, Syrah and a Merlot/Cabernet Sauvignon blend.

The Reserve Range: Only produced when vintage conditions are ideal. Includes the classic varietals Chardonnay, Cabernet Sauvignon/Merlot, Noble Sémillon.

Joseph Soler: One of New Zealand's pioneering winemakers, Joseph Soler was the key influence in Anthony Joseph Vidal's decision to migrate to New Zealand. During the 1998 vintage, winemaker Rod McDonald saw a small parcel of Cabernet Sauvignon as being particularly distinctive. Released as the Joseph Soler label it has become a truly exceptional wine that wine writers applaud as one of the best reds in New Zealand.

RECENT AWARDS

Vidal Reserve Cabernet Sauvignon 2002 & Reserve Merlot Cabernet Sauvignon 2000 – Gold: Royal Easter Show Wine Awards 2005; Unwooded Chardonnay 2004, Reserve Chardonnay 2002, Marlborough Pinot Noir 2002, Reserve Merlot Cabernet Sauvignon 2002 – Gold: Air New Zealand Wine Awards 2004; 18 of the 22 Vidal wines entered in the Air New Zealand Wine Awards 2004 received medals, winning four gold, seven silver and seven bronze

Alpha Domus

Church Road Winery

Black Barn Vineyard

Black Barn Vineyard

Wairarapa

WAIRARAPA, occupying a large area in the south-eastern North Island, is New Zealand's fifth largest wine region, producing some 1.7 per cent of the national crop. Its vineyards are scattered from near the city of **Masterton** south to around the town of **Martinborough**, the oldest and best-known sub-region. Sheltered in the west by the Rimutaka and Tararua ranges, and in the east by rolling hills, the broad valley of the Wairarapa enjoys a sunny, dry climate with vines planted on free-draining, low-vigour soils. This results in intensely flavoured grapes, especially powerful Pinot Noirs, the variety that makes up 60 per cent of plantings. Sauvignon Blanc, Chardonnay and Pinot Gris are also key wines. Most of the vineyards are boutique owner-operated businesses producing small quantities. The reputation of their wines, however, is impressive. The Wairarapa's location just over the Rimutaka Range from Wellington has made it a great weekend getaway for city dwellers keen on the restaurants and wine trails of this booming area.

For more information visit:
www.wairarapanz.com or contact

Martinborough i-SITE Visitor Information Centre
18 Kitchener St, Martinborough
Tel: (06) 306 9043
Email: martinborough@wairarapa.co.nz

Masterton i-SITE Visitor Information Centre
316 Queen St, Masterton
Tel: (06) 370 0900
Email: info@wairarapanz.com

Murdoch James

HISTORY

Wairarapa's first vines were planted in Masterton in 1883 by wealthy landowner William Beetham, and although the region showed early promise, little planting occurred until the 1970s. Publisher Alister Taylor established the first commercial venture on river terraces in Martinborough, and the following year Dr Neil McCallum of Dry River planted his small Martinborough vineyard. Others soon followed.

SOILS

Preferred sites in the region have free-draining, shallow loams with gravelly subsoils. The Masterton vineyards sit on light loams and heavy gravels. The sub-region of Gladstone and East Taratahi south of Masterton are chiefly free-draining river terraces. The best-known soils are those of the Martinborough Terraces, containing shallow loam topsoils above deep alluvial gravel subsoils laid down by the Huangarua River. The Te Muna sub-region south of Martinborough has similar soils.

CLIMATE

Climatically Wairarapa is more aligned to Marlborough than to any of the North Island regions. It has warm summer temperatures and a cool, dryish autumn. Cool nights help preserve the grapes' acidity and fruity characters. Exposure to strong north-westerly winds reduces yields, and spring frosts are a danger.

GRAPE VARIETIES AND WINE STYLES

Pinot Noir is Wairarapa's most planted and certainly most acclaimed grape variety, its success having helped drive the region's rapid development. Wairarapa Pinots are powerful wines with concentrated fruit flavours. Sauvignon Blanc is the next most planted variety and is produced in styles similar to Marlborough's aromatic wines. Rich styles of Chardonnay are produced along with Pinot Gris in a range of styles from light to rich.

SUB-REGIONS

Martinborough, in and around the township, with vineyards (including the earliest) planted on silty loams over gravelly river terrace soils. Produces acclaimed Pinot Noir and excellent Sauvignon Blanc, Riesling, Chardonnay and Pinot Gris.

Te Muna, south-east of Martinborough, sharing similar soils, is a new sub-region, chiefly producing Pinot Noir.

South Martinborough, further south than Te Muna, sitting up against the foothills, produces mainly Pinot Noir.

Masterton, with chiefly silt loam soils over gravelly river terraces, is producing Pinot Noir, Sauvignon and Riesling. Many new vineyards are planted here.

Gladstone and East Taratahi (Dakins Road), south of Masterton and the site of some of the Wairarapa's earliest plantings, is expanding rapidly, with many new vineyards set to come on stream. Chief varieties are Sauvignon Blanc, Riesling, Pinot Noir and Pinot Gris.

Murdoch James

Schubert Wines

Schubert Wines

Schubert Wines

Tirohana Estate

Margrain Vineyards

Margrain Vineyards

Events

- **Toast Martinborough.** Wairarapa's premier wine and food festival that celebrates new-release Martinborough wines. Events are held at participating wineries and vineyards around the township. Held annually on the third Sunday in November. www.toastmartinborough.co.nz
- **Martinborough Country Fair.** Set in and around the town square includes art, craft and food stalls from all over NZ. Held on the first Saturday in February and March. www.martinboroughfair.org.nz

For more information on events visit: www.wairarapanz.co.nz

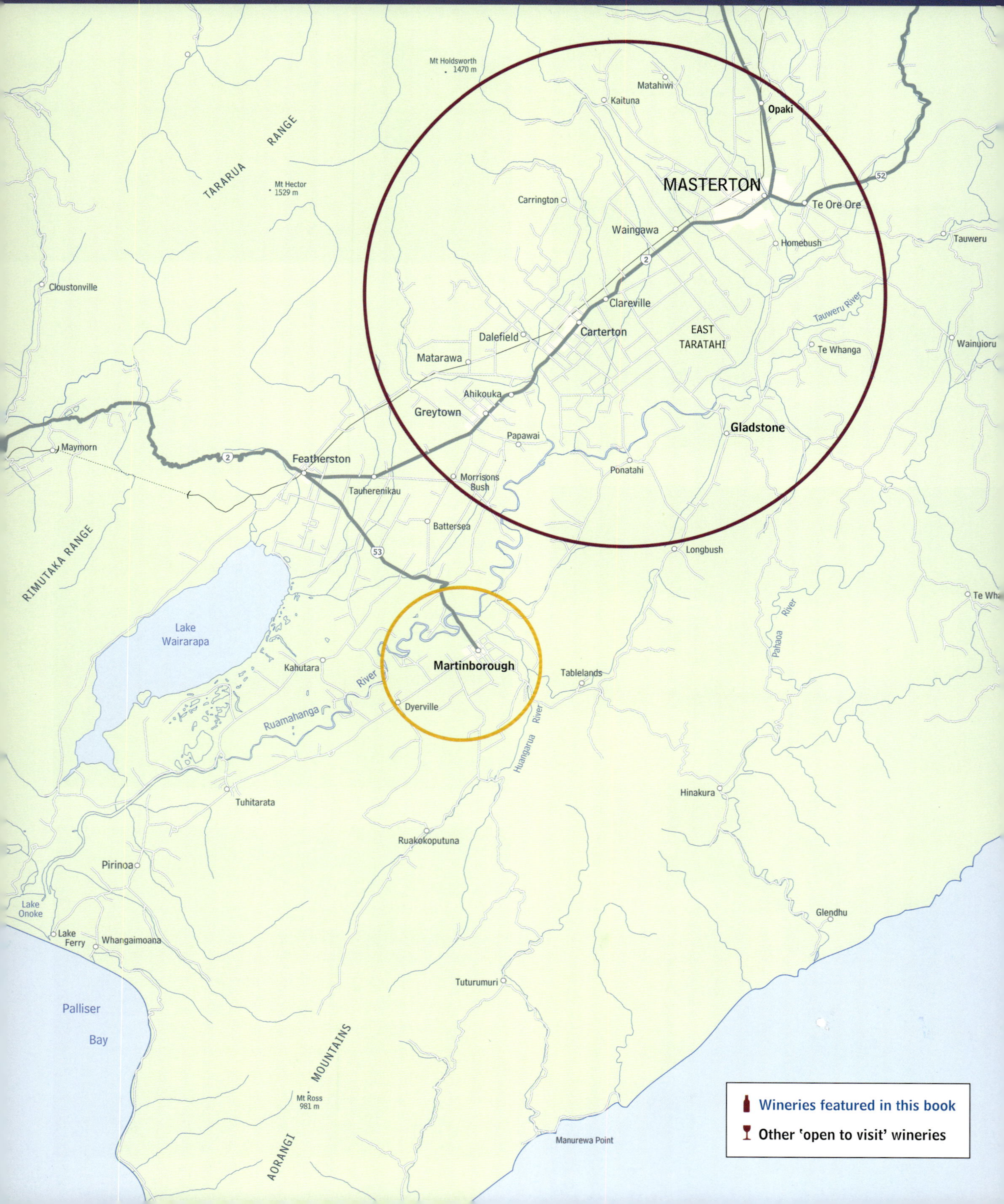

MASTERTON
Opaki
Matahiwi
Kaituna
Mt Holdsworth 1470 m
TARARUA RANGE
Mt Hector 1529 m
Carrington
Te Ore Ore
Waingawa
Homebush
Tauweru
Cloustonville
Clareville
Carterton
EAST TARATAHI
Tauweru River
Dalefield
Matarawa
Te Whanga
Wainuioru
Ahikouka
Greytown
Gladstone
Papawai
Maymorn
Featherston
Morrisons Bush
Ponatahi
Tauherenikau
Battersea
Longbush
RIMUTAKA RANGE
Te Wha
Lake Wairarapa
Pahaoa River
Martinborough
Kahutara
Tablelands
Ruamahanga River
Dyerville
Huangarua River
Tuhitarata
Hinakura
Ruakokoputuna
Pirinoa
Lake Onoke
Glendhu
Lake Ferry
Whangaimoana
Tuturumuri
Palliser Bay
AORANGI MOUNTAINS
Mt Ross 981 m
Manurewa Point
Wineries featured in this book
Other 'open to visit' wineries

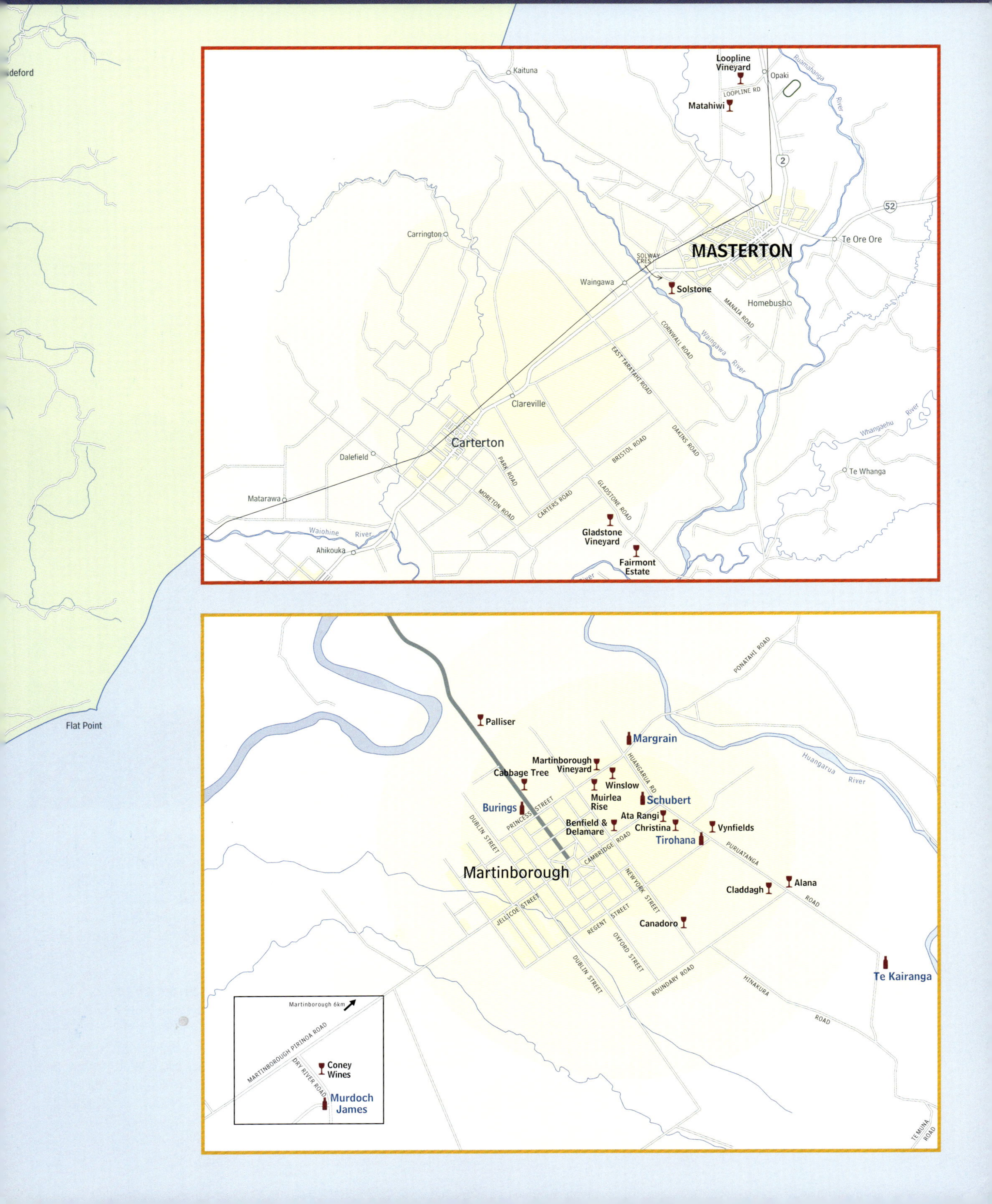

deford
Flat Point
Loopline Vineyard
Opaki
LOOPLINE RD
Ruamahanga River
Matahiwi
Kaituna
2
52
Carrington
MASTERTON
Te Ore Ore
SOLWAY CRES
Waingawa
Solstone
Homebush
MANAIA ROAD
CORNWALL ROAD
Waingawa River
EAST TARATAHI ROAD
Clareville
Carterton
Whangaehu River
DAKINS ROAD
BRISTOL ROAD
Dalefield
Te Whanga
PARK ROAD
MORETON ROAD
GLADSTONE ROAD
CARTERS ROAD
Matarawa
Waiohine River
Ahikouka
Gladstone Vineyard
Fairmont Estate
PONATAHI ROAD
Palliser
Margrain
Huangarua River
Martinborough Vineyard
Cabbage Tree
Winslow
HUANGARUA RD
Muirlea Rise
Schubert
Burings
PRINCESS STREET
Ata Rangi
DUBLIN STREET
Benfield & Delamare
Christina
Vynfields
Tirohana
PURUATANGA
CAMBRIDGE ROAD
Martinborough
NEW YORK STREET
Alana
Claddagh
ROAD
JELLICOE STREET
REGENT STREET
Canadoro
OXFORD STREET
DUBLIN STREET
BOUNDARY ROAD
HINAKURA ROAD
Te Kairanga
Martinborough 6km
MARTINBOROUGH PIRINOA ROAD
DRY RIVER ROAD
Coney Wines
Murdoch James
TE MUNA ROAD

WAIRARAPA
Martinborough

Margrain Vineyard

In the heart of the Martinborough vineyard area, Margrain Vineyard was born from the passion for fine wine, good food and the country lifestyle held by owners Daryl and Graham Margrain. From the outset, the company's aim has been to grow top-quality grapes and produce wines of excellence. A four-hectare vineyard was planted in 1992 using only the most successful grape varieties and clones grown from the Martinborough region. Three years later the first wines from the estate were produced, coinciding with the opening of the Margrain Vineyard Villas. With 15 luxury accommodation units set on the edge of the picturesque terrace vineyard and close to other world-renowned Martinborough wineries, the villas offer a unique 'stay amongst the vines' experience and are particularly suitable for a distinctive executive retreat. In 2000 an adjacent vineyard was purchased where the cellar shop and The Old Winery Café are located. Modern New Zealand cuisine is the speciality, which visitors can enjoy in rustic and relaxed surroundings.

Cnr Ponatahi & Huangarua Rds
Martinborough
Tel: (06) 306 9202
Fax: (06) 306 9297
Email: wine@margrainvineyard.co.nz
Website: www.margrainvineyard.co.nz

DIRECTIONS
Near the intersection of Huangarua Rd and Princess St, a few minutes' drive from Martinborough Square.

OPENING HOURS
Cellar door: Fri/Sat/Sun & public holidays, 11am–5pm. Café: all year, lunch Fri–Sun, dinner Fri–Sat. Functions by arrangement.

WINERY SALES
Cellar door, retail, mail order, Internet

PRICE RANGE $20–$46

TASTING
Tasting fee: $4 refundable on purchase.

CAFÉ
The Old Winery Café. Reservations: (06) 306 8333

ACCOMMODATION
Margrain Vineyard Villas: deluxe accommodation tastefully decorated, each with its own individual style. Equipped with tea/coffee making facilities, SKY TV, clock radios, en suites and private balconies.

OTHER FACILITIES
Informal conference facilities are available. 'The Woolshed' seats up to 35 people and 'The Boardroom' up to 20 people with fabulous views of the Tararuas.

OWNERS
Graham & Daryl Margrain

WINEMAKER
Strat Canning

DATE ESTABLISHED 1992

WINES
Margrain Pinot Noir, Merlot, Chardonnay, Chenin Blanc, Gewürztraminer, Petit Pinot Noir, Pinot Gris, Riesling, Botrytis Selection Riesling

RECENT AWARDS
2001 Pinot Noir – Gold: Royal Easter Show 2002; 2000 Pinot Noir – Blue-Gold: Sydney International Wine Competition 2001; 1999 Pinot Noir – Silver: Air NZ Wine Awards 2000; 1998 Pinot Noir – Gold: Air NZ Wine Awards 1999

Murdoch James

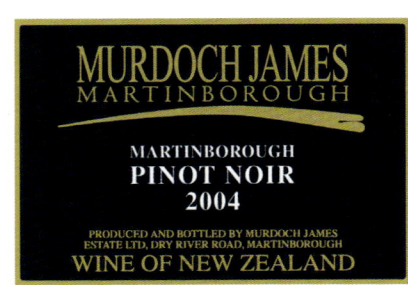

Established in 1986 by Roger and Jill Fraser, Murdoch James Estate is a family owned and run boutique producer of premium award-winning wines. From their initial purchase of a 2.5-hectare vineyard, over 30 hectares have now been planted and for the last four vintages they have operated on a fully organic basis, only making wine from their Martinborough-grown grapes.

Amid beautiful surroundings on the north-facing terraces of the Dry River, visitors are offered the 'complete wine experience' with tasting, a range of tours to cater for all interests, delicious lunches, and accommodation in the beautifully restored Winemaker's Cottage. The café has a wonderful outlook across the Dry River to Lake Wairarapa and the snow-capped Tararua mountain ranges. During summer large bi-fold doors open onto an extensive outdoor eating area, while in the winter you can relax indoors in front of the fire while still enjoying the view. The kitchen team places emphasis on sourcing local produce to create a café experience to remember.

WINES
Three Pinot Noirs are made, two single-vineyard wines ('Blue Rock' and 'Fraser') and a regional blend ('Martinborough'), plus Syrah, Pinot Gris, Cabernet Franc, Chardonnay (unoaked), Sauvignon Blanc, Riesling worldwide. In recent years, the Pinot Noir (Fraser & Blue Rock), Cabernet Franc and Syrah have won 5 trophies and 38 medals at the Air NZ Wine Shows, the London Wine Challenge and the International Wine & Spirit Competition (UK)

RECENT AWARDS
Murdoch James has an outstanding record of trophies and medals (both domestically and overseas) across their full range of wines, along with many accolades from wine critics

ACCOMMODATION
The Winemaker's Cottage – a fully restored self-contained cottage set amongst the vineyard with beautiful views, furnished with antiques, 2 double bedrooms, $150–$200 per night.

WAIRARAPA
Martinborough

Dry River Rd, Martinborough
Tel: (06) 306 9165
Fax: (06) 306 9120
Email: info@murdoch-james.co.nz
Website: www.MurdochJames.co.nz

DIRECTIONS
From Martinborough Village Square, follow Jellicoe St towards Lake Ferry for 6km. Turn left into Dry River Rd and continue 3km to the winery entrance on the right.

OPENING HOURS
Wine tasting and sales: 7 days, 11am–5.30pm. Café: Summer: 6 days (closed Wed), 12pm–3pm. Winter: Fri–Sun, 12pm–3pm. Closed Christmas Day and New Year's Day.

WINERY SALES
Cellar door, retail, mail order, Internet

PRICE RANGE $19–$60

TASTING & TOURS
Hosted wine tasting: $3 pp, includes a 20-min talk and sampling of up to five wines. A variety of tours are available, including the tours of barrel caves and vineyards, finishing with a tasting. Fee: $15–$50 pp (depending on format). Phone for bookings.

CAFÉ
The Riverview Café

PICNIC AREA
By the vines and lake.

OTHER FACILITIES & ACTIVITIES
Wine and Food Match dinners, blind tastings and wine appreciation classes can be organised for groups. Available for weddings and conferences. To assist with planning there is a comprehensive co-ordination service.

OWNERS
Roger & Jill Fraser

WINEMAKER
James Walker

DATE ESTABLISHED 1986

WAIRARAPA
Martinborough

Puruatanga Rd, Martinborough, Wairarapa
Tel: (06) 306 9933
Fax: (06) 306 9943
Email: info@tirohanaestate.com
Website: www.tirohanaestate.com

DIRECTIONS
Entering Martinborough on Kitchener Street, turn left (following grape signage) into Princess Street (Catholic church on corner). Continue along Princess Street and turn right in to Huangarua Rd (following grape signage). Proceed along this road, which changes into Puruatanga Rd. Tirohana Estate is on your right.

OPENING HOURS
7 days, 9am–6pm (closed Christmas Day, Good Friday and Anzac Day morning)

WINERY SALES
Cellar door, mail order, Internet

PRICE RANGE
$24–$165

TASTING & TOURS
Small charge for tastings (refundable on purchase). Individual passing traveller and larger groups welcome.

FOOD OPTIONS
Gourmet snacks, teas, coffees and soft drinks. Also pre-ordered gourmet packed picnics.

PICNIC AREA
Several landscaped picnic areas and umbrella tables are available – all with breathtaking views. BBQ facilities by prior arrangement. Picnic blankets and fully equipped baskets can also be arranged for a unique picnic experience among the vines.

OWNER
The Raymond Thompson Family Trust

WINEMAKER
Consultant Head Winemaker: Gary Voss
Apprentice Winemaker: Saranne James

DATE ESTABLISHED 1988

Tirohana Estate

Tirohana Estate is a critically acclaimed premium boutique vineyard in the heart of the picturesque wine-growing region of Martinborough. The Estate is an interesting venue to visit for both the passing tourist as well as the wine connoisseur. The exclusive Tasting Area houses interesting artefacts and historical information and photographs. The Cellar Door has distinctive charm and character along with an intriguing range of goods on offer as well as the distinctive selection of Tirohana wines.

The landscaped grounds offer picnic and seating areas with breathtaking views across the vineyard to the hills beyond. If you can't bear to leave then stay at the beautiful Tirohana House, which has received a 5-star Qualmark rating reflecting the high standard and unique range of services and facilities available.

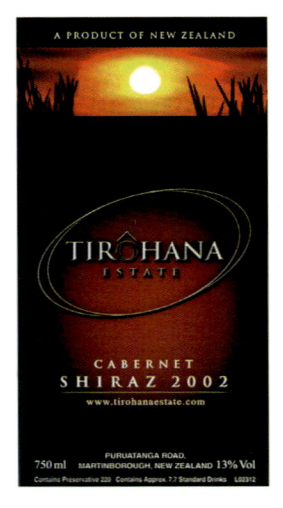

WINES
Tirohana Estate Sauvignon Blanc, Chardonnay, Riesling, Late Harvest Riesling, Cabernet Shiraz, Pinot Noir

OTHER FACILITIES
The Cellar Door is full of atmosphere and charm with unique artefacts, offering a range of gifts and locally made preserves, produce and jewellery, gourmet snacks, teas, coffees and soft drinks along with Tirohana's range of wines. The Tasting Area is entrenched in mystery and character with a variety of interesting historical furnishings on display. The vineyard concierge is available to arrange tours and wine talks as well as all manner of local activities from fishing to hot-air ballooning, golf to pony trekking.

OTHER PRODUCTS
Tirohana Estate gourmet preserves, pickles and chutneys; Tirohana Estate exclusive hand-made jewellery.

ACCOMMODATION
Nestled within the photogenic grounds of Tirohana Estate – Tirohana House is available as a vinestay for between 2–10 guests. Self-contained and/or serviced facilities are available. Modelled on a traditional colonial French farmhouse, the property is elegantly furnished to a high standard with spectacular views across the vineyard and hills beyond. Tirohana House has also been awarded 5-star classification by the official New Zealand tourism authority, Qualmark.

EVENTS & ACTIVITIES
Tirohana Estate is not only an ideal and interesting venue for the passing traveller but can also accommodate groups for weddings and conferences. Throughout Tirohana's calendar there are numerous other events such as food and art weekends, interweaving everything from opera to live string quartets to guest chefs who will conjure up gourmet delicacies to complement wine tasting.

WAIRARAPA
Martinborough

Schubert Wines

Schubert is a new winery founded by German winemakers Kai Schubert and Marion Deimling whose dream was to establish their own vineyard and winery. After searching the world for an ideal place to grow premium Pinot Noir, in 1998 they acquired a small, established vineyard in Martinborough and 40 hectares of bare land just north of Martinborough, at Dakins Road. On the land at Dakins Road high-density planting started in 1999 and now 12 hectares are under vines with the main focus on Pinot Noir. Since the first release in 2001 their wines have won numerous awards internationally and now more than 80 per cent are exported.

WINES
Labels: Schubert
Wine styles: Pinot Noir, Cabernet Sauvignon/Merlot, Cabernet Sauvignon, Syrah, Tribianco (Chardonnay/Pinot Gris/Müller-Thurgau blend), Sauvignon Blanc and the Dolce (dessert wine)

RECENT AWARDS
Schubert Pinot Noir *2003* – Gold: 'Mondial du Pinot Noir', Switzerland, Gold: Air New Zealand Wine Awards; Schubert Cabernet Sauvignon 2002 – Gold: 'Vinalies Internationales, Paris'

57 Cambridge Rd, Martinborough
Tel: (06) 306 8505
Fax: (06) 306 8506
Email: info@schubert.co.nz

DIRECTIONS
From Martinborough Town Square drive to the end of Cambridge Rd, turn left on to Huangarua Rd and left again into first driveway, where the tasting room is located.

OPENING HOURS
Most days, 11am–3pm

WINERY SALES
Cellar door, mail order, retail

PRICE RANGE
$20–$50

TASTING
Open most days for tasting between 11am–3pm
Tasting is free of charge.
No large groups please.

EVENTS & ACTIVITIES
Participant in Toast Martinborough held 3rd Sunday in November.

OWNERS
Kai Schubert & Marion Deimling

WINEMAKERS
Kai Schubert & Marion Deimling

DATE ESTABLISHED 1998

WAIRARAPA
Martinborough

Te Kairanga Wines

Te Kairanga is a popular point of call for anyone visiting the Martinborough area. At this popular country vineyard cellar-door sales are available year round from the historic 130-year-old farmhouse. Visitors are encouraged to taste the wines before buying, and the staff are more than happy to guide you through the range. The weekend tours are a great way to see what happens behind the scenes, showing how the vineyard and winery operate before finishing off with a wine tasting. Visitors are welcome to use the very attractive picnic spot nearby the cellar door.

WINES
Labels: Reserve Wines: Flagship wines only made when conditions are ideal. Premium Wines: High-quality wines at an affordable price. Castle Point Range: Easy-drinking, soft styles ready to be enjoyed now.
Wine styles: Pinot Noir, Chardonnay, Sauvignon Blanc, Riesling, Pinot Gris, Merlot, Cabernet Sauvignon.

RECENT AWARDS
Reserve Pinot Noir 2001 – Trophy & Blue-Gold: Sydney International Wine Challenge 2003, Top 100: Royal International 2003, Gold: Air New Zealand Wine Awards 2002

Martins Rd, Martinborough
Tel: (06) 306 9122
Fax: (06) 306 9322
Email: info@tekairanga.co.nz
Website: www.tkwine.co.nz

DIRECTIONS
From Martinborough Town Square, drive to the end of Cambridge Rd, turn into Puruatanga Rd and travel to the end, veer right into Martins Rd. Te Kairanga is on this corner.

OPENING HOURS
7 days, 10am–5pm

WINERY SALES
Cellar door, retail, mail order

PRICE RANGE $14–$65

TASTING & TOURS
Tasting is free of charge. Wine tours (45min–1hr): Sat & Sun, 2pm.
Fee: $5 pp (deductible from wine purchases). Large groups by prior arrangement, $5 fee non-refundable.

FOOD OPTIONS
Deli items are available for picnics.

PICNIC AREA
By the Cellar Door there is an attractive grassy picnic area shaded by trees with tables.

EVENTS & ACTIVITIES
Annual TK Day — Wellington Anniversary Weekend Sunday: Live music, food and wine.

OWNER
Te Kairanga Wines Limited

WINEMAKER
Peter Caldwell

DATE ESTABLISHED 1983

WAIRARAPA
Martinborough

Open By Appointment

Burings of Martinborough

After making wine for various Martinborough wineries, Chris Buring established his own winemaking business. Together with his wife, Polly, they converted a barn into a boutique winery on their Oak House bed and breakfast property. Grapes are purchased from growers in the southern Wairarapa to make a Riesling, Rosè, and Pinot Noir. The label, "Burings of Martinborough", is so named to avoid confusion with the Australian brand "Leo Buring" but gives reference to the rebirth of the Buring name, made famous in Australia by Chris' great-uncle, Leo Buring, who produced a string of outstanding Rieslings. Their characterful eighty-year-old Californian bungalow, only minutes from Martinborough Square and vineyards, offers gracious bed and breakfast accommodation which also runs residential 'gourmet weekends' which include cooking demonstrations and tutored wine tastings.

Wines: Pinot Noir, Riesling, Chardonnay, Rosé.
Winery sales: Cellar door, mail order, retail, Internet
Price range: $15 to $45

Oak House, 45 Kitchener St,
Martinborough
Tel: (06) 306 9198
Fax: (06) 306 8198
Email: chrispolly.oakhouse@xtra.co.nz
Website: www.burings.co.nz
Owners: Chris & Polly Buring

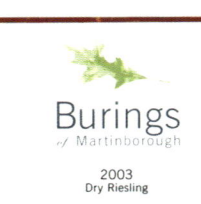

WAIRARAPA

Te Kairanga Wines

Schubert Wines

Schubert Wines

Nelson

Veronique Cornille

NELSON lies in the north-west of the South Island, the country's eighth largest wine region with around 3 per cent of the national crop, and an area of great natural beauty including three national parks. **Nelson** city, on the seaside in Tasman Bay, is the biggest urban centre, the hub of the local horticultural and viticultural industries, and with an energetic community of craftspeople and artists. Bordered on three sides by hills, the Nelson region enjoys a warm, sunny climate, cooled by sea breezes. Most grape-growing takes place on the free-draining alluvial soils of the broad **Waimea Plains** that stretch to the coast, with a number of wineries around the town of **Richmond** and in the **Brightwater** district. A wide range of varieties is produced in chiefly fruit-driven styles. Above the north-western edge of the plains, the heavier clay and gravel soils of the **Upper Moutere** hills produce complex, minerally wines. Further north-west, new grape-growing areas are developing around **Motueka** and at **Golden Bay**.

Nelson is well known for its food, wine, arts and crafts, as well as a diverse range of adventure activities.

For more information visit:
www.nelsonnz.com, www.nelsonwines.co.nz or contact

Nelson i-SITE Visitor Information Centre
Cnr Trafalgar & Halifex Streets
Nelson
Tel: (03) 548 2304
Email: vin@nelsonnz.com

Woollaston Estates

HISTORY
German immigrant winemakers arrived in the region in the 1840s but moved on instead to South Australia. Nelson became dominated by horticultural crops and no serious attempts at grape-growing were made until Rod Neill planted a small vineyard at Stoke, south of Nelson, in the late 1960s, making his first wines in 1972. Austrian-born Hermann Seifried planted a couple of hectares of grapes at Upper Moutere in 1973 and he was to become an important figure in the area, advising beginning grape-growers in the late 1970s. Most of Nelson's wine companies have been centred on the Upper Moutere, but in recent times clusters of wineries have emerged on the Waimea Plains.

SOILS
Alluvial loam covers the Waimea Plains while soils in the Upper Moutere district are predominantly clay loams and gravels over hard clay subsoil.

CLIMATE
Nelson enjoys warm summers with very high sunshine hours (the country's highest) and cold, crisp winters. The proximity to the sea helps moderate temperature extremes, and frosts are extremely rare. The Waimea Plains can be windy, more so than the Moutere Hills district. Most of Nelson's rain falls in the autumn and winter.

GRAPE VARIETIES AND WINE STYLES
Nelson winemakers specialise and excel in grape varieties that respond to cooler growing conditions. Pinot Noir, Sauvignon Blanc, Chardonnay and Riesling are the major varieties. The region's temperate climate is ideal for making plummy Pinot Noir and ripe, fruit-flavoured Sauvignon Blanc. Chardonnay is produced in a wide range of rich, creamy, oaked styles and crisp, fresh unoaked styles.

SUB-REGIONS
Waimea Plains, unfurling from the surrounding ranges inland and spreading to the sea. Its alluvial soils are known for producing Chardonnay, Sauvignon Blanc, Pinot Noir and Riesling in fruit-driven styles. Most wineries are clustered around the towns of Richmond and Brightwater.

Moutere Hills, surrounding the fruit-growing town of Upper Moutere to the west of Nelson city. Its heavier clay and gravel soils produce minerally wines, principally Chardonnay, Pinot Noir and Sauvignon Blanc.

Woollaston Estates

Kahurangi Estate

Te Mania Estate

Stafford Estate

Te Mania Estate

Woollaston Estates (Grant Stirling)

Waimea Estate

Events

- **Sealord Nelson Summer Festival.** A two-month-long festival from December to February incorporating a variety of events. www.nelsonfestivals.co.nz
- **Hooked on Seafood.** Nelson's premier wine and seafood event showcases the best of regional offerings. Held annually in March.
- **Last of the Summer Fare.** A twilight gathering of the region's vineyards and gourmet food producers. Held at Richmond in March.
- **Nelson Arts Festival.** An annual week-long celebration of art in the region. Held in October.

For more information on events visit:
www.nelsonnz.com or www.nelsonfestivals.co.nz

Kaiteriteri
Takaka River
Riwaka
Motueka River
Cobb River
Umukuri
Brooklyn
Motueka
Port Motueka
Lower Moutere
Jacket Island
Mariri
Moutere Inlet
Pangatotara
Kina
Braeburn
Tasman
Ngatimoti
Pokororo
Harakeke
Orinoco
Ruby Bay
Rosedale
Himmelsfeld
Neudorf
Glovers
Mapua
Neudorf
Woodstock
Blackbird Valley
Upper Moutere
Mahana
Bronte
Woollaston Estates
Rimu Grove
Kahurangi Estate
Thorpe
Dovedale
Moutere Hills
Sunset Valley
Redwoods Valley
60
Stafford Lane
Stanley Brook
Brightwater
6
Spring Grove
Tapawera
Rakau
Wai-iti River
Wakefield

TASMAN BAY

Whangamoa Head
Delaware Bay
Pepin Island
Whangamoa
Glenduan
Wakapuaka
Hira
Marybank
Atawhai
Tui Glen
Dodson Valley
Brooklands
Port Nelson
NELSON
Tahunanui
Bishopdale
Enner Glynn
Stoke
Rabbit Island

Te Mania
Waimea Estate
Richmond
Hope
Fossil Ridge
Brightwater Vineyards

BRYANT RANGE

Wineries featured in this book
Other 'open to visit' wineries

NELSON

Kahurangi Estate

Kahurangi is the Maori word meaning, 'treasured possession'. The majestic peaks of Mt Arthur and The Twins in the nearby Kahurangi National Park, New Zealand's second largest national park, provide a dramatic backdrop to Kahurangi Estate, a New Zealand family-owned boutique vineyard specialising in hand-made wines. Located in the historic village of Upper Moutere, the Estate has two vineyards with the home block planted with some of the oldest vines in the South Island. The café at the Cellar Door offers alfresco dining, and specialises in vineyard platters and antipasti using fresh local produce and Kahurangi Estate Olive Oil.

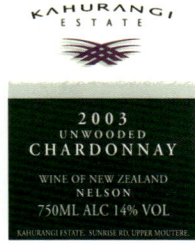

WINES
Kahurangi Estate
Gewürztraminer, Riesling, Sauvignon Blanc, Chardonnay, Pinot Gris, Pinot Noir, Montepulciano

RECENT AWARDS
Kahurangi Estate Mt Arthur Chardonnay 2003 – Silver: Air New Zealand Wine Awards 2004; Heaphy Series Moutere Riesling 2003 – Silver: Bragato Wine Awards 2004; Kahurangi Estate Late Harvest Riesling 2002 – Silver: Bragato Wine Awards 2003

OTHER PRODUCTS
Kahurangi Estate Olive Oil

Sunrise Rd, RD1
Upper Moutere
Tel: (03) 543 2980
Fax: (03) 543 2981
Email: wine@kahurangiwine.com
Website: www.kahurangiwine.com

DIRECTIONS
Located in the Upper Moutere Village on the Moutere Highway, 33km from Nelson.

OPENING HOURS
Cellar door & cafe: Sept–May: 7 days, 11am–5pm; Jun–Aug: Thurs–Sun, 11am–5pm

WINERY SALES
Cellar door, mail order, retail

PRICE RANGE
$17.90–$25

TASTING
Tasting fee: $2 pp for a range of wines, refundable on purchase.

CAFÉ
Vineyard Platters and antipasti available. Weekend wine & food matching. Atomic Coffee and Cakes. Tel: (03) 543 2980

ACCOMMODATION
Luxury, self-contained, two-bedroom cottage in a working vineyard setting. Tel: (03) 543 2980. Fax: (03) 543 2981

OTHER FACILITIES
The Banquet Room is available for large groups and private tastings.

EVENTS/ACTIVITIES
Weekend wine & food matching; Art Exhibitions

OWNERS
Greg & Amanda Day

WINEMAKER
Daniel Schwarzenbach

DATE ESTABLISHED
1973

NELSON

Stafford Lane Estate

Stafford Lane is a family-owned boutique winery, olive grove and orchard located on the beautiful Waimea Plains. Unique soil conditions and the region's favourable climate combine to produce an abundance of fruit perfect for their wide range of quality products. Their first Sauvignon Blanc produced in 2002 was a sellout and the owners have increased their planting from the original tiny 0.5-hectare site to 6.5 hectares with new plantings of Sauvignon Blanc, Pinot Gris, Pinot Noir and Gewürztraminer. Gourmet preserves are made from the feijoas, apples and pears grown on the property using traditional recipes. Their olive oil is pressed from over 10 varieties of olives grown on their property and is sold as varietal extra virgin olive oil throughout New Zealand.

WINES
Stafford Lane Estate Nelson Sauvignon Blanc, Riesling, Chardonnay, Pinot Noir, Late Harvest Chardonnay

RECENT AWARDS
Sauvignon Blanc 2002 – 4 stars: *Cuisine* magazine

OTHER PRODUCTS
Varietal extra virgin olive oil and olives; dukkah, gourmet preserves

80 Moutere Highway
Richmond
Tel: (03) 544 2851
Fax: (03) 544 2051
Email: mike.carol.mcgrath@xtra.co.nz

DIRECTIONS
800m from the intersection of the Coastal Highway (SH60) and the Moutere Highway; 8km from Richmond.

OPENING HOURS
7 days, 11am –5pm

WINERY SALES
Cellar door, retail, mail order

PRICE RANGE
$13.95–$19.95

TASTING
Tasting fee: $3, includes five wines, two olive oils, dukkah, olives, chutney and bread; refundable on purchases over $15.

FOOD OPTIONS
Tasting platters of olive oil, dukkah, olives, chutney and bread.

PICNIC AREA
Picnic tables are set amongst the olives and feijoa trees.

OTHER FACILITIES
Private tasting functions can be organised at the cellar door.

OWNERS
Mike & Carol McGrath

WINEMAKER
Sally Albrecht

DATE ESTABLISHED
2001

Seifried's Vineyard Restaurant & Winery

Seifried Estate is a family owned and operated company that has been making stylish, food-friendly wine since 1976 — all three children now work in various areas of the winery carrying on the family tradition. Success continues year after year with awards and accolades for their exquisite, intensely varietal hand-crafted wines, all made from their own estate-grown fruit.

The winery complex includes a tasting area, shop and restaurant and is a great place to visit. At the cellar door, located in the Rabbit Island vineyard, the knowledgeable staff will assist you in tasting the range of wines and answer any questions. You can enjoy simply delicious food at the Vineyard Restaurant complemented by the fine food-friendly wines. Specialising in the wonderful range of fresh produce that Nelson has to offer, the restaurant provides indoor dining facilities as well as a spacious and pretty outdoor garden with a well-equipped playground to keep the children occupied while you dine at leisure.

WINES
Labels: Winemakers Collection, Seifried, Old Coach Road
Wine Styles: Sauvignon Blanc, Riesling, Chardonnay, Gewürztraminer, Pinot Gris, Pinot Noir, Cabernet Sauvignon, Merlot, Zweigelt, Syrah

RECENT AWARDS
Winemakers Collection Sauvignon Blanc 2004 — Blue-Gold: 2005 Sydney International Wine Competition, Gold: 2004 Liquorland Top 100; Winemakers Collection Barrique 2003 Fermented Chardonnay — Gold: 2005 Royal Easter Wine Show, Gold & Best in Class: 2004 Bragato Wine Awards, Silver: 2004 International Chardonnay Challenge & 2004 Air New Zealand Wine Awards; Seifried Nelson Chardonnay 2004 — Gold: 2005 Royal Easter Wine Show; Old Coach Road Chardonnay 2003 — Gold: 2005 Royal Easter Wine Show, Silver: 2004 Bragato Wine Awards

OTHER PRODUCTS
A selection of wine-related souvenirs and clothing is available at the Cellar Door.

NELSON

Corner SH60 & Redwood Rd
Appleby
Tel: (03) 544 5599
Fax: (03) 544 5522
Email: wines@seifried.co.nz
Website: www.seifried.co.nz

DIRECTIONS
Located just 20 minutes from central Nelson City, on the Coastal Highway (SH60) towards Motueka. Look for the winery on the right, at the Rabbit Island intersection.

OPENING HOURS
7 days (closed Christmas Day, Boxing Day and Good Friday)
Cellar door: 10am–5pm
Restaurant: lunch daily and dinner by reservation

WINERY SALES
Cellar door, retail, mail order, Internet

PRICE RANGE $10–$35

TASTING
A small fee applies, refundable on purchase.

WINERY TOURS
By appointment only.

RESTAURANT
Seifried's Vineyard Restaurant is open year round. Lunch: 7 days; Evening dining: 7 days during summer, by reservation only during winter. For reservations Tel: (03) 544 1555

OTHER FACILITIES
Two beautiful function rooms are available: 1) 'Applebys' opens into an intimate garden area, with a beautiful hand-crafted fireplace to add to the cosy atmosphere. 2) 'Vines' has panoramic views over the vineyard and surrounding countryside from a spacious balcony.

OWNERS
Hermann & Agnes Seifried

WINEMAKER
Chris Seifried

DATE ESTABLISHED
1973

NELSON

Te Mania Estate

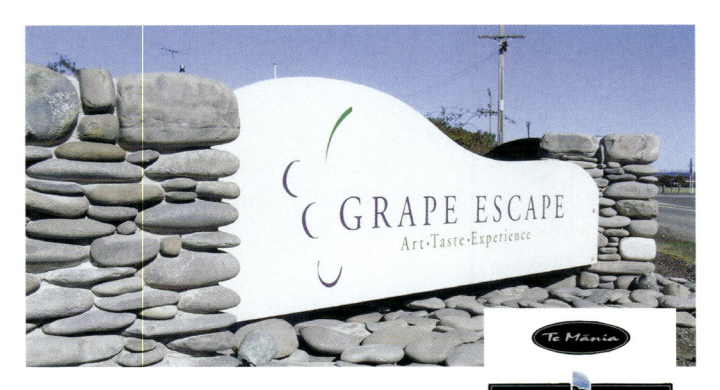

Te Mania Estate, pronounced Te Mar-nee-a and meaning 'The Plains', is a small family-owned vineyard established by Jon and Cheryl Harrey in 1990. Their range of quality, award-winning wines is available at their cellar door tasting room within the historic, refurbished buildings of the Grape Escape complex. Here you will experience the taste of fine wine, regional food, local art and more. Enjoy a leisurely lunch or coffee in a delightful garden setting, taste a wide selection of premium-quality wines, and view superb, hand-crafted artworks and jewellery. Ensure you allow plenty of time to browse the many attractions of this 'must visit' destination.

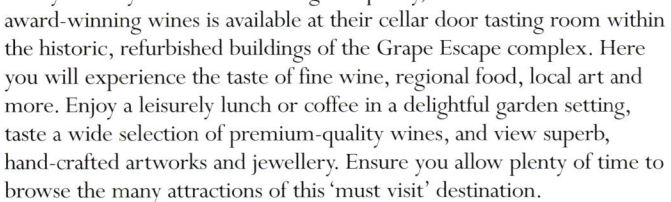

WINES
Te Mania Riesling, Sauvignon Blanc, Chardonnay, Reserve Chardonnay, Pinot Noir, Reserve Pinot Noir; **Three Brothers** Merlot/Malbec/Cabernet blend, and dessert wines

RECENT AWARDS
Te Mania wines consistently achieve award-winning success in both wine competitions and magazine tastings. Current highlights include a top-ranking 5 stars & 93/100 by Bob Campbell in *Gourmet Traveller Wine* magazine for the Te Mania Reserve Pinot Noir 2003.

OTHER PRODUCTS
Local olive oils, organic soaps, gourmet sauces and dressings.

McShanes Rd, RD1, Richmond
Tel/Fax: (03) 544 4054
Email: temania@ts.co.nz
Website: www.temaniawines.co.nz

DIRECTIONS
On the corner of McShane Rd and SH60 (Appleby Highway). A 3-minute drive from Richmond and 15 minutes from Nelson.

OPENING HOURS
7 days.
Summer: 10.30am–5pm
Winter: 11am–4pm

WINERY SALES
Cellar door, retail, mail order

PRICE RANGE
$15–$30

TASTING & TOURS
Tasting fee: 50c per wine, refundable on purchase. Group tastings by arrangement.

OTHER FACILITIES
Escape Gallery, Living Light candles, Prenzel Liqueur tasting room, children's playground, cottage gardens. Private functions may be arranged through the Grape Escape Café & Winebar.

OWNERS
Jon & Cheryl Harrey

WINEMAKER
Tania O'Sullivan

DATE ESTABLISHED 1990

NELSON

Waimea Estates

Since their first vintage in 1997, Waimea Estates have been creating award-winning Nelson wines. Their philosophy is that 'good wine is made in the vineyard' and their belief in intensive canopy management and low cropping ensures ripe and highly concentrated fruit. The three words winemaker Michael Brown uses to sum up his aims in his wines are: 'concentration, texture, balance'. At their celebrated 'Café in the Vineyard', you can sample and purchase Waimea wines including some hard-to-find back vintages. Or you can enjoy the seasonal menu that features superb cuisine based on local ingredients. There is a mix of indoor and outdoor dining with live music in the weekends throughout the summer.

WINES
Labels: Spinyback, Waimea, Signature Vineyard & Bolitho Reserve (prestige range)
Wine Styles: Sauvignon Blanc, Riesling, Chardonnay, Gewürztraminer, Pinot Gris, Rosé, Pinot Noir, Cabernet Sauvignon/Merlot

RECENT AWARDS
'Winemaker Michael Brown has a gift for producing ultra-clean, ultra-pure fruit and densely textured, food-friendly wines' – *Gourmet Traveller Wine* Jun/Jul 2005; 'For summer dining it doesn't get much better than this …' – *Michael Guy's Eating Out 2005*

EVENTS AND ACTIVITIES
Annual Vintage Open Day held Anzac Day, Annual Winemaker Dégustation Dinner (spring), Wine Appreciation Workshops, exhibitions of local artists.

Appleby Highway, Hope
Tel: (03) 544 6385
Fax: (03) 544 6385
Email: office@waimeaestates.co.nz
Website: www.waimeaestates.co.nz

DIRECTIONS
At the start of the Appleby Highway to Motueka and Golden Bay.

OPENING HOURS
Summer: 7 days, 10am–5pm
Winter: Wed–Sun, 11am–4pm

WINERY SALES
Cellar door, retail, mail order, Internet

PRICE RANGE $14.95–$39.95

TASTING & TOURS
50 cents per tasting, refundable up to $2. Tours by appointment only. Tour fee varies according to the size and needs of a group. Please phone ahead to arrange.

CAFÉ
Café in the vineyard
Reservations: (03) 544 4963

OTHER FACILITIES
Evening functions and wedding receptions are a speciality of the café and cater to a wide range of tastes and budgets.

OWNERS
Trevor & Robyn Bolitho

WINEMAKER Michael Brown

DATE ESTABLISHED 1993

Woollaston Estates

The Woollaston Estates winery at Mahana in the Upper Moutere has 360-degree panoramic views across Tasman Bay from D'Urville Island to Nelson City in the east and of the majestic Mt Arthur range to the west.

Committed to producing high-quality distinctive wines, the owners of Woollaston Estates believe passionately that these are defined in the vineyard and subtly enhanced in the winery. Varieties and clones are carefully matched to their vineyards' sites and soils: Pinot Noir and Pinot Gris on the Moutere clays, Sauvignon Blanc and Riesling from the gravels of the Waimea Plains of Nelson. A unique gravity-fed, four-level winery is built into the hillside and has a 'living roof' of soil and vegetation.

Fine art complements fine wine at Woollaston Estates Gallery, which features works by Toss Woollaston and other contemporary New Zealand artists. Acknowledged as one of New Zealand's foremost 20th-century painters, Woollaston lived and painted nearby. A vineyard walk and sculpture park is being developed under the guidance of leading New Zealand sculptor, Andrew Drummond.

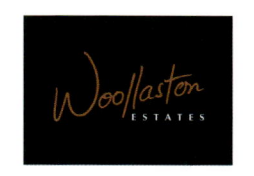

2004
Pinot Noir
NELSON

WINE OF NEW ZEALAND

WINES
Woollaston Estates Sauvignon Blanc, Chardonnay, Riesling, Pinot Noir, Pinot Gris, Pinot Rosé

OTHER FACILITIES
The Woollaston art gallery (at the Cellar Door). A sculpture walk is scheduled to open in 2006. The winery complex has function and banqueting facilities for up to 200 guests. The Estates' courtyard and lawn, with sweeping vineyard, mountain and sea views, is also available.

NELSON

243 Old Coach Rd
Upper Moutere
Tel: (03) 543 2817
Fax: (03) 543 2317
Email: mail@woollaston.co.nz
Website: www.woollaston.co.nz

DIRECTIONS
The best way to get to Woollaston is on the road to Mapua. Turn left onto Dominion Rd just after passing Nile Rd. Follow Dominion Rd 2km to the top of the hill and turn left onto Old Coach Rd. Travel for approx. 1km before turning right onto School Rd, the winery entrance is on the right a few metres into School Rd.

OPENING HOURS
Jan & Feb: 7 days, 11am–4.30pm. Other months by appointment only.

WINERY SALES
Retail, mail order (Cellar Club), Internet, Cellar Door. To enquire about becoming a Cellar Club member contact: cellar@Woollaston.co.nz or phone the winery.

PRICE RANGE $18–$45

TASTING
A small tasting fee, refundable on purchase, applies. Groups welcome by appointment.

WINERY TOURS
By appointment only.

PICNIC AREA
Picnic facilities are being developed.

OWNERS
Philip & Chan Woollaston
Glenn Schaeffer

WINEMAKER
Andrew Sutherland

DATE ESTABLISHED 2000

Marlborough

MARLBOROUGH, in the north-eastern corner of the South Island, is the largest grape-growing and winemaking region in New Zealand with over 85 wineries and 275 grape-growers producing 57.1 per cent of the national crop. The region boasts three distinct landscapes: the breathtaking Marlborough Sounds, the stunning high country rolling down to the Pacific coast, and central Marlborough which is known as vineyard country. At the heart of this central area is the region's main urban centre of **Blenheim**, and the satellite wine country village of **Renwick**. Between the **Wither Hills** and the **Richmond Ranges** (made famous by the Cloudy Bay label) you'll find the heartland of Sauvignon Blanc across the **Wairau River plains**.

Wine lovers and foodies come to tour Marlborough wineries and they discover culinary paradise. Not only can you taste a variety of award-winning wines at the region's many vineyards, you can also sample fresh Sounds oysters with the world's best Sauvignon Blanc, taste local lamb or game in a first-class restaurant, or discover salmon secrets in a top cooking school.

For more information visit:
www.destinationmarlborough.com or contact

Marlborough Information & Travel Centre
Blenheim Railway Station
Grove Rd, Blenheim
Tel: (03) 577 8080

Mike Hollman

Cloudy Bay

HISTORY

In the early 1970s, Montana Wines were looking for more land on which to expand their North Island grape-growing and winemaking enterprise. They decided on Marlborough. When the first Marlborough vines were planted in 1973 few people predicted that the region would become New Zealand's largest and best-known wine-growing area in little more than 20 years. The distinctive qualities of the first wines captured the imagination of the country's winemakers and wine drinkers alike and sparked an unparalleled boom in vineyard development. Although Montana triggered this 20th-century boom in Marlborough, wine was in fact being produced here much earlier with the first commercial harvests in the 1870s.

SOILS

The free-draining alluvial loams over gravelly subsoils in the Wairau and Awatere River Valleys provides ideal growing conditions.

CLIMATE

Marlborough regularly claims the highest sunshine hours in New Zealand. This sunshine, coupled with cool nights and a long growing season, helps to build and maintain the vibrant fruit flavours for which Marlborough is now renowned. The region has relatively low rainfall during the ripening season which helps protect the thin-skinned and tight-clustered bunches of Sauvignon Blanc grapes from developing botrytis and other fungal diseases.

GRAPE VARIETIES AND WINE STYLES

Sauvignon Blanc is the most planted grape variety with Chardonnay in second place, followed by Pinot Noir and Riesling. Sauvignon Blanc may be the star but Marlborough has also earned an enviable reputation for Méthode Traditionnelle sparkling wines as well as a wide range of both white and red table wines.

SUB-REGIONS

Wairau Valley, surrounding Blenheim and predominantly south of the Wairau River, bounded by the Richmond Ranges and the Wither Hills. The heartland of Sauvignon Blanc.

Awatere Valley, south of Blenheim, stretches right along the lower Awatere River. The town of Seddon is in the centre of the region. Sauvignon Blanc, Riesling and Chardonnay are produced here.

Hunter's Wines

Isabel Estate

Wine and Food Festival

Highfield Estate

Wairau River Wines

Fromm Clayvin Vineyard

Events

- **The BMW Wine Marlborough Festival.** New Zealand's premier wine and food event showcasing over 40 wineries and gourmet food producers with entertainment from New Zealand's leading performers. Wine workshops and culinary demonstrations. Second Saturday in February. www.bmw-winemarlborough-festival.co.nz

- **Blues, Brews & Barbecues.** Showcases boutique beers from around New Zealand. First Saturday in February.

- **Pinot at Cloudy Bay.** For lovers of Pinot Noir, NZ's most sophisticated wine-tasting event with over 20 Pinot Noirs from around the world and fine food. Held in June. www.cloudybay.co.nz

- **Kaikoura Seafeast.** Annual celebration of the abundance of the ocean. Features entertainment, wine and fine food from Kaikoura, Marlborough and North Canterbury. First Saturday of October. www.seafest.co.nz

- **Marlborough Farmers Market.** Every Sunday 9am–12pm. A & P Showgrounds Blenheim

For more information on events visit:
www.destinationmarlborough.com

View to Wither Hills

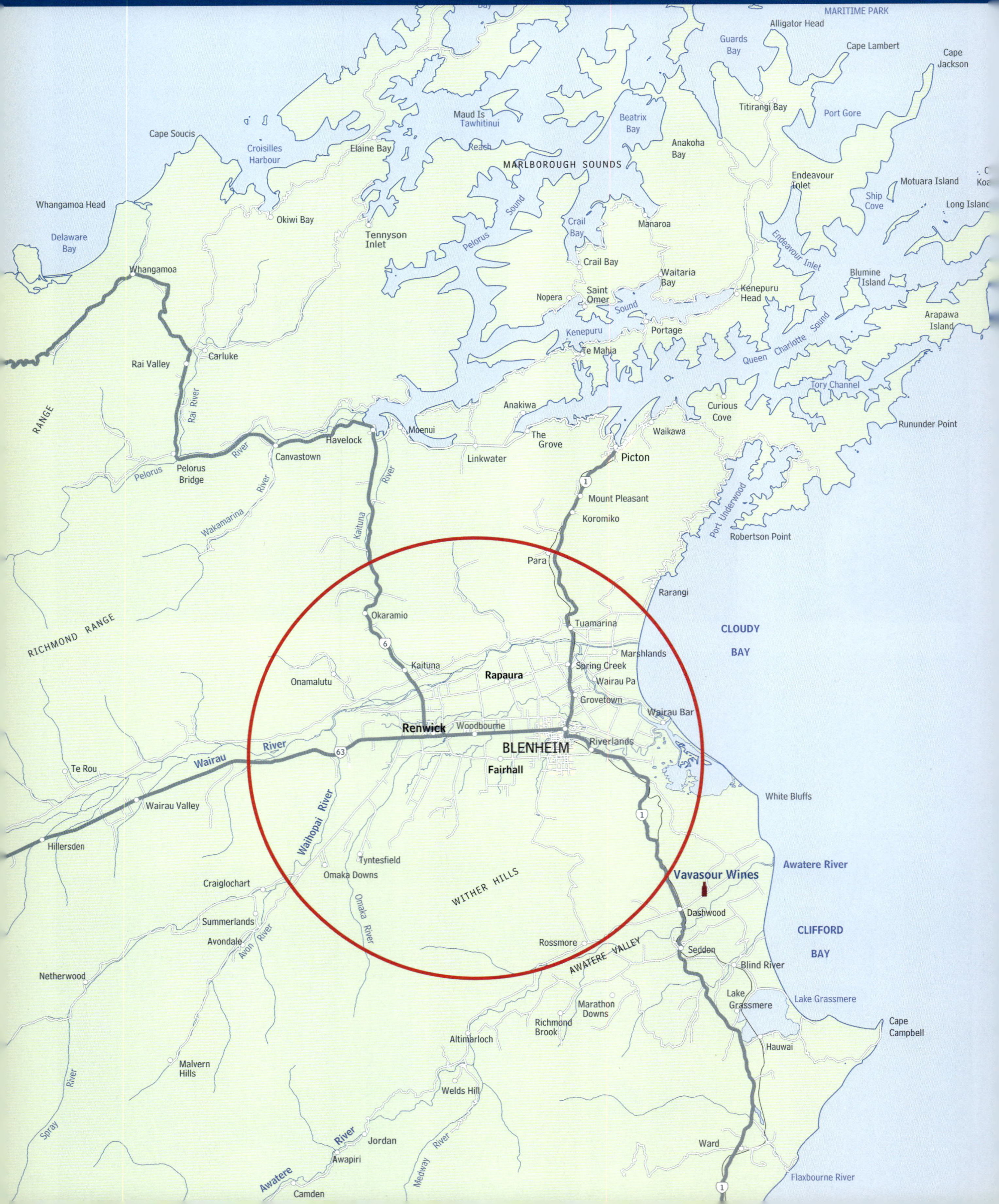
MARITIME PARK
Alligator Head
Guards Bay
Cape Lambert
Cape Jackson
Titirangi Bay
Port Gore
Maud Is
Tawhitinui
Reach
Beatrix Bay
Cape Soucis
Croisilles Harbour
Elaine Bay
Anakoha Bay
MARLBOROUGH SOUNDS
Endeavour Inlet
Motuara Island
Whangamoa Head
Ship Cove
Long Island
Okiwi Bay
Crail Bay
Manaroa
Endeavour Inlet
Delaware Bay
Tennyson Inlet
Pelorus Sound
Crail Bay
Waitaria Bay
Blumine Island
Whangamoa
Nopera
Saint Omer
Kenepuru Head
Kenepuru Sound
Portage
Arapawa Island
Queen Charlotte Sound
Carluke
Te Mahia
Rai Valley
Tory Channel
Rai River
Anakiwa
Curious Cove
RANGE
Rununder Point
Havelock
Moenui
The Grove
Waikawa
Canvastown
Linkwater
Picton
Pelorus River
Pelorus Bridge
Kaituna River
Mount Pleasant
Wakamarina River
Koromiko
Port Underwood
Robertson Point
Para
Rarangi
Okaramio
Tuamarina
CLOUDY BAY
RICHMOND RANGE
Marshlands
Kaituna
Spring Creek
Rapaura
Onamalutu
Wairau Pa
Grovetown
Wairau Bar
Renwick
Woodbourne
BLENHEIM
Riverlands
Wairau River
Fairhall
Te Rou
White Bluffs
Wairau Valley
Waihopai River
Hillersden
Tyntesfield
Awatere River
Omaka Downs
Vavasour Wines
Craiglochart
WITHER HILLS
Dashwood
Summerlands
Omaka River
CLIFFORD BAY
Avondale
Avon River
Rossmore
Seddon
AWATERE VALLEY
Blind River
Netherwood
Marathon Downs
Lake Grassmere
Lake Grassmere
Richmond Brook
Cape Campbell
Altimarloch
Hauwai
Malvern Hills
Spray River
Welds Hill
Awatere River
Jordan
Ward
Awapiri
Medway River
Flaxbourne River
Camden

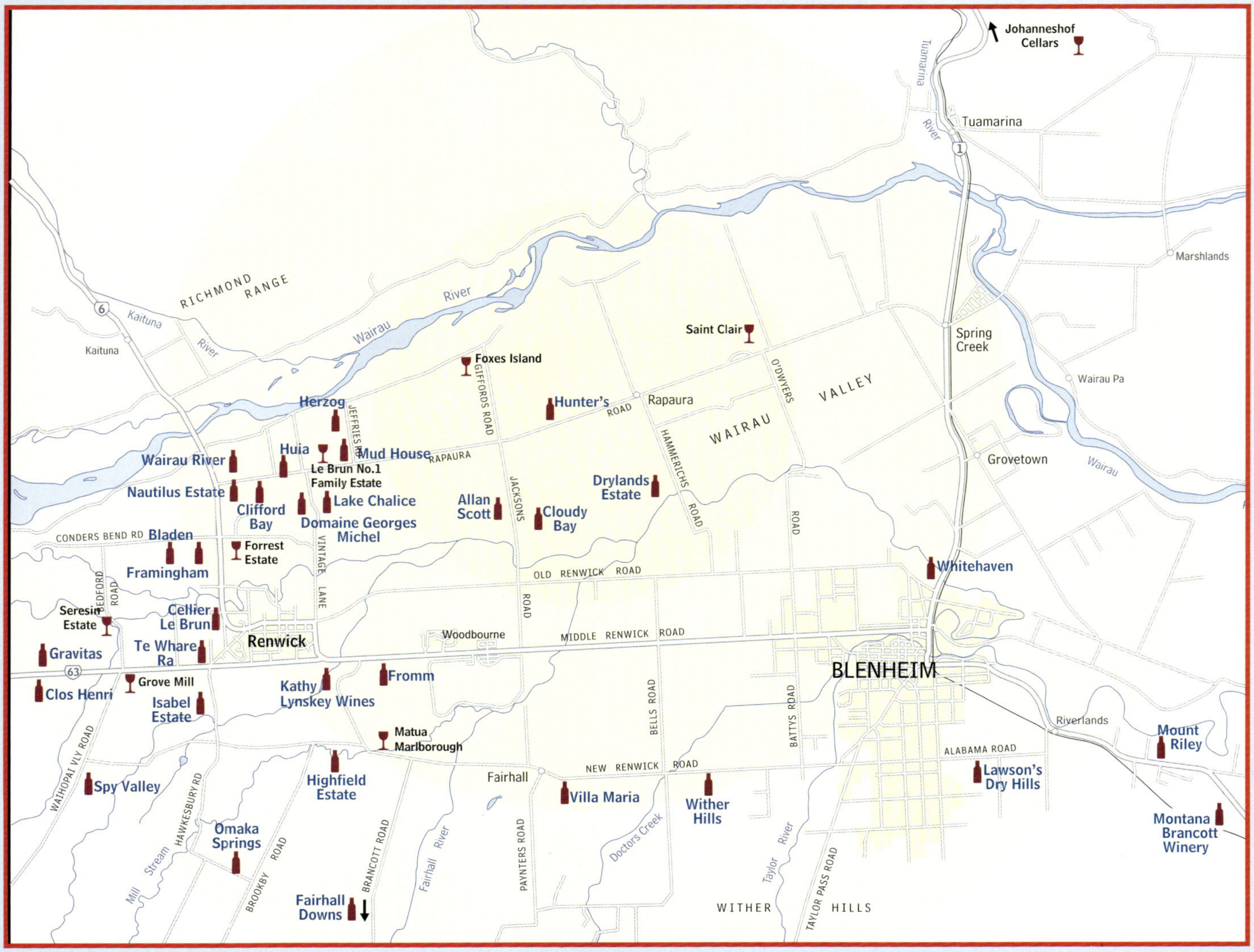

Wineries featured in this book

Other 'open to visit' wineries

MARLBOROUGH
Awatere Valley

Redwood Pass Rd
Awatere Valley
Tel: (03) 575 7481
Fax: (03) 575 7240
Email: vavasour@vavasour.com
Website: www.vavasour.com

DIRECTIONS
Turn off SH1 into Redwood Pass Rd just north of Seddon. The winery is 4km on the right.

OPENING HOURS
Oct–Apr: 7 days, 10am–5pm
May–Oct: Sun–Fri, 10am–5pm

WINERY SALES
Cellar door, retail, mail order, Internet

PRICE RANGE $12–$25

TASTING & TOURS
Tasting is free of charge. Tours by appointment.

PICNIC AREA
Next to the winery in the garden with picnic tables.

OWNER
New Zealand Wine Fund

WINEMAKER
Glenn Thomas

DATE ESTABLISHED 1986

Vavasour Wines

You will find Vavasour Wines on the banks of the magnificent Awatere River, south of Blenheim — it was here in 1986 that they became the pioneers of winemaking in the Awatere Valley. A harsh and dramatic environment — Mt Tapuae-o-Uenuku's 2900-metre peak rises to the south, and to the north lies the ocean reducing the risk of frosts — the rainfall is lower, the soil less fertile and the wind helps reduce the risk of diseases.

The terraced banks of the Awatere River provide an ideal soil structure for the vineyard. Wines are produced from low-yielding vines, which ensure the highest possible concentration of flavours. This is a very hands-on vineyard — they often hand-pick to ensure only the best fruit makes it into the bottle, and whole-bunch press. Extra grapes are sourced from contract growers based in both the Wairau and Awatere Valleys.

The winery is located in the vineyard and offers an authentic cellar-door experience, the tasting table set on a couple of wine barrels is inside the winery. Visitors are also welcome to picnic in the sunny and sheltered garden out front.

WINES
Vavasour Sauvignon Blanc, Chardonnay, Pinot Gris, Riesling, Pinot Noir
Dashwood Sauvignon Blanc, Chardonnay, Pinot Noir

The premium Vavasour range is made predominantly from estate-grown Awatere grapes creating elegant finely textured wines designed to improve with age. The Dashwood range, a lighter, more approachable style designed for early drinking, is made from blended fruit from the Wairau and Awatere Valleys.

RECENT AWARDS
Vavasour Sauvignon Blanc 2002 – Gold: International Wine and Spirit Competition, London

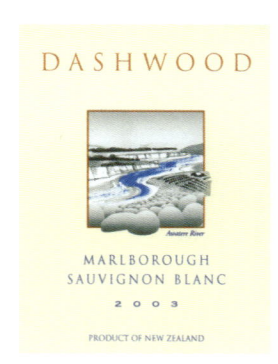

MARLBOROUGH
Wairau Valley

Allan Scott Wines & Estates

A family owned and operated winery and vineyard, Allan Scott Wines and Estates has a solid reputation as one of the region's top wine producers. Surrounded by 60 hectares of prime vineyard in Jacksons Road are the winery, cellar door and restaurant. Specialising in providing the company's range of wines for tasting and purchases, the Cellar Door shop is tastefully designed and decorated with a wide range of unique gifts and local produce. Twelve Trees Restaurant is a popular luncheon venue, celebrating the best in the province in a superb indoor/outdoor garden restaurant. Diners can choose between the sheltered outdoor garden with water features and life-size chess or inside open-plan dining area.

WINES
Allan Scott Chardonnay, Sauvignon Blanc, Riesling, Pinot Gris, Gewürztraminer, Méthode Traditionnelle, Pinot Noir, Merlot

RECENT AWARDS
Champion Méthode Traditionnelle: NZ Wine Society Royal Easter Show Wine Awards 2004

Jacksons Rd, RD3, Blenheim
Tel: (03) 572 9054
Fax: (03) 572 9053
Email: scott.wines@xtra.co.nz
Website: www.allanscott.com

DIRECTIONS
Jacksons Rd runs between Middle Renwick Rd, across Old Renwick Rd, to Rapaura Rd. Allan Scott is at the Rapaura Rd end.

OPENING HOURS
Cellar Door: 7 days, 9am–4.30pm. Closed Christmas Day, New Year's Day, ANZAC Day and Good Friday. Restaurant: lunch, 7 days from 9am

WINERY SALES
Cellar door, mail order, retail

PRICE RANGE
$17.50–$38

TASTING & TOURS
A nominal charge applies for tastings, refundable on purchase. Tours by arrangement.

RESTAURANT
Twelve Trees Restaurant offers a constantly changing menu created to reflect seasonal specialities and complement Allan Scott wines. Reservations: (03) 572 7123

OTHER FACILITIES
Wedding venue and functions by arrangement

OWNERS
Allan & Catherine Scott

WINEMAKER
Jeremy McKenzie & Josh Scott

DATE ESTABLISHED 1990

MARLBOROUGH
Wairau Valley

Bladen Estate

One of the smallest and friendliest tasting rooms in Marlborough, Bladen Estate is a boutique family owned and run vineyard that offers the special experience of meeting and tasting with the owners. Chris and Dave are passionate about the wines they produce and their belief that 'wine is made on the vine' ensures that quality is foremost at every step of their winemaking process. Best known for their Aromatics, though Pinot Noir is their latest planting venture, the wines reflect the individuality and personality of this small vineyard. Every year these highly sought after wines that are often exclusive to the cellar door sell out very quickly.

WINES
Bladen Marlborough Gewürztraminer, Pinot Gris, Riesling, Sauvignon Blanc, Pinot Noir, Merlot/Malbec

RECENT AWARDS
Pinot Gris 2004 – Gold & Champion Pinot Gris Trophy: The Royal Easter Show Wine Awards 2005; Sauvignon Blanc 2003 – 5 Stars & Top 5 in its class: 'Wine of the Year' *Winestate* magazine; Riesling 2000 – Gold: Liquorland Top 100

Bladen Estate
Conders Bend Rd, Renwick
Tel: (03) 572 9417
Fax: (03) 572 9217
Email: info@bladen.co.nz
Website: www.bladen.co.nz

DIRECTIONS
Turn into Conders Bend Rd on the western side of SH6, 1km north of Renwick. Bladen Estate is 500m on the left.

OPENING HOURS
October (commencing Labour Weekend) to Easter: 7 days, 11am–5pm

WINERY SALES
Cellar door, retail, mail order, Internet

PRICE RANGE $18–$35

TASTING
Tasting is free of charge.

OWNERS
Dave Macdonald & Christine Lowes

WINEMAKER
Simon Waghorn

DATE ESTABLISHED 1989

MARLBOROUGH
Wairau Valley

Cellier Le Brun

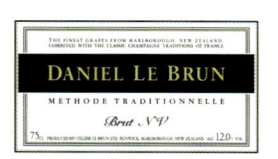

Daniel Le Brun Méthode Traditionnelle is a name synonymous with superb, consistent and very stylish wine produced from premium Marlborough grapes. A small and dedicated team craft the Daniel Le Brun wines acknowledging the traditional techniques particular to Méthode Traditionnelle production, and the modern winemaking practices associated with producing quality table wines under the Terrace Road label. Visitors can learn more about how these wines are crafted from the friendly and knowledgeable staff whilst tasting the wines at the Cellar Door, and enjoying an informative tour of the underground cellars. Cuisine at Le Brun operated by chef Chris Fortune affords guests the best of local, fresh, honest cuisine in an ambient vineyard setting.

WINES
Daniel Le Brun range of Méthode Traditionnelle wines include Brut NV, Taché, Blanc de Blancs, and Vintage premium styles.
Terrace Road features distinctive still wines: Sauvignon Blanc, Chardonnay, Riesling, Pinot Gris and Pinot Noir. Also the Classic Brut Méthode Traditionnelle.

RECENT AWARDS
Daniel Le Brun Blanc de Blancs 1997 – Gold: Royal Easter Show Wine Awards 2005; Terrace Road Sauvignon Blanc 2004 – Gold: Royal Easter Show Wine Awards 2005

Contact details
Terrace Rd, Renwick
Tel: (03) 572 8859
Fax: (03) 572 8814
Email: sales@lebrun.co.nz
Website: www.lebrun.co.nz

DIRECTIONS
Terrace Rd is located on the northern outskirts of Renwick township off SH6.

OPENING HOURS
Cellar Door: 7 days, 9.30am–4.30pm
Restaurant: Summer: 7 days, from 9am for breakfast, brunch and lunch. Dinner by arrangement. Winter: reduced hours.

WINERY SALES
Cellar door, retail, Internet

PRICE RANGE
$18.50–$40

TASTING & TOURS
Tasting is free of charge. Tours daily, on demand.

RESTAURANT
Cuisine at Le Brun with Chris Fortune. Reservations: (03) 572 9953

OWNER
Resene Paints Ltd

WINEMAKER
Consultant Winemaker: Mark Inglis
Resident Winemaker: Zelda Neil

DATE ESTABLISHED 1980

MARLBOROUGH
Wairau Valley

Clifford Bay Estate

Growing on the terraces above the Awatere River near the coast are the Sauvignon, Chardonnay and Riesling vines that produce the wonderful grapes for Clifford Bay Estate wines. Since their first vintage in 1997 when the Sauvignon Blanc was awarded three gold medals and numerous other credits, Clifford Bay Estate wines have continued to receive significant accolades in New Zealand and overseas. The distinctive 'Tuscan-style' cellar door is conveniently located on Rapaura Road for wine tastings and sales and includes a very popular restaurant that features fresh local produce. Diners can enjoy the Marlborough sunshine at sheltered courtyard tables set around a central water feature, or indoors beside a cosy open fire on cooler days. Private functions are also available.

WINES
Clifford Bay Sauvignon Blanc, Chardonnay, Riesling, Pinot Noir

RECENT AWARDS
Sauvignon Blanc 2004 – 5 stars: *Winestate* magazine Best of Recent Releases Nov/Dec 04; Riesling 2004 – Silver: Canterbury A&P Show International Aromatic Wine Competition; Chardonnay 2002 – 4 stars: *Winestate* magazine, May/Jun 04; Pinot Noir 2003 – 4 stars: *Gourmet Traveller Wine* Top 100 New Releases Nov 04

Clifford Bay Estate
26 Rapaura Rd, Renwick
Tel: (03) 572 7148
Fax: (03) 572 7138
Email: wine@cliffordbay.co.nz
Website: www.cliffordbay.co.nz

DIRECTIONS
Located just east of the intersection of SH6 and Rapaura Rd, next to Nautilus Estate.

OPENING HOURS
Cellar Door & Restaurant:
7 days, summer from 9.30am, winter from 10am

WINERY SALES
Cellar door, retail, mail order, Internet

PRICE RANGE $16–$30

TASTING
Tasting fee: $2 (refundable on purchase).

RESTAURANT
Popular restaurant with indoor/outdoor dining offering fresh local produce. Open 7 days. Bookings recommended.
Tel: (03) 572 7132

OWNER
Clifford Bay Estates Ltd

WINEMAKER
Glenn Thomas (Vavasour Wines)

DATE ESTABLISHED 1994

MARLBOROUGH
Wairau Valley

Clos Henri

Clos Henri is owned by the internationally recognised winemaking family of Henri Bourgeois of Sancerre, France. For ten generations the family has crafted premium-quality Sauvignon Blanc and Pinot Noir wines and in 2000 chose 100 hectares of Marlborough land to continue their passion abroad.

Tastings are held by appointment in Ste Solange, a quaint old country church complete with steeple which was moved onto the property.

Visitors can partake in the fabulous hillside views the site offers with the new Clos Henri self-guided 'Flavours in the Vines' vineyard tour or purchase a tasters picnic basket filled with wine, Clos Henri home-made cheeses and bread and while away a relaxing few hours in the sunshine amongst the vines.

WINES
Clos Henri Marlborough Sauvignon Blanc, Pinot Noir

Clos Henri
639 SH63, Renwick
Tel: (03) 572 7923
Fax: (03) 572 7926
Email: wine@closhenri.com
Website: www.closhenri.com

DIRECTIONS
Travel 6km west of Renwick on SH63; Clos Henri (No. 639) is on the left — look for the church and head towards it.

OPENING HOURS
By appointment

WINERY SALES
Cellar door only

PRICE RANGE $20–$40

TASTING & TOURS
By appointment. 'Flavours in the Vines': self-guided walking vineyard tour.

PICNIC AREA
Purchase a tasters picnic basket and picnic amongst the vines.

OTHER FACILITIES
Available for private functions and weddings.

OWNER
Bourgeois family

WINEMAKERS
Sally & Jasper Raats

DATE ESTABLISHED 2001

MARLBOROUGH
Wairau Valley

Cloudy Bay Vineyards

One of the original wineries in the region, Cloudy Bay quickly became recognised internationally as a benchmark producer of Marlborough Sauvignon Blanc. Innovation, meticulous attention to detail and regional expression are the guiding principles of Cloudy Bay. Headed since inception by chief winemaker Kevin Judd, the Cloudy Bay team is committed to producing 'wines of region' and strives to enhance the pure, bracing flavours and stunning vibrancy naturally afforded by the climate and soils of Marlborough. Traditional vinification techniques are combined with modern winemaking technology to produce a range of wines that individually express the flavour, balance and spirit of the Cloudy Bay estate style. Visitors to the cellar door are welcome to picnic in the picturesque winery grounds.

WINES
Pelorus NV, Pelorus Vintage
Cloudy Bay Sauvignon Blanc, Te Koko, Chardonnay, Gewürztraminer, Pinot Noir, Late Harvest Riesling

Jacksons Rd, Blenheim
Tel: (03) 520 9140
Fax: (03) 520 9040
Email: info@cloudybay.co.nz
Website: www.cloudybay.co.nz

DIRECTIONS Jacksons Rd runs between Middle Renwick Rd, across Old Renwick Rd, to Rapaura Rd; Cloudy Bay is at the Rapaura Rd end.

OPENING HOURS
7 days, 10am–4.30pm; closed Christmas Day and Good Friday

WINERY SALES Cellar door, retail, mail order

PRICE RANGE $26–$40

TASTING & TOURS
Tastings of all currently released wines and the occasional limited release are available. Group tours available by appointment (max. 20 persons), some charges may apply. Enquiries: info@cloudybay.co.nz.

PICNIC AREA Visitors are welcome to picnic on the winery lawns.

EVENTS/ACTIVITIES
'Pinot at Cloudy Bay' third Saturday every June.

OWNER
Moët Hennessy Wine Estates

WINEMAKERS
Chief Winemaker: Kevin Judd
Winemaker: Eveline Fraser

DATE ESTABLISHED 1985

MARLBOROUGH
Wairau Valley

Domaine Georges Michel

Georges Michel established Domaine Georges Michel Wine Estate in 1997 to focus on the production of top-quality Sauvignon Blanc, Chardonnay and Pinot Noir. Consultant winemaker, Guy Brac de la Perrière, blends years of French winemaking experience with the fresh flavours of Marlborough to produce triumphant wines.

In 2005 Georges' daughter, Swan, joined the winemaking team after qualifying in winemaking. She brings new vision and enthusiasm as well as overseas and local vintage experience. The picturesque winery with its wine, gift and gourmet shop are open to the public. The original restaurant has been rebuilt into "La Veranda", a huge rotund Victorian villa.

WINES
Golden Mile Sauvignon Blanc, Chardonnay, Pinot Noir; **La Reserve** Chardonnay, Pinot Noir; **Summer Folly** Rosé and Autumn Folly Dessert Wine; **Marc of Marlborough** grape spirit (traditional French style)

RECENT AWARDS
Winners of numerous medals and awards including: Liquorland Top 100, Air NZ Wine Awards, Royal Easter Wine Show, *Cuisine* recommendations and many international awards.

56 Vintage Lane
Rapaura, Blenheim
Tel: (03) 572 7230
Fax: (03) 572 7231
Email: georgesmichel@xtra.co.nz
Website: www.georgesmichel.co.nz

DIRECTIONS Vintage Lane is off Rapaura Rd at the Renwick end. The vineyard is on the right.

OPENING HOURS
Cellar Door: Mid-Oct–mid-Apr: 7 days, 10.30am–4.30pm; Mid-Apr–mid-Oct. Phone for details. Restaurant: Summer, 7 days, 12–4pm; Fri & Sat night for dinner. Winter: phone for details.

WINERY SALES
Cellar door, retail, mail order

PRICE RANGE $16–$49

TASTING & TOURS
Tasting is free of charge. Tours by appointment.

RESTAURANT La Veranda: indoor and outdoor dining, serving modern à la carte cuisine. Res: (03) 572 9177

OTHER PRODUCTS
Gourmet French products, fine French imported wines including Georges' own and those made by Guy Brac de la Perrière.

OWNER Georges Michel

WINEMAKERS
Guy Brac de la Perrière, Swan Michel, Peter Saunders

DATE ESTABLISHED 1997

MARLBOROUGH
Wairau Valley

Drylands Marlborough

Nestled in the picturesque sun-drenched area of the renowned Marlborough wine-growing region, Drylands produces wines of the finest quality and individual character. The cellar door is looked after by knowledgeable, friendly staff, and visitors can taste and purchase Drylands' extensive selection of varietals, all exclusively from Marlborough. And as part of the Nobilo Wine Group, they also offer an extensive range of Nobilo, Selaks and other imported brands. The Drylands philosophy is 'Searching for the Best' — resulting in the finest wines, sourced from only their best vineyards. This endeavour for quality was recently acknowledged at the prestigious 2003 International Wine & Spirit Competition in London, when Nobilo Wine Group was awarded Best New Zealand Wine Producer of the Year.

WINES
Labels: White Cloud, Fernleaf, Fall Harvest, Station Road, House of Nobilo, Nobilo Icon, Selaks Premium Selection, Selaks Founders Reserve, Drylands, Castle Cliffs
Wine styles: Sauvignon Blanc, Chardonnay, Riesling, Pinot Gris, Pinot Noir, Syrah, Merlot, Cabernet Sauvignon, Sparkling, Dessert Wines, Port

RECENT AWARDS
Best New Zealand Wine Producer of the Year Trophy: International Wine & Spirit Competition London 2003; Highest Awarded Winery Trophy: International Chardonnay Challenge 2003; Champion of Champions Winemaker Trophy: Hawke's Bay A&P Mercedes-Benz Wine Show 2003

Hammerichs Rd, Blenheim
Tel: (03) 570 5252
Fax: (03) 570 5272
Email: drylands@nobilo.co.nz
Website: www.drylands.co.nz

DIRECTIONS
Less than 5 minutes from Blenheim and the airport, Hammerichs Rd runs between Rapaura and Old Renwick Rds.

OPENING HOURS
7 days, 10am–5pm

WINERY SALES
Cellar door, retail and mail order

PRICE RANGE $8–$100

TASTING & TOURS
Tasting is free of charge. Tours by appointment.

OTHER PRODUCTS
Comprehensive range of imported wines from Australia and South Africa.

OWNER
Constellation Brands Inc.

WINEMAKER
Chief Winemaker: Darryl Woolley

DATE ESTABLISHED
Vineyards 1980
Winery 1995

MARLBOROUGH
Wairau Valley

Fairhall Downs Estate Wines

Epitomising the 'small is beautiful' philosophy, Fairhall Downs Estate is a family owned and operated Marlborough wine company specialising in premium, single vineyard wines. First planted in 1982 and now covering 32ha the vineyard is one of the more established in the Marlborough region. A picturesque country road leads to the Cellar Door with its range of superbly crafted wines. Quality there speaks for itself and visitors can taste the vineyard's internationally renowned Sauvignon Blanc, Chardonnay, Pinot Gris and Pinot Noir. From the tasting room, views of Marlborough's Brancott Valley dropping down to the Wairau Plains enhance the Fairhall Downs wine-tasting experience.

WINES
Fairhall Downs Sauvignon Blanc, Pinot Gris, Chardonnay, Pinot Noir

RECENT AWARDS
An array of gold medals and trophies have been awarded to many of the wines produced since 1996.

70 Wrekin Rd,
Brancott Valley, Blenheim
Tel: (03) 572 8356
Fax: (03) 572 8357
Email: enquiries@fairhalldowns.co.nz
Website: www.fairhalldowns.co.nz

DIRECTIONS
On Wrekin Rd, just 12km from Blenheim and 8km from the airport. Follow the signs from the New Renwick Rd / Brancott Rd turnoff.

OPENING HOURS
Mon–Fri, 10am–4pm

WINERY SALES
Cellar door, mail order (free delivery throughout New Zealand)

PRICE RANGE
$18–$30

TASTING & TOURS
Tasting is free of charge. Vineyard tours are available by appointment.

OWNERS
Julie & Stuart Smith,
Jill & Ken Small

CONSULTANT WINEMAKER
David Freschi

DATE ESTABLISHED
Vineyard established 1982. First wine produced for the Fairhall Downs label 1996.

MARLBOROUGH
Wairau Valley

Framingham Wine Company

Framingham has become one of the most regularly recommended 'must see' wineries on the Marlborough wine trail and it certainly lives up to its promise to deliver the best, not only with their much awarded aromatic wines but also with their facilities. Through the gatehouse entranceway, the Rosé-planted walled courtyard leads to an elegant tasting room with native timber panels and a marble fireplace for cold winter days. A staircase leads to underground cellars where vintages past and present are aged in perfect conditions and there is a museum of wine-related memorabilia. You will be given a warm welcome to taste and purchase these wines at the cellar door year round.

WINES
Framingham Sauvignon Blanc, Gewürztraminer, Riesling (several styles), Pinot Gris, Pinot Noir, Chardonnay and a Merlot/Malbec blend. Occasionally wines of special interest are released through the cellar door.

RECENT AWARDS
Chardonnay 2003 – Gold: 2004 Air New Zealand Wine Awards; Classic Riesling 2003, Dry Riesling 2003, Pinot Gris 2004 – Gold: *NZ Home & Entertaining* 2004

Framingham Wine Company
Conders Bend Rd, Renwick
Tel: (03) 572 8884
Fax: (03) 572 9884
Email: sales@framingham.co.nz
Website: www.framingham.co.nz

DIRECTIONS
Turn into Conders Bend Rd on the west side of SH6, 1km north of Renwick. Framingham is immediately on the left.

OPENING HOURS
Oct–Apr: 7 days, 10am–5pm
May–Sept: 7 days, 11am–4pm

WINERY SALES
Cellar door, retail, mail order, Internet

PRICE RANGE
$18.50–$35

TASTING & TOURS
Tasting is free of charge. Tours by appointment only.

OTHER ACTIVITIES
Underground wine cellar, native gardens and courtyard

OWNER
Orlando Wyndham

WINEMAKER
Andrew Hedley

DATE ESTABLISHED
1994

MARLBOROUGH
Wairau Valley

Fromm Winery — La Strada

Set in the middle of the five-hectare home vineyard, Fromm Winery is a specialist red wine producer founded by Swiss winemaker Georg Fromm, whose experience dates back four generations of winegrowers. La Strada means 'the way'. It is a symbolic name for the winery and its wines; the notion behind it means 'to move forward'. You will find some exceptional Pinot Noirs and Bordeaux varieties at the cellar door. More recently, the boutique winery also made a name for itself with deliciously zingy low alcohol Rieslings. Low cropping, sustainable viticulture, and hand tending in the vineyard contribute to the exceptional wines the winery is known for.

WINES
Labels: La Strada, Fromm Vineyard, Clayvin Vineyard
Wine styles: Chardonnay, Gewürztraminer, Riesling Dry, low alcohol Rieslings, Rosé, Pinot Noir, Syrah, Malbec, Merlot, Merlot/Malbec

OTHER PRODUCTS
Spiegelau wine glasses

Godfrey Rd, Blenheim
Tel: (03) 572 9355
Fax: (03) 572 9366
Email: lastrada@frommwineries.com
Website: www.frommwineries.com

DIRECTIONS
On the corner of Godfrey and Middle Renwick Rd, near Renwick.

OPENING HOURS
Summer: 7 days, 11am–5pm
Winter (late Apr–Oct): Fri–Sun, 11am–4pm. Closed Christmas Day and Good Friday

WINERY SALES
Cellar door, mail order, retail

PRICE RANGE
$17–$60

TASTING
Tasting is free of charge

OWNERS
Georg Fromm & Pol Lenzinger

WINEMAKERS
Hätsch Kalberer & William Hoare

DATE ESTABLISHED 1991

MARLBOROUGH
Wairau Valley

Herzog Winery & Luxury Restaurant

Hans and Therese Herzog come from a wine-growing family that dates back to 1482. They moved their winery and Michelin-starred restaurant from their native Switzerland to Marlborough where they run one of New Zealand's leading boutique estates. The vineyard's unique microclimate and extremely low yields allow Hans to create rare and precious wines of extraordinary depth and structure. The restaurant was built out of pure passion, giving locals and visitors to New Zealand the opportunity to experience the Herzog wines with world-class food as they were intended. This is destination dining at its best in a stunning secluded location, overlooking the estate's 11-hectare vineyard and mountains beyond.

WINES
Herzog Marlborough Merlot/Cabernet Sauvignon — 'Spirit of Marlborough', Pinot Noir, Montepulciano, Pinot Gris, Chardonnay, Viognier, FeatherWhite

RECENT AWARDS
Herzog wines are not entered in competitions; recent accolades include: 'The Herzog Pinot Noir is the best I have tasted in New Zealand', Huon Hooke, *Sydney Morning Herald*

81 Jeffries Rd, Blenheim
Tel: (03) 572 8770
Fax: (03) 572 8730
Email: info@herzog.co.nz
Website: www.herzog.co.nz

DIRECTIONS
Turn into Jeffries Rd, off Rapaura Rd. Herzog is at the end of the road.

OPENING HOURS
Cellar Door: Mon–Fri, 11am–5pm; weekends 11am–4pm. Cellar Door Bistro: Oct–May, Tues–Sun for lunch. Luxury Restaurant: Oct–May, Tues–Sun from 7pm

WINERY SALES
Cellar door, retail, mail order and from the restaurant

PRICE RANGE $29–$59

TASTING & TOURS
Tasting fee: $10 for 3 wines (refundable on purchase of 3 bottles). Tours by appointment only.

ACCOMMODATION
Luxury cottage in Herzog's beautiful vineyard.

RESTAURANT
Herzog Luxury Restaurant. Reservations: (03) 572 8770

EVENTS & ACTIVITIES
Cooking classes, kitchen tours and themed dégustation dinners.

OWNERS
Hans & Therese Herzog

WINEMAKER Hans Herzog

DATE ESTABLISHED 1994

MARLBOROUGH
Wairau Valley

45 Lanark Lane, Renwick
Tel: (03) 572 2731
Fax: (03) 572 2732
Email: vineyard@new-zealand-wines.com
Website: www.new-zealand-wines.com

DIRECTIONS
7km west of Renwick on SH63, turn right into Lanark Lane, the vineyard is on the left.

OPENING HOURS
By appointment only.

WINERY SALES
Tasting facilities, retail (Cellar Select chain and some fine wine outlets), mail order, Internet

PRICE RANGE $19–$35

TASTING & TOURS
Tastings and tours around the vineyard and hill site by appointment only. A tasting fee may apply (refundable on purchase).

OWNERS
Pam & Martyn Nicholls and their three children, Garth, Bryony & Hugo

WINEMAKER
Chris Young

DATE ESTABLISHED 1994

Gravitas Wines

The Gravitas name comes from the Latin word denoting something of great stature, quality and elegance — words that summarise the company's philosophy and practice. Their impressive rise to global fame in a few short years is one of the great stories of the New Zealand wine industry. Gravitas has recently been described as 'setting the standard for the antipodean wine industry, the most exciting wine producer in New Zealand' by *Swig* (UK). Its Chardonnay has been rated as one of the world's top 25 white wines (Burgundy/aromatic) by Jancis Robinson MW, Europe's foremost wine writer and judge; its Sauvignon Blanc the best in New Zealand by Bob Campbell MW.

Gravitas has been described as being 'on the lunatic fringe end of the quality control spectrum', with all wines meticulously crafted and made only from estate-grown grapes. The grapes are picked by hand over a one-month period, at extremely low yields. This, along with the cooler climate in the lower Wairau Valley, gives Gravitas wines their legendary concentration.

While Gravitas has traditionally exported 100 per cent of its wines, tasting is available by appointment at the vineyard. In mid-2005 Gravitas obtained Resource Consent for construction of a boutique winery, barrel hall, and new tasting room on a hill formed by the confluence of the Wairau and Waihopai Rivers. From this site spectacular panoramic views of Marlborough delight visitors.

WINES
Gravitas Sauvignon Blanc, Reserve (oaked) and Unoaked Chardonnay, Pinot Noir, Riesling and a Vin de Paille dessert wine

RECENT AWARDS
In the last two years, Gravitas has won a total of 40 medals in competitions around the world, including gold at the International Wine & Spirit Competition in London, and trophy for the best Sauvignon Blanc at France's prestigious Citadelle du Vins. Michael Cooper, author of the *Wine Atlas of New Zealand*, rated Gravitas 2003 Oaked Chardonnay and 2004 Sauvignon Blanc 4½ and 5 stars respectively. The new Pinot Noir is currently creating a storm overseas.

MARLBOROUGH
Wairau Valley

Highfield Estate

To form a lasting impression of Marlborough as a unique winemaking region Highfield Estate is a must-see. With unsurpassed views across the Wairau Valley vineyards from their dramatic viewing tower this is one of Marlborough's most visited sites. Enjoy wine tasting at the cellar door, dine at the restaurant or play pétanque. Offering indoor and outdoor dining the restaurant specialises in matching fresh local cuisine with their food-friendly wines to give you one of the best culinary experiences in the Wairau Valley. Highfield's winery specialises in making wines using only Marlborough grapes grown on their chosen vineyards. Sold in seven countries these award-winning wines, made only when vintage quality permits, are emerging as an ultra-premium New World wine brand.

WINES
Highfield Marlborough Sauvignon Blanc, Pinot Noir, Chardonnay, Riesling, Elstree Cuvée Brut

RECENT AWARDS
Sauvignon Blanc 2004 – Blue-Gold: Sydney International Wine Competition 2005, Gold: Winpac Wine Competition Hong Kong 2005, Gold: Air NZ Wine Awards & Royal Easter Show 2004; Pinot Noir 2002 – Best Pinot Noir Trophy, Gold, Top 100 Winner: Sydney International Wine Competition 2005

OTHER PRODUCTS
Art exhibitions (art for sale), local craft

Brookby Rd, Blenheim
Tel: (03) 572 9244
Fax: (03) 572 9257
Email: winery@highfield.co.nz
Website: www.highfield.co.nz

DIRECTIONS
Turn off SH6 onto Godfrey Rd, turn right into Dog Point Rd then left into Brookby Rd.

OPENING HOURS
Cellar Door: 7 days, 10am–5pm
Restaurant: 7 days, 11.30am–3.30pm

WINERY SALES Cellar door, retail, mail order, Internet

PRICE RANGE $24–$38

TASTING Tasting is free of charge. Tours by appointment only.

RESTAURANT Highfield Restaurant. Reservations: (03) 572 9244 ext 3

ACCOMMODATION
Luxury, single-bedroom, self-contained apartment with unsurpassed views of the Wairau Valley. $250 per night.

OWNERS
Shin Yokoi & Tom Tenuwera

WINEMAKER
Alistair Soper

DATE ESTABLISHED 1988

MARLBOROUGH
Wairau Valley

Huia Vineyards

Mike and Claire Allen were drawn to Marlborough by the intense fruit flavours in the wines. Here they established Huia, a boutique-sized private company committed to the production of hand-crafted and high-quality Marlborough wines that are aromatic, elegant and food-friendly. Huia wines are now in demand worldwide – currently 85 per cent of their wines are exported.

The owners chose the name Huia as an intrinsically New Zealand name and to reflect the feel of the South Pacific. The Huia was a unique New Zealand bird, now extinct, but still revered for its unusual beauty.

WINES
Huia Sauvignon Blanc, Riesling, Pinot Gris, Gewürztraminer, Chardonnay, Pinot Noir, Vintage Brut

RECENT AWARDS
Some recent accolades include: Sauvignon Blanc 2004 – 4 stars+: Ron Wiegand, *Restaurant and Wine*; Pinot Gris 2004 – Exceptional: Dan Berger's *Vintage Experiences*; Pinot Noir 2002 – 4 stars: *Michael Cooper's Buyer's Guide to NZ Wines*

22 Boyces Rd, Blenheim
Tel: (03) 572 8326
Fax: (03) 572 8331
Email: wine@huia.net.nz
Website: www.huia.net.nz

DIRECTIONS
Turn off Rapaura Rd into Boyces Rd; 100m along turn right to the winery.

OPENING HOURS
10.30am–5pm. Summer: Labour Weekend–1 May, 7 days. Winter: 1 May–Labour Weekend, 5 days, Mon–Fri.

WINERY SALES
Cellar door, retail, mail order

PRICE RANGE $20–$36

TASTING
Tasting free of charge.

OTHER PRODUCTS
Huia-branded wine knives, sparkling stoppers, T-shirts, caps & hats, wine glasses

OWNERS
Mike & Claire Allen

WINEMAKERS
Mike & Claire Allen

DATE ESTABLISHED 1990

Hunter's Wines

It was the late Ernie Hunter and his wife Jane who put Marlborough on the world map when their Sauvignon Blanc was voted Best White Wine by the London *Sunday Times* Vintage Festival in 1986. Now one of New Zealand's most established wineries, Jane continues to build on the company's formidable reputation producing award-winning wines based on the intense fruit flavours of the region. Recent expansion has seen the vineyard increase by two and a half times and production grow to around 60,000 cases, nearly half of which is exported. Jane Hunter has been awarded an OBE and an honorary doctorate for services to the wine industry, and recently received the inaugural 'Women in Wine Award' at the International Wine & Spirit Competition (UK).

The winery is set amongst native gardens where a vine-covered trellised walkway links the restaurant, wine shop and gallery where the artist in residence has his studio. Set in the vineyard, Hunter's Restaurant is renowned for its gourmet fare and is a winner of numerous culinary awards. The outdoor dining area includes a pool and children's play area, or during winter relax indoors by the open fire in the farmhouse-style dining room.

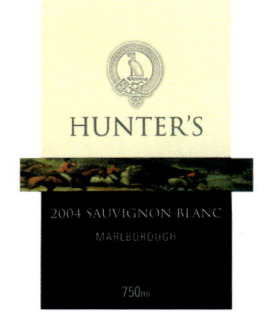

WINES
Hunter's Marlborough Sauvignon Blanc, Chardonnay, Riesling, Gewürztraminer, Rosé, Pinot Noir, Merlot and Miru Miru™ (Maori for 'bubbles') Miru Miru™ Reserve Sparkling Wine

RECENT AWARDS
Over the past 20 years Hunter's Wines have won numerous international awards and medals including the Marquis de Goulaine Trophy for 'Best Sauvignon Blanc in the World' at the 1992 International Wine & Spirit Competition and a Black Diamond award (3 golds in one year) in 1995 at Intervin New York. More recently in 2003 the Hunter's 2002 Sauvignon Blanc won the Old Ebbitt Bar & Grill Wines for Oysters Competition.

ACTIVITIES
Hunter's Garden: A unique tourist attraction, the garden features rare and interesting New Zealand flora. Regular sculpture exhibitions in the gardens. Artist in residence: visit Clarry Neame in his studio.

MARLBOROUGH
Wairau Valley

Rapaura Rd, Blenheim
PO Box 128
Renwick
Tel: (03) 572 8489
Fax: (03) 572 8457
Email: wine@hunters.co.nz
Website: www.hunters.co.nz

DIRECTIONS
Located on the north side of Rapaura Rd between Jacksons and Hammerichs Rds.

OPENING HOURS
Cellar Door: 7 days, 9am–5pm
Restaurant: lunch 7 days, 12pm–3pm; dinner Thurs–Sun from 6pm

WINERY SALES
Cellar door, retail, mail order, Internet

PRICE RANGE $12–$28

TASTING
Wine tasting available 7 days, 9am–5pm

OTHER PRODUCTS
Marlborough olive oils

RESTAURANT
Hunter's Garden Restaurant. Open all year. Bookings are advised for dinner. Reservations: (03) 572 8803.

PICNIC AREA
Set amongst an extensive native garden.

EVENTS
Hunters Garden Marlborough: A programme of garden workshops, tours and social events held each Nov.
www.garden-marlborough.co.nz

OWNER
Jane Hunter

WINEMAKERS
Chief Winemaker: Gary Duke
Winemaker: Andrew Parley

DATE ESTABLISHED 1979

MARLBOROUGH
Wairau Valley

72 Hawkesbury Rd
Renwick
Tel: (03) 572 8300
Fax: (03) 572 8383
Email: info@isabelestate.com
Website: www.isabelestate.com

DIRECTIONS
Turn into Hawkesbury Rd, off West Coast Highway 63 near Renwick and the winery is 500m on the right (signposted).

OPENING HOURS
Mon–Fri, 11am–4pm. Open weekends during summer.

WINERY SALES
Cellar door, fine wine stores, mail order, Internet

PRICE RANGE $20–$49

TASTING & TOURS
Tasting and tours by appointment. Please note: during busy periods the cellar may be unavailable to visit.

OTHER PRODUCTS
Isabel estate-grown olive oil, Isabel shirts, aprons and wine accessories

OWNERS
Michael & Robyn Tiller

WINEMAKERS
Michael Tiller & Patricia Miranda

DATE ESTABLISHED 1982

Isabel Estate

Set on the elevated Omaka Terrace, Isabel Estate is one of the largest privately owned estates in Marlborough, containing some of the oldest vines in the region. Producing grapes of exceptional quality, yields are restricted by pruning to low bud numbers and, where necessary, shoot and bunch thinning. Isabel Estate's terroir combines deep free-draining gravel with a narrow layer of calcium-rich clay. The modern winery situated in the middle of the vineyard combines the very best of high- and low-tech equipment to maximise vineyard flavours.

Recognised internationally as a producer of fine wines, most of the estate's production is destined for export markets. However, a small amount of wine is retained at the winery where visitors can enjoy a tasting in the stylish and purpose-built tasting salon that has superb views of the vineyards. For the complete vineyard experience you can stay on the estate in their cosy and rustic self-contained lodge.

WINES
Isabel Marlborough Sauvignon Blanc, Chardonnay, Dry Riesling, Pinot Gris, Pinot Noir, Noble Sauvage

RECENT AWARDS
Sauvignon Blanc 2004 – 91 points: *The Wine Review* (USA), Ranked in Top 10 of 114 NZ Sauvignon Blancs: Joelle Thomson; Sauvignon Blanc 2003 – 5 stars: *Winestate* magazine (Aust); Pinot Gris 2004 – Ranked one of the best NZ Pinot Gris yet: Joelle Thomson, *WineNZ* magazine; Chardonnay 2002 – Gold: International Wine Challenge 2004, 90 points: *Wine Spectator* (USA); Pinot Noir 2001 – 5 stars: *Winestate* magazine (Aust)

ACCOMMODATION
Located on the estate, Isabel Lodge has a spacious, rustic feel with a large stone fireplace, a well-equipped kitchen and private access. With views of the Richmond Ranges, it accommodates couples or a small group comfortably. Marlborough Airport is 5 minutes away by car and the village of Renwick is just 2 minutes away. For details and bookings visit: www.isabelestate.com or Tel: (03) 572 8300.

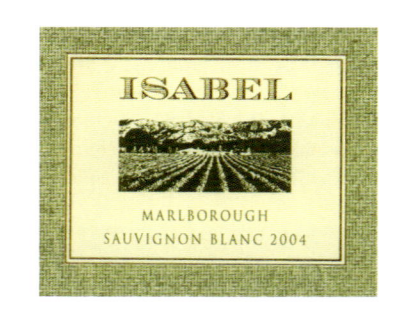

MARLBOROUGH
Wairau Valley

Kathy Lynskey Wines

Kathy Lynskey & Kent Casto

Kathy Lynskey Wines is a privately owned boutique Marlborough wine company producing only 6000 cases of single vineyard and reserve wines annually. Because the owners are passionate about creating varietal wines which reflect true fruit characters for each variety, all the wines produced are unblended and 100 per cent of the varietal. The company's estate vineyard comprises nine hectares planted on old riverbed soils adjoining the Omaka River.

Owners Kathy Lynskey and Kent Casto live on the vineyard, which allows them to adopt a 'hands on' approach to vineyard management. Vines are cropped at levels that maximise the intense fruit flavours and all grapes with the exception of Sauvignon Blanc are hand-picked. Since releasing its first Sauvignon Blanc in 1998 the company has achieved excellent recognition in New Zealand and the United States, winning awards in major competitions and receiving regular 4- and 5-star ratings.

Their tasting room is located on the vineyard. You may sample all available varietals, providing they have not sold out, as well as their estate-grown, hand-picked extra virgin olive oil. If you are a passionate gardener, you may ask to walk through the private cottage garden behind the tasting room.

WINES
Kathy Lynskey Wines Marlborough Vineyard Select Sauvignon Blanc, Single Vineyard Gewürztraminer, Single Vineyard Pinot Gris, Godfrey Reserve Chardonnay, Block 36 Reserve Pinot Noir, 15 Rows Reserve Merlot

RECENT AWARDS
15 Rows Reserve Merlot – Trophy Champion Classical Red Table Wine: Romeo Bragato Wine Awards 2004, 5-star honours: Best of the Bunch *Cuisine* magazine 2004; Godfrey Reserve Chardonnay 2002: 91/100 points *Wine Spectator* (USA) 2003; Block 36 Reserve Pinot Noir 2003 – Gold: Riverside International Wine Competition 05, Gold: Dallas Morning News Wine Competition 05; Vineyard Select Sauvignon Blanc 2004 – Double Gold: Eastern International Wine Competition USA 05, Gold: West Coast Wine Competition USA 05; Single Vineyard Gewürztraminer 2004 – Gold: New World International Wine Competition USA, 5 stars: *Winestate* magazine Oct 05

36 Godfrey Rd, Blenheim
Tel: (03) 572 7180
Fax: (03) 572 7181
Email: lynskeys.wines@xtra.co.nz
Website: www.kathylynskeywines.co.nz

DIRECTIONS
On the corner of Godfrey and Middle Renwick Rd, near Renwick.

OPENING HOURS
7 days, 10.30am–4pm

WINERY SALES
Cellar door, retail, mail order, Internet

PRICE RANGE $20–$55

TASTING
Tasting fee: $3 pp

OTHER PRODUCTS
Estate-grown extra virgin olive oil

OWNERS
Kathy Lynskey & Kent Casto

WINEMAKERS
Consulting Winemaker: Alan McCorkindale

DATE ESTABLISHED 1998

MARLBOROUGH
Wairau Valley

Lake Chalice Wines

Chris Gambitsis bought the Falcon Vineyard in 1989, an abandoned vineyard that needed complete overhaul. He also rehabilitated the adjacent quarry block, turning wasteland into valuable vineyards, winning a Ministry of the Environment Green Ribbon Award. Visitors are amazed that vines flourish in the extremely stony ground which produces low yields with intense flavours. Lake Chalice isn't the prettiest vineyard in Marlborough but you can't deny the quality of the wines produced.

Lake Chalice Wines is a proud sponsor of the Wingspan Birds of Prey Charitable Trust (www.wingspan.co.nz), dedicated to the preservation of New Zealand's endangered raptors. Their emblem, appearing on every bottle, is the native New Zealand falcon — the karearea.

WINES
Lake Chalice Platinum (Reserve) Chardonnay, Chardonnay, Unoaked Chardonnay, The Raptor Sauvignon Blanc, Sauvignon Blanc, Pinot Gris, Rosé, Merlot, Pinot Noir, Botrytised Late Harvest Riesling

RECENT AWARDS
Sauvignon Blanc 2004 – 2 Trophies (Best Lighter Bodied White Wine & Best White Table Wine): Sydney International Wine Competition 2005; Sauvignon Blanc 2002 – Gold: Royal Easter Wine Show 2003

93 Vintage Lane, Renwick
Tel: (03) 572 9327
Fax: (03) 572 9327
Email: wine@lakechalice.com
Website: www.lakechalice.com

DIRECTIONS
Near the Renwick end of Rapaura Rd. Turn south into Vintage Lane, proceed for 1km and look for the two blue towers.

OPENING HOURS
Labour Day (Oct)–Easter: 7 days, 11am–4pm. Rest of the year: by appointment

WINERY SALES
Cellar door, retail, mail order, Internet

PRICE RANGE $17–$150

TASTING
Tasting is free of charge.

PICNIC AREA
BYO picnic and enjoy the quiet, sheltered and shady dell.

OWNERS
Phil Binnie, Chris Gambitsis (Gambo) & Matt Thomson

WINEMAKER
Matt Thomson

DATE ESTABLISHED 1989

MARLBOROUGH
Wairau Valley

Lawson's Dry Hills

Lawson's Dry Hills is committed to the production of premium Marlborough wines and has received many accolades and show successes. Grapes are harvested from right across the spectrum of soil types, ranging from light stony soils to heavy loams, including clay-based. As one of the pioneers in the New Zealand screwcap initiative they are committed to ensuring the quality and integrity of all their wines by using screwcap closures. The winery has a modern cellar door and there is an attractive picnic area. You can meet Tomi, the owners' Golden Labrador who in 2002 achieved international celebrity status for being able to pick when the harvest should start just by sniffing the grapes.

WINES
Lawson's Dry Hills Marlborough Sauvignon Blanc, Riesling, Gewürztraminer, Pinot Gris, Chardonnay, Pinot Noir, Pinot Rosé, Late Harvest Sémillon

RECENT AWARDS
Sauvignon Blanc 2004 – Blue-Gold & Top 100: Sydney International Wine Challenge; Gewürztraminer 2004 – Trophy: Liquorland International Top 100

Alabama Rd, Blenheim
Tel: (03) 578 7674
Fax: (03) 578 7603
Email: wine@lawsonsdryhills.co.nz
Website: www.lawsonsdryhills.co.nz

DIRECTIONS
From Blenheim any of the roads to the Wither Hills. Turn left into Alabama Rd. The winery is on the right, 1km from Redwood St intersection.

OPENING HOURS
7 days, 10am–5pm

WINERY SALES
Cellar door, retail, mail order

PRICE RANGE $16.50–$28

TASTING & TOURS
Tasting is free of charge. Tours can be arranged.

FOOD OPTIONS
Cheese platters can be organised to accompany tastings.

PICNIC AREA
Vine-enclosed courtyard adjacent to the cellar door.

OTHER PRODUCTS
Clothing from Merino Mink, Snowy Peak & Lawson's Dry Hills, locally made gold & silver jewellery, Gewürztraminer brandy

OWNERS
Barbara & Ross Lawson

WINEMAKERS
Marcus Wright & Dean Boyce

DATE ESTABLISHED 1992

MARLBOROUGH
Wairau Valley

Montana Brancott Winery

The Montana Brancott Winery is home to some of New Zealand's finest wines and is one of Marlborough's top tourist attractions. This building is designed for the celebration of life and what's best about it — food and wine, music and crafts. Visitors can pop in for a quick coffee, a meal with a distinct Marlborough flavour or a winery tour and tasting. Its spacious downstairs restaurant and outdoor area can cater for large groups, and the exclusive Tower Room is perfect for more intimate gatherings.

A tour of the winery is de rigueur. Montana planted the first vineyards in Marlborough in 1973 and this is the oldest working winery in the region. The giant grape-tipping tanks are the first of their kind in the world, the French Coquard grape press the first in the Southern Hemisphere, and the large traditional wooden cuves remain a rarity in New Zealand. This winery makes some of New Zealand's best — including the Montana Reserve range and the Montana Terraces, Brancott, Fairhall and Renwick Estate wines.

Montana Brancott Winery, SH1
Riverlands, Blenheim
Tel: (03) 578 2099
Fax (03) 578 0463
Website: www.montana.co.nz

DIRECTIONS
Five minutes south of Blenheim on SH1.

OPENING HOURS
Cellar door: 7 days, 9am–5pm
Restaurant: 9am–5pm

WINERY SALES
Cellar door, retail, and mail order (through subscription to the winery newsletter 'Brancott Brio')

PRICE RANGE $13–$99

TASTING & TOURS
Tasting trays available for $5 and $7. Daily tours, 10am–3pm. Bookings are advisable. Tour fee: $10, with a discount for group bookings.

RESTAURANT
Brancott Winery Restaurant is one of the region's leading winery restaurant/cafés offering premium Marlborough fare. Bookings advisable: (03) 577 5776

OTHER FACILITIES
Conference and private function facilities. With its unique ambience, award-winning wines, fabulous cuisine and picture-perfect setting this is one of Marlborough's premier wedding venues.

OWNER
Allied Domecq Wines (NZ) Ltd

SENIOR WINEMAKER
Patrick Materman

DATE ESTABLISHED 2000

WINES
Montana Classic Sauvignon Blanc, Riesling, Pinot Noir
Montana Reserve Sauvignon Blanc, Chardonnay, Pinot Noir, Merlot, Riesling, Pinot Gris
Montana Estate Terraces Pinot Noir, Brancott Sauvignon Blanc, Fairhall Cabernet Sauvignon, Renwick Chardonnay

RECENT AWARDS
Montana Sauvignon Blanc 2004 – Best Value Dry White, Top 100 & Blue-Gold: Sydney International Wine Competition 2005; Montana Reserve Chardonnay 2002 – Gold: Japan Wine Challenge 2003 & 2004, Sydney International Wine Competition 2004; Montana Brancott Estate Sauvignon Blanc 2002 – Gold: International Wine Competition Asia 2004 & Japan Wine Challenge 2003; Montana Terraces Estate Pinot Noir 2002 – Gold: Japan Wine Challenge 2003, 4½ stars: *Sunday Star-Times* Mar 04

MARLBOROUGH
Wairau Valley

193 Rapaura Rd, Blenheim
Tel: (03) 572 7170
Fax: (03) 572 7170
Email: info@mudhousevillage.co.nz
Website: www.mudhousevillage.co.nz

DIRECTIONS
On Rapaura Rd. Turn right off SH1 at Spring Creek if coming from Picton, or left off SH6 just over the Waihopai River Bridge if coming from the Nelson direction.

OPENING HOURS
7 days, 10am–5pm
(closed Christmas Day)

WINERY SALES
Cellar door, retail, mail order, Internet

PRICE RANGE $18.50–$45

TASTING
Tasting is free of charge but there may be a small fee for large groups (this is refundable on purchase). Large groups by appointment only.

CAFÉ
The Mud House Village Café offers indoor and outdoor dining and serves an excellent range of snacks, vineyard platters, salads, seasonal soups, delicious desserts, ice creams and coffee, all home-made on the premises.

OTHER ATTRACTIONS
The Olive Shop has a range of award-winning local olive oils and gifts, including locally made jewellery and gourmet foods.

ACCOMMODATION
Off-site: Waterfall Lodge is a luxury, 2-bedroom, self-contained mud-brick cottage set amongst the vines at the Le Grys vineyard with stunning views over the vineyard and the Richmond Ranges. Reservations: (03) 572 9490 or 021 313 208 or stay@legrys.co.nz

OWNERS
Mud House Wine Company:
John & Jennifer Joslin
Mud House Village: Andy & Adele Joslin

WINEMAKERS
Allan Hedgeman & Matt Thomson (consultant)

DATE ESTABLISHED 1996

The Mud House Village

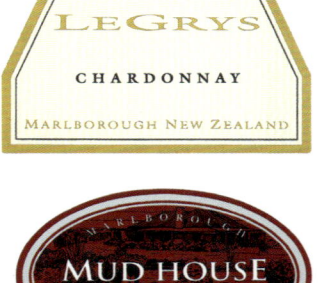

Situated in the heart of the Rapaura wine district, the Mud House Village has become a 'must visit' for locals and tourists alike offering a wide variety of activities on-site. Visitors to the mud-brick cellar door have the opportunity to taste all the Mud House wines, the main label in New Zealand, and the highly sought after Le Grys range, only available here or by mail order as most is exported. Lovers of bubbles can taste the No.1 Family Estate and No. 8 Méthode Traditionnelle owned and produced by Daniel and Adele Le Brun.

Adjoining the cellar door is the Village Café, which offers seasonal home-made cuisine with excellent coffee and treats to tempt anyone. Sometimes during the summer there are BBQ lunches with live music. With a lake and landscaped native garden this forms the perfect setting for alfresco dining, enjoying a glass of wine. Or you can be deciding what gifts or special mementoes to purchase from the various shops on-site.

WINES
Mud House Sauvignon Blanc, Riesling, Pinot Gris, Late Harvest Riesling, Merlot, Vineyard Selection Pinot Noir; **White Swan** Reserve Sauvignon Blanc and Chardonnay; **Black Swan** Reserve Pinot Noir; **Le Grys** Chardonnay, Sauvignon Blanc, Home Vineyard Pinot Noir

RECENT AWARDS
Mud House White Swan Reserve Sauvignon Blanc 2004 & Le Grys Sauvignon Blanc 2004 – Blue-Gold: Sydney International Wine Awards; Mud House Sauvignon Blanc & Marlborough Pinot Gris 2004 – 4 stars: *Winestate* magazine Best of Recent Releases May/Jun 05; Mud House Sauvignon Blanc 2004 – 4 stars: *Cuisine* magazine Best of the Bunch July 05

MARLBOROUGH
Wairau Valley

Nautilus Estate
12 Rapaura Rd, Renwick
Tel: (03) 572 9364
Fax: (03) 572 9374
Email: sales@nautilusestate.com
Website: www.nautilusestate.com

DIRECTIONS
Located at 12 Rapaura Rd, approximately 100m east of the intersection of SH6 and Rapaura Rd.

OPENING HOURS
7 days, 10am–4.30pm

WINERY SALES
Cellar door, retail, mail order

PRICE RANGE $14.50–$35.90

TASTING & TOURS
Tasting is free of charge. Tours by appointment only.

OTHER PRODUCTS
Speciality South Island cheeses

OWNER
The Hill Smith family

WINEMAKER
Clive Jones

DATE ESTABLISHED 1985

Nautilus Estate

Nautilus Estate is named after the beautiful *Nautilus pompillius*, a native of the South Pacific Ocean, the shell of which is their brand emblem and appears on every label. The stylish cellar door makes extensive use of the natural curves found in the shape of the Nautilus shell, with the tones and colours reflecting the local environment — the river gravels of the Wairau River and the natural timbers. The winery incorporates an underground library cellar and by appointment you can tour the specialised Pinot Noir winery — a unique facility designed specifically for small-batch winemaking.

All wines are produced exclusively from Marlborough fruit with approximately 60 per cent of the production exported to 28 countries. Winemaker Clive Jones produces stylish, concentrated wines that cellar well and go nicely with food. Premium wines are available to taste and for sale under the Nautilus brand and a range of fruit-driven easy-drinking wines that are good value for money under the Twin Islands label. As well, a wide variety of speciality South Island cheeses are available for sale.

WINES
Nautilus Estate Cuvée Marlborough Brut NV, Sauvignon Blanc, Chardonnay, Pinot Gris, Pinot Noir
Twin Islands Sauvignon Blanc, Chardonnay, Pinot Noir, Merlot/Cabernet

RECENT AWARDS
An array of awards and gold medals including the International Wine Challenge 'Sparking Wine of the Year' and 'Sauvignon Blanc of the Year'.

MARLBOROUGH
Wairau Valley

Mount Riley Wines

Mount Riley is the dominant peak in the Richmond Ranges, the mountains that overlook Marlborough. Mount Riley owns six vineyards in the Wairau Valley, each site carefully chosen for its unique attributes and ability to produce grapes of outstanding quality. Mount Riley produces a broad portfolio of exceptional wines. Its 100 per cent bottle fermented sparkling Sauvignon Blanc, Savée, is particularly popular with visitors as an innovative product, unique to Mount Riley. The stylish new glass and concrete winery and cellar door has a glass frontage allowing views of its state-of-the-art winemaking equipment and tanks. As well as wine tasting visitors are welcome to picnic in the grounds.

WINES
Mount Riley Sauvignon Blanc, Saveé (Sparkling Sauvignon Blanc), Riesling, Chardonnay, Rosé, Pinot Noir, Merlot/Malbec; **Seventeen Valley** (flagship range) Chardonnay, Pinot Noir, Sauvignon Blanc

RECENT AWARDS
All wines have achieved notable success in wine shows both in NZ and overseas. The first release of Seventeen Valley Chardonnay in 1998 was awarded NZ's only Chardonnay Gold Medal at the London International Wine and Spirit Competition. Every vintage since has received a gold medal.

Cnr Malthouse Lane & SH1, Riverlands, Blenheim
Tel: (03) 577 9900
Fax: (03) 577 9901
Email: info@mountriley.co.nz
Website: www.mountriley.co.nz

DIRECTIONS
Five minutes south of Blenheim on the corner of Malthouse Rd and SH1 opposite Cobb Cottage.

OPENING HOURS
Oct–March: 7 days, 10am–4pm
Rest of the year: by appointment

WINERY SALES
Cellar door, retail

PRICE RANGE $15–$34

TASTING & TOURS
Tasting is free of charge. Tours by appointment only.

PICNIC AREA
Situated in the vineyard with picnic tables, umbrellas and a pétanque court.

OTHER ACTIVITIES
Historic New Zealand photography collection by acclaimed photographer Marti Friedlander.

OWNER Buchanan family

WINEMAKER Digger Hennessy

DATE ESTABLISHED 1991

MARLBOROUGH
Wairau Valley

Omaka Springs Estates

Located on 71 hectares in the heart of the picturesque Omaka Valley, Omaka Springs Estates specialises in producing premium cool-climate varietal grapes. Owners Geoff and Robina Jensen and winemaker Ian Marchant produce their entirely estate-grown, classic medal-winning wines at the on-site winery, where their aim and philosophy is to produce only 'high quality wines at affordable prices'. As a result, the Omaka Springs Estates label is growing in reputation and demand all over the world. Included on the estate is one of the country's largest commercial olive groves with over 2500 trees, including 23 different varieties. These trees produce high-quality olives that are processed on the estate into fine extra virgin olive oil.

WINES
Omaka Springs Sauvignon Blanc, Riesling, Chardonnay, Pinot Gris, Pinot Noir, Merlot, Dog Rock Red, Jaime (Sparkling)

RECENT AWARDS
Sauvignon Blanc 2004 – Gold: Wine Style Asia Awards Singapore, Royal Hobart International Wine Show, Silver: Air NZ Wine Awards; Riesling 2004 – Best Buy: *Wine NZ* magazine; Winemakers Selection Chardonnay 2002 – 3½ stars: *Cuisine* magazine, Bronze: International Chardonnay Challenge

OTHER PRODUCTS
Omaka Springs Extra Virgin Olive Oil, walnuts

Kennedys Rd, Renwick
Tel: (03) 572 9933
Fax: (03) 572 9934
Email: wine@omaka.co.nz
Website: www.omaka.co.nz

DIRECTIONS
Turn into Brookby Rd off Dog Point Rd. Travel 3km then turn right into Kennedys Rd. The vineyard is 500m on the right.

OPENING HOURS
October (commencing Labour Weekend) to end of February: Mon–Fri, 10am–4pm

WINERY SALES
Cellar door, retail, Internet

PRICE RANGE $17–$50

TASTING
Tasting by appointment, free of charge. Tours by appointment.

OWNERS
Geoff & Robina Jensen

WINEMAKER
Ian Marchant

DATE ESTABLISHED 1992

MARLBOROUGH
Wairau Valley

Spy Valley Wines

Spy Valley is the local nickname for the Waihopai Valley where a satellite communications monitoring base is located. Situated amongst the rolling hills of the valley, 125 hectares of estate vineyards planted with eight varieties of grapes producing premium-quality fruit surround the Spy Valley winery. Owning their vineyards ensures total control of the winemaking process and true single-vineyard estate production. Adorning the landscape considered too hard for grapes are 3000-plus olive trees, which produce impressive yields of olive oil. A striking new state-of-the-art winery designed in sympathy with the landscape incorporates a stunning tasting room with picnic tables outside. Marvellous views extend over the vineyards and olive groves to the nearby hills.

RECENT AWARDS
20 Best New Wineries: *USA Food & Wine* magazine, Oct 04: 'Hundreds of exciting new wineries have opened around the world in recent years defying the worldwide economic slump … Innovative new wineries that would be impossible for any oenophile to ignore … The planet's 20 most notable new producers. .

ACCOMMODATION
Luxurious and private Timara Lodge is situated on 600 acres of land with 25 acres of beautiful gardens; 4 rooms available (8 guests max.), www.timara.co.nz

37 Lake Timara Rd
Blenheim
Tel: (03) 572 9840
Fax: (03) 572 9830
Email: info@spyvalley.co.nz
Website: www.spyvalleywine.co.nz

DIRECTIONS
Turn into Waihopai Valley Rd off SH63 just south of Renwick. The winery is 2km on the left.

OPENING HOURS
Summer: 7 days, Mon-Fri, 10am–4pm

WINERY SALES Cellar door, retail, mail order, Internet

PRICE RANGE $16.95–$28.95

TASTING & TOURS
Tasting fee: $3 for groups of 10 or more (refundable on purchase). Groups are advised to make an appointment. Tours by appointment only.

PICNIC AREA Picnic tables are situated outside the tasting room, commanding views and maximising sunshine.

OWNER Family owned

WINEMAKERS
Ant Mackenzie & Jayne Cosgrove

DATE ESTABLISHED 1991

MARLBOROUGH
Wairau Valley

Wairau River Wines

The Wairau River cellar door with its distinctive mud-brick construction, wide verandahs and stunning views is a perfect place to visit year round. You can relax on the sun-drenched lawns under shady umbrellas or inside next to the roaring open fire. Their innovative seasonal menu utilises the freshest local produce matched with their superb wines. Wairau River is one of the oldest and largest family-owned estate wineries in Marlborough. All wines are made on-site in their state-of-the-art winery from 100 per cent estate-grown grapes planted on the alluvial banks of the Wairau River. Their philosophy is one of elegance, fruit power and small-batch vintning to produce award-winning, classical styles of wines.

WINES
Wairau River Sauvignon Blanc, Riesling, Chardonnay, Pinot Gris, Gewürztraminer, Pinot Noir

RECENT AWARDS
Consistent high performer in all media tastings, numerous domestic and international awards & medals.

Cnr Rapaura Rd & SH6
Renwick
Tel: (03) 572 9800
Fax: (03) 572 9885
Email: office@wairauriverwines.com
Website: www.wairauriverwines.com

DIRECTIONS
On the corner of SH6 and Raparua Rd.

OPENING HOURS
7 days, except Christmas Day and Good Friday. Cellar door: 10am–5pm. Restaurant: 12pm–3pm

WINERY SALES
Cellar door (includes exclusive wine specials), retail, mail order

PRICE RANGE $17–$40

TASTING
Tasting available 7 days, 10am–5pm. Tasting fee: $2 for groups of more than 10 (refundable on purchase).

CAFÉ Open for lunch 7 days, 12pm–3pm. Bookings recommended.

OTHER PRODUCTS
Home-made relishes and jams

OWNERS
Phil & Chris Rose

WINEMAKER
Allan McWilliams

DATE ESTABLISHED 1978

MARLBOROUGH
Wairau Valley

56 Anglesea St
PO Box 70
Renwick
Tel: (03) 572 8581
Fax: (03) 572 8518
Email: tewharera@xtra.co.nz
Website: www.te-whare-ra.co.nz

DIRECTIONS
Located in Anglesea St, Renwick near the corner of SH63.

OPENING HOURS
Summer & public holidays:
7 days, 10am–5pm
Winter & public holidays:
Thurs–Sun, 10am–4pm
Other times by appointment.

WINERY SALES
Cellar door, retail, mail order, Internet

PRICE RANGE $19–$28

TASTING & TOURS
Tasting is free of charge and is available by appointment outside of normal opening hours. Tutored tastings can be arranged for groups. Tours by appointment.

OWNER
Flowerday family

WINEMAKERS
Jason & Anna Flowerday

DATE ESTABLISHED 1979

Te Whare Ra Wines

Founded in 1979, Te Whare Ra is the oldest boutique winery in Marlborough. The name that translates from Maori to mean 'The House in the Sun' reflects its sunny Renwick location. The owners and winemakers Jason and Anna Flowerday both come from extensive family involvement in the Australian and New Zealand wine industries, and their winemaking philosophy is centred on producing premium estate-grown, hand-crafted wines which express a 'somewhere-ness rather than a same-ness'.

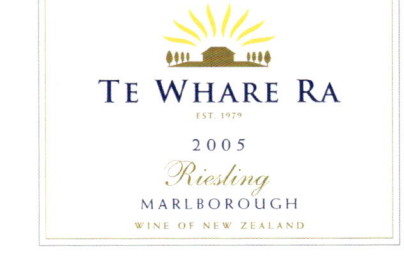

Early plantings in this vineyard are some of the oldest in Marlborough, which together with long summer sunlight hours, free-draining river shingle soils and cool winters contribute to Te Whare Ra's winemaking successes. They have won many awards over the past few years, in particular with the Gewürztraminer sourced from a 25-year-old block of vines.

The winery at Te Whare Ra is constructed from mud-bricks. The cellar door is above the winery tanks so that you can see the vintage in progress, and the view from the balcony is magnificent — right over the vineyards to the surrounding Wairau and Richmond Ranges.

WINES
Te Whare Ra Sauvignon Blanc, Riesling, Gewürztraminer, Chardonnay and Pinot Noir, from current plantings. There are plans to introduce Pinot Gris and Syrah in the next few years.

RECENT AWARDS
Te Whare Ra Duke of Marlborough Gewürztraminer 2002 – Gold & P&O Nedlloyd Trophy for Champion Gewürztraminer: 2002 Air NZ Wine Awards, rated a Potential Classic by Michael Cooper in 2005 *Buyer's Guide to NZ Wines*, rated one of the top 5 Gewürztraminers produced in New Zealand by Bob Campbell in *Cuisine* magazine (100th issue); Te Whare Ra Sauvignon Blanc 2004 – 3 Gold medals: 2004 Romeo Bragato Wine Awards, 2004 Liquorland Top 100 and 2004 Royal Hobart Wine Show

MARLBOROUGH
Wairau Valley

Corner Paynters & New Renwick Rds
Phone: (03) 577 9530
Email: enquiries@villamaria.co.nz
Website: www.villamaria.co.nz

DIRECTIONS
Corner of New Renwick and Paynters Rds, beside the Fairhall Golf Club.

OPENING HOURS
7 days, 10am–5pm

WINERY SALES
Cellar door, retail, mail order

PRICE RANGE Starting at $14

TASTING & TOURS
Tasting is free of charge. Tours by appointment only (contact the cellar door).

OWNER
George Fistonich

WINEMAKERS
Group Winemaker: Alastair Maling
Senior Winemaker: George Geris

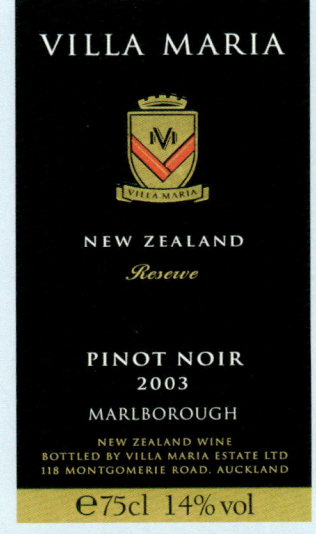

DATE ESTABLISHED 1961

Villa Maria Estate Marlborough

Founded in 1961 by owner and Managing Director George Fistonich, Villa Maria is New Zealand's largest privately owned winery and produces New Zealand's most awarded wines.

At the picturesque Villa Maria Marlborough winery you can taste some of the superb wines derived from this region. The Marlborough winery is state-of-the-art and has received awards for its architectural design. Built to cope with an increased grape tonnage, the winery now crushes the majority of Villa Maria's Marlborough harvest from its vineyards and contract growers throughout the region.

The winery and cellar shop were designed to blend into the surrounding landscape, set amongst the vines with the Wither Hills providing a stunning backdrop with views over the Wairau Valley towards the Richmond Ranges.

WINES
Villa Maria produces four distinctive ranges of wine:

Private Bin – A popular selection of varietal wines, which are well structured and display true varietal characteristics.

Cellar Selection – An emphasis on fruit quality and minimal handling results in intensely flavoured, elegant, food-friendly wines.

Reserve – Only produced from the best vineyards in New Zealand's top wine-growing areas to ensure they exhibit the finest regional characteristics possible. Wines must be of exceptional quality to justify the 'Reserve' marque.

Single Vineyard: These wines are created from vineyards of exceptional quality and only when vintage conditions allow these sites to fully express their individual characteristics.

Wines across the ranges: Chardonnay, Sauvignon Blanc, Riesling, Pinot Gris, Gewürztraminer, Late Harvest Riesling, Late Harvest Gewürztraminer, Noble Riesling, Pinot Noir, Merlot, Merlot/Cabernet Sauvignon

RECENT AWARDS
Four Trophies, 10 gold and 11 silver medals: Royal Easter Show Wine Awards 2005. Eight trophies, 14 gold and 11 silver medals: Air New Zealand Wine Awards 2004. Villa Maria Reserve Pinot Noir 2003 – Champion Wine of the Show (twice) & Best Pinot Noir Trophy: Royal Hobart Wine Show 2004. Owner George Fistonich was short-listed for three consecutive years as one of 50 prominent figures in the wine industry by UK *Wine International* magazine 2003–05, was named New Zealander of the Year by *National Business Review* in 2004, was named a 'top ten New Zealander' by the *New Zealand Herald* in 2004, and was awarded with a Distinguished Companion of the New Zealand Order of Merit in 2005.

MARLBOROUGH
Wairau Valley

Whitehaven Winery & Restaurant

Whitehaven Wine Company is a family-owned business, which from modest beginnings has rapidly achieved a reputation for producing quality wines that are now exported to six countries. The cellar door and café is located in a historic 142-year-old building on the outskirts of Blenheim. Here you can taste a range of wines crafted by a winemaker focused on quality rather than quantity. Popular for lunches and dinners, you can enjoy the cosy ambience of the log fire or bask in the sunshine in the secluded cottage garden. The fabulous wines can be enjoyed with the well-priced menu that includes a tempting array of Marlborough cuisine — this is a very pleasurable place to idle away the hours.

WINES
Whitehaven Sauvignon Blanc, Pinot Gris, Gewürztraminer, Chardonnay, Reserve Chardonnay, Riesling, Pinot Noir, Single Vineyard Reserve Pinot Gris & Gewürztraminer

RECENT AWARDS
Sauvignon Blanc 2004 – Gold: Air NZ Wine Awards 2004 & Royal Easter Wine Show 2005. All wines have won numerous awards in NZ and overseas.

1 Dodson St, Blenheim
Tel: (03) 577 6634
Fax: (03) 577 6634
Email: café@whitehaven.co.nz
Website: www.whitehaven.co.nz

DIRECTIONS Heading north towards Picton, turn right just before the bridge into Dodson St.

OPENING HOURS
Cellar door and café: 7 days.
Lunch: 11.30am–3pm
Dinner: 6pm–9pm

WINERY SALES Cellar door, retail, mail order, Internet and at the Whitehaven Restaurant

PRICE RANGE $10–$32

TASTING
Tasting fee is $2 for three wines.

RESTAURANT
Lunch & dinner. Booking advisable: (03) 577 6634.

OTHER ACTIVITIES
Exhibitions of up-and-coming local artists; children's play area; pétanque

OTHER FACILITIES
Available for private functions.

OWNERS Whitehaven Wine Company: Greg & Sue White
Whitehaven Café: Nikki Andrews & Helen Winstanley

WINEMAKER Simon Waghorn

DATE ESTABLISHED 1994

MARLBOROUGH
Wairau Valley

Wither Hills Vineyards

Wither Hills is founded on the sincere belief that the finest wines are always created from exceptional vineyards. The commitment to produce only the highest quality fruit is reflected in the wines — hence the statement 'Created in the Vineyard'.

The 'no compromise' approach to winemaking has carried through to their iconic Tasting Room and Cellar where the Wither Hills experience is relaxed, sophisticated and welcoming. You are invited to linger in the sumptuous Tasting Room, or sit outside and enjoy the delicious wines beside the delightful lawn. With a fully equipped boardroom and 5 gorgeous dining rooms, the team at Wither Hills can cater for a complete range of special occasions.

WINES
Wither Hills Sauvignon Blanc, Chardonnay, Pinot Noir

RECENT AWARDS
Wither Hills has amassed 23 trophies and 62 gold medals in just 10 years, with just 3 wines. Some of the most recent include: Sauvignon Blanc 2004 – Double Gold: San Francisco Wine Competition 2004; Chardonnay 2003 – Gold: Royal Easter Show 2005; Pinot Noir 2003 – Gold & Trophy: Japan Wine Challenge 2005

211 New Renwick Rd, RD2, Blenheim
Telephone: (03) 578 4036
Fax: (03) 578 4039
Email: winery@witherhills.co.nz
Website: www.witherhills.co.nz

DIRECTIONS
5 minutes' drive from Blenheim along New Renwick Rd.

OPENING HOURS
7 days, 10am–4.30pm

WINERY SALES
Cellar door, retail, mail order, Internet

PRICE RANGE
$17–$39

TASTING & TOURS
Tasting is free of charge. Tours by prior arrangement.

PICNIC AREA
Outside the tasting room in a sheltered courtyard.

OTHER FACILITIES
Fully equipped, multi-capable event facilities include a boardroom and 5 dining rooms

OWNER
Lion Nathan Limited

WINEMAKERS
Brent Marris & Ben Glover

DATE ESTABLISHED
Wither Hills: 1994; Tasting Room & Cellar: 18 March 2005

Spy Valley Wines

Wine and Food Festival

Framingham Wine Company

Wairau River Wines

Fairhall Downs Estate Wines

Highfield Estate

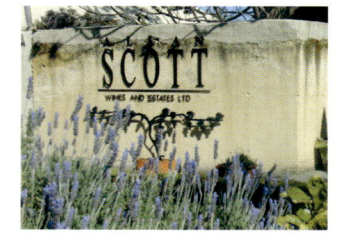

Allan Scott Wines and Estates

121

Canterbury

Mari Schuster

CANTERBURY has two major wine areas: the vast **Canterbury Plains** around the South Island city of **Christchurch**, and the smaller, sheltered **Waipara Valley**, 65 kilometres north of Christchurch. This is New Zealand's sixth largest wine region, producing some 1.8 per cent of the national crop. The Canterbury Plains were first planted commercially in the 1970s, and vineyards are now scattered from **Amberley** in the north to **Timaru** in the south. Soils consist of mainly alluvial silt loams over gravel subsoils and produce generally lighter-bodied, elegant styles of chiefly Pinot Noir and Chardonnay. The more recently developed Waipara Valley, with vineyards around the towns of **Waipara** and **Omihi**, is warmer than the plains, and has predominantly chalky loam soils that can be rich in limestone. Its wines, which often display rich, ripe fruit flavours, include Pinot Noir, Chardonnay and Riesling, with Merlots and Cabernet Sauvignons in warmer vintages.

Christchurch has a reputation for its 'Englishness', with its old stone buildings and punts gliding on the tree-lined Avon River. It is the gateway to the rivers of the Canterbury Plains and the mountains and skifields of the Southern Alps.

For more information visit:
www.christchurchnz.net, www.canterburyfare.co.nz or contact

Christchurch Canterbury i-SITE Visitor Information Centre
Old Chief Post Office Building
Cathedral Square West, Christchurch
Tel: (03) 379 9629
Email: info@christchurchnz.net

Daniel Schuster Wines

HISTORY

French immigrants brought grapes to Akaroa on Banks Peninsula in 1840 but its modern winemaking era began much later after trials at Lincoln University in the 1970s showed which varieties best suited Canterbury's cool-climate conditions. The region's first commercial winery was St Helena, planted by Robin and Norman Mundy at Belfast, just north of Christchurch in 1978. Their success inspired other pioneering producers.

SOILS

The Canterbury Plains has variable soils, mostly free-draining silty loams overlying river gravels as well as moderately fertile soils with good water-holding ability. The Waipara Valley includes stony soils, gravelly loams over alluvial subsoils, as well as chalky limestone-derived clays and loams.

CLIMATE

Abundant sunshine, warm, dry summers followed by long, dry autumns, along with relatively cool growing conditions are a feature in both the Waipara Valley and the Canterbury Plains. Waipara, however, being sheltered from the coast by a low range of hills, can be significantly warmer although late spring frosts can be a danger in both sub-regions. The hot summer days followed by cool nights help preserve the grapes' acidity, while the favourably dry autumns minimise fungal infections.

Pegasus Bay

GRAPE VARIETIES AND WINE STYLES

The major variety is Pinot Noir, usually full-bodied wines rich in fruit characters. The region has a wide range of Chardonnay styles, from cool, crisp fruity wines to full-bodied ones. Pinot Noir and Chardonnay make up some 60 per cent of the crop. The third most planted variety is Riesling, made in dry, elegant styles or richer and fruitier examples. Late-harvest and botrytised wines are also popular. Other varieties include riper styles of Sauvignon Blanc, and Pinot Gris.

SUB-REGIONS

Canterbury Plains, from Amberley in the north to Timaru in the south. The scattered vineyards on the plains produce mostly lighter-bodied, elegant styles of chiefly Pinot Noir and Chardonnay.

Waipara Valley, some 65km north of Christchurch, is the scene of much recent development. Its wines show rich, ripe fruit flavours.

Banks Peninsula, east of Christchurch, was the birthplace of Canterbury's wine industry, and now produces small quantities of mainly Pinot Noir and Chardonnay from boutique wineries.

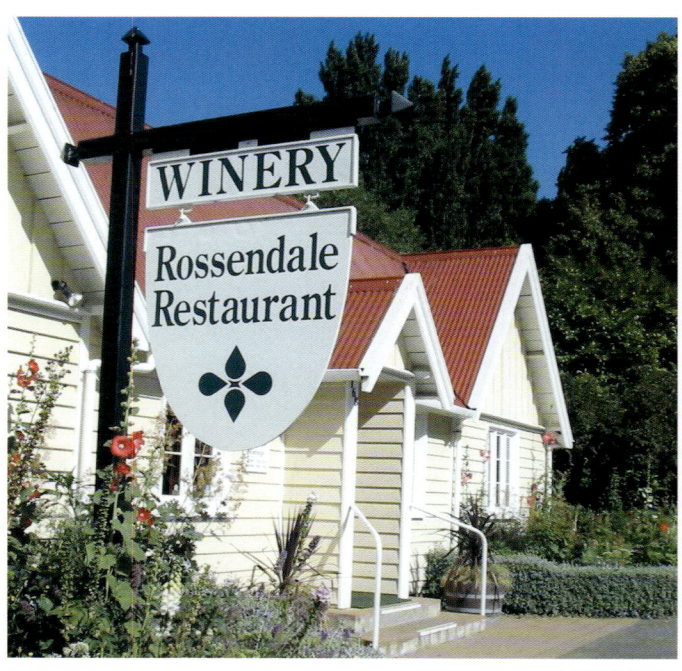

Rossendale Winery

Muddy Water

Cracroft Chase (Lyn McKinnon)

Events

- **Waipara Wine & Food Celebration.** The region's wine and food producers gather to show their wares in a festival held in the historic Glenmark Church grounds. Held annually in March.
- **Jade Wine & Food Festival of Canterbury.** All the offerings of the region. Held in Christchurch annually on the third Sunday in February.
- **New Zealand Organic Food & Wine Festival.** The country's premier organic produce festival, held in Oamaru annually in March.

For more information on events visit:
www.christchurchnz.net

Wineries featured in this book

Other 'open to visit' wineries

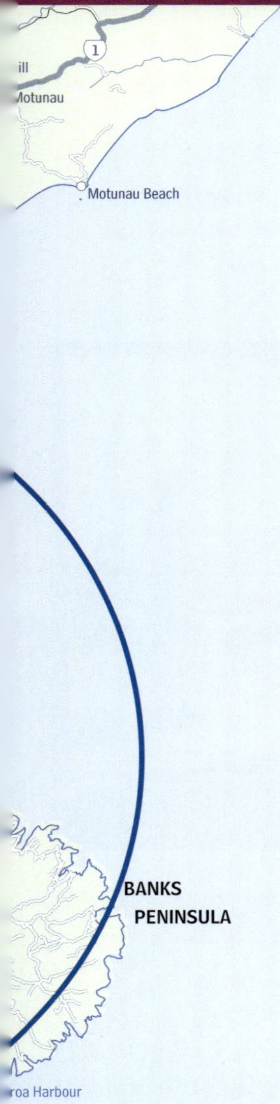
1
Motunau
Motunau Beach
BANKS
PENINSULA
roa Harbour

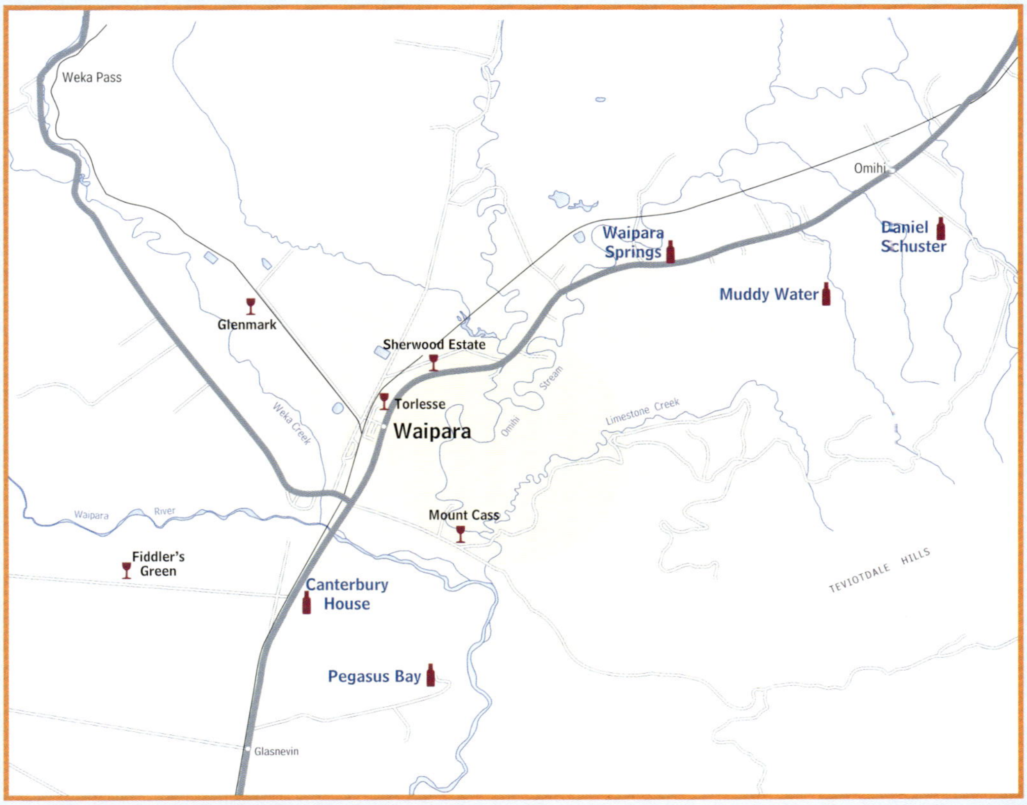
Weka Pass
Omihi
Waipara
Springs
Daniel
Schuster
Muddy Water
Glenmark
Sherwood Estate
Torlesse
Waipara
Weka Creek
Omihi
Stream
Limestone Creek
Waipara
River
Mount Cass
Fiddler's
Green
Canterbury
House
TEVIOTDALE HILLS
Pegasus Bay
Glasnevin

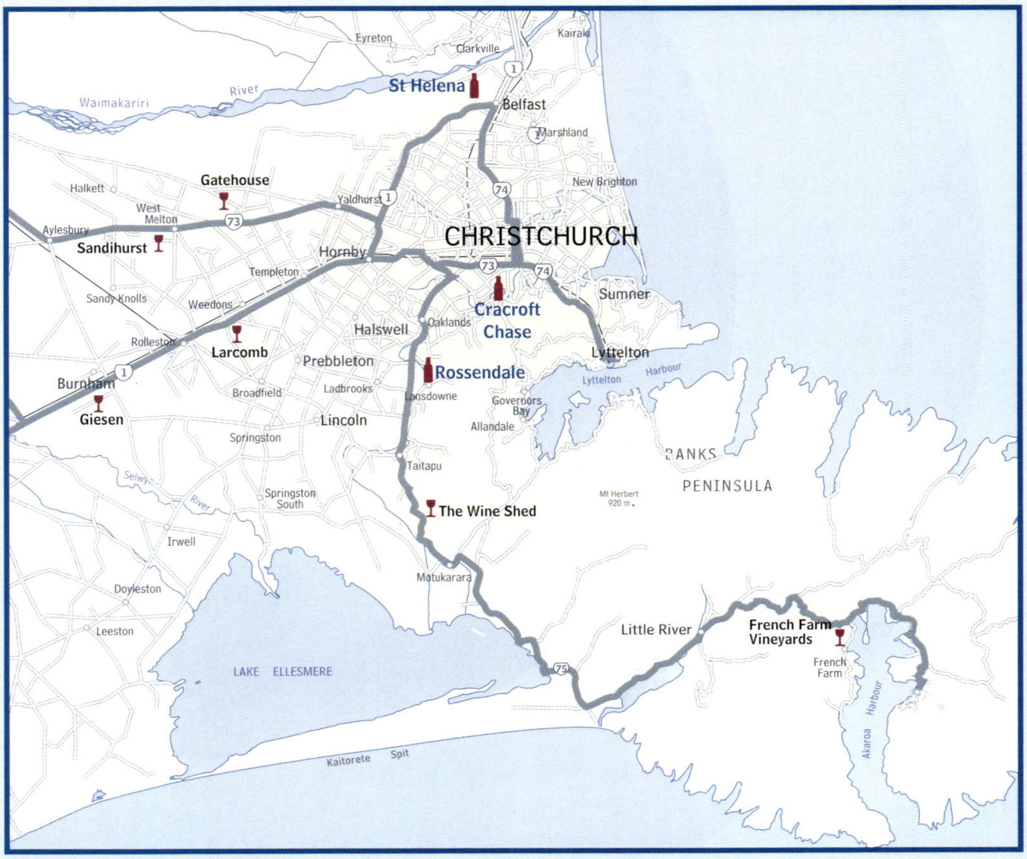
Eyreton
Clarkville
Kairaki
1
St Helena
Waimakariri
River
Belfast
Marshland
New Brighton
Halkett
Gatehouse
74
West
Melton
Yaldhurst
1
Aylesbury
73
Sandihurst
CHRISTCHURCH
Hornby
73
74
Templeton
Sumner
Cracroft
Chase
Sandy Knolls
Weedons
Halswell
Oaklands
Rolleston
Larcomb
Lyttelton
Prebbleton
Rossendale
Lyttelton
Harbour
Burnham
1
Ladbrooks
Broadfield
Lansdowne
Governors
Bay
Giesen
Lincoln
Allandale
Springston
Taitapu
BANKS
PENINSULA
Selwyn
River
Springston
South
Mt Herbert
920 m
The Wine Shed
Irwell
Motukarara
Doyleston
Little River
French Farm
Vineyards
Leeston
French
Farm
75
LAKE ELLESMERE
Akaroa
Harbour
Kaitorete
Spit

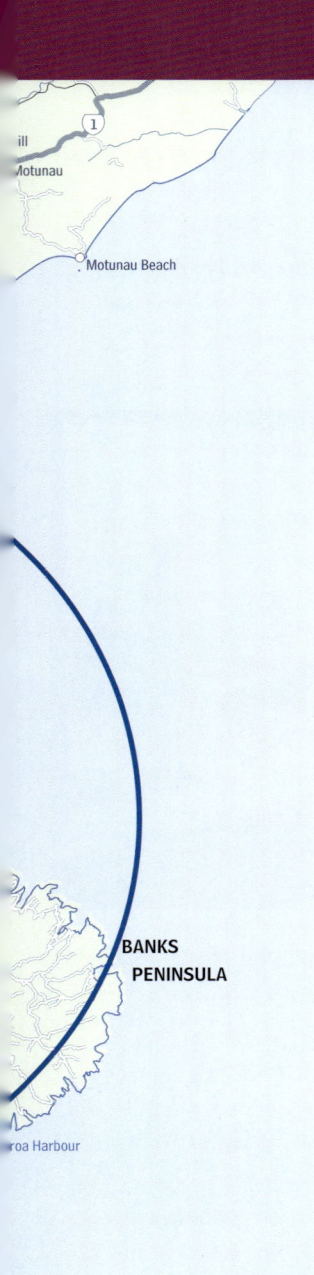

CANTERBURY
Waipara

Canterbury House

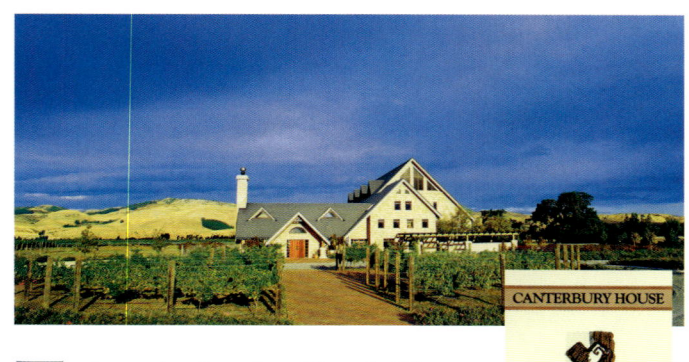

The impressive Canterbury House building incorporates a restaurant, tasting room and state-of-the-art winery built to handle a planned annual production of 125,000 cases of premium estate-grown wines. Surrounded by beautifully landscaped gardens and vineyards, the building with its vaulted ceiling, large fireplace, antique furniture and tapestries evokes images of the fine baronial halls and wine chateaux of Europe. The gourmet menu takes advantage of the season's freshest fare and includes a selection of dishes to suit every appetite and budget. During harvest in April there is a unique opportunity to taste fresh grape juice from the varieties grown in the Canterbury House vineyard before it completes its fermentation into wine.

WINES
Canterbury House Riesling, Noble Riesling, Sauvignon Blanc, Chardonnay, Pinot Gris, Late Harvest Pinot Gris, Pinot Noir, Merlot, Méthode Traditionnelle

RECENT AWARDS
Chardonnay Reserve 2002 – Gold: Bragato Wine Awards 2003; Pinot Gris 2003 – Gold: NZ Wine Society Royal Easter Wine Show 2004; Riesling 2002 – Gold: Liquorland Top 100 2003; Noble Riesling 2002 – Gold & Trophy for Best Sweet Wine: Liquorland Top 100 2003

780 Glasnevin Rd, SH1
Amberley
Tel: (03) 314 6900
Fax: (03) 314 6905
Email: info@canterburyhouse.co.nz
Website: www.canterburyhouse.com

DIRECTIONS
50km north of Christchurch on SH1.

OPENING HOURS
Cellar door, wine tasting and snacks: 7 days, 10am–5pm
Lunch: 7 days, 11.30am–3pm
Dinner: group bookings and by reservation only

WINERY SALES
Cellar door, retail, mail order, Internet

PRICE RANGE
$14.90–$28.90

TASTING & TOURS
Group bookings: $3 per person, otherwise free of charge. Tours by appointment only.

RESTAURANT
Daily à la carte lunch menu, morning and late afternoon snacks and special blended coffees.
Reservations: (03) 314 6900

OTHER FACILITIES
Available for weddings and functions, to suit personal requirements.

OWNER
Dr Michael Reid

WINEMAKER
Alan McCorkindale

DATE ESTABLISHED
1994

CANTERBURY
Waipara

Daniel Schuster Wines

One of the earliest planted vineyards in the region, Daniel Schuster Wines produce a range of traditionally crafted, classical Pinot Noir, Chardonnay and Riesling wines. Their philosophy encompasses integrated farming methods in the vineyard with continuous green cover year round and many native shrubs and wildflowers providing a healthy biological vineyard environment. This practice allows them to eliminate the use of chemical sprays which, along with their policy of limiting crop levels, creates wines of intensity and character that proudly promote the terroir from which they derive.

Only one hour north of Christchurch, visitors are welcome at the newly built, architecturally designed tasting room to share the passion in the wines proudly produced under the Daniel Schuster label.

WINES
Omihi Hills Vineyard 'Selection' Pinot Noir, **Petrie Vineyard** 'Selection' Chardonnay, **Waipara** Pinot Noir and Riesling, **Twin Vineyards** Pinot Noir, **Hull Vineyard** Late Harvest Riesling

RECENT AWARDS
One of New Zealand's Top 10 Wineries: *NZ Herald*, Feb 2004; Petrie Vineyard Selection Chardonnay 1999 – 'The best New Zealand Chardonnay I've tasted to date': Robert Parker's *Wine Advocate* (USA); Omihi Hills Vineyard Selection Pinot Noir 2001 – 5 Stars: *Michael Cooper's Buyer's Guide to NZ Wines 2005*

192 Reeces Rd, Omihi
Tel: (03) 314 5901
Fax: (03) 314 5902
Email: info@danielschusterwines.com
Website: www.danielschusterwines.com

DIRECTIONS
Drive approx. 1 hour north of Christchurch on SH1 until you reach Omihi (20 minutes north of Amberley). Turn right into Reeces Rd and continue for 2km to the gate.

OPENING HOURS
Daily, 10am–5pm

WINERY SALES
Cellar door, retail, mail order, Internet

PRICE RANGE
$12–$60

TASTING & TOURS
Tasting fee: $5, refundable on purchase. Barrel tasting and winery tour conducted by winemaker by prior arrangement.

EVENTS
Participant in the Waipara Wine & Food Celebration held the last Sunday in March each year.

OWNERS
Danny & Mari Schuster, Tim & Edith Hull

WINEMAKER
Danny Schuster

DATE ESTABLISHED
1986

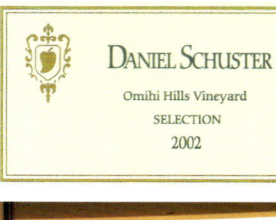

CANTERBURY
Waipara

Pegasus Bay

Pegasus Bay is a small family owned and operated winery whose aim is to produce wines of the highest quality that fully express the features of their vineyard. In a picturesque setting with an extensive outdoor dining area among lakes and beautiful gardens, Pegasus Bay offers a memorable experience to wine & food enthusiasts, whether it be tasting their highly regarded estate-grown wines, viewing the barrel hall and wine cellars or indulging the appetite with delectable local produce in the winery restaurant. The menu has an emphasis on freshness and simplicity and is designed to complement the wines. The atmosphere inside is warm, with a large open fire, and contemporary works from some of New Zealand's leading artists hang on the recycled native timber walls.

WINES
Pegasus Bay Riesling, Sauvignon/Sémillon, Chardonnay, Pinot Noir, Cabernet/Merlot. Reserve Wines (produced only in exceptional vintages): Aria — late-picked Riesling, Maestro — Merlot/Malbec, Prima Donna — Pinot Noir, Finale — Noble Chardonnay (barrique-fermented)

RECENT AWARDS
Pegasus Bay does not enter shows but recent accolades include: Pinot Noir 2002 — 5 stars: *Winestate* magazine; NZ's Best Casual Dining Restaurant 2005: *Cuisine* magazine

Stockgrove Rd
RD2 Amberley, Waipara
Tel: (03) 314 6869
Fax: (03) 314 6861
Email: info@pegasusbay.com
Website: www.pegasusbay.com

DIRECTIONS 45 minutes north of Christchurch. Turn right down Stockgrove Rd which is about 5 minutes past Amberley.

OPENING HOURS Wine tasting & sales: 7 days, 10.30am–5pm
Restaurant: 7 days, 12 noon–4pm

WINERY SALES
Cellar door, winery restaurant, retail, mail order, Internet

PRICE RANGE
$21.50–$70

TASTING & TOURS
Tasting fee: $2, refundable on purchase. Tours by appointment.

RESTAURANT
Bookings recommended: (03) 314 6869

OWNER
The Donaldson family

WINEMAKERS
Matthew Donaldson & Lynnette Hudson

DATE ESTABLISHED 1985

CANTERBURY
Waipara

Waipara Springs Wines

Waipara Springs is a boutique vineyard and winery producing premium-quality wines that have received acclaim in New Zealand and internationally since opening in 1990. Originally planted with four hectares of grapes, this has now been expanded to 20 hectares. The café and winery are housed in attractive old farm buildings originally built as stables and a grain shed. Visitors can enjoy tasting at the wine bar with an informative and friendly commentary or dine at the café, now one of the most popular in the region. With indoor and outdoor seating, the eclectic menu features a wonderful array of tempting dishes using as many local ingredients as possible, including salmon, lamb, cheeses, asparagus and other seasonal produce.

WINES
Waipara Springs Barrique Chardonnay, Lightly Oaked Chardonnay, Sauvignon Blanc, Riesling, Gewürztraminer, Pinot Blush, Botrytised Riesling, Pinot Noir, Reserve Pinot Noir, Cabernet Sauvignon

RECENT AWARDS
Waipara Springs 2003 Reserve Pinot Noir has won the Regional NZ Pinot Noir Trophy in the Decanter World Wine Awards

409 Omihi Rd, SH1, Waipara
Tel: (03) 314 6777
Fax: (03) 314 6777
Email: wine@waiparasprings.co.nz
Website: www.waiparasprings.co.nz

DIRECTIONS
On SH1, a 50-minute drive north of Christchurch and 4km past the turn-off to Hanmer Springs (SH7).

OPENING HOURS
Wine tasting, sales & café: 7 days, 11am–5pm (closed 24/25/26 December & 1 Jan). Café closed June, July & August

WINERY SALES Cellar door, retail, mail order, Internet

PRICE RANGE $16–$36

TASTING Tasting fee $3, refundable on purchase.

CAFÉ
Waipara Springs Café
Reservations: (03) 314 6777

ACTIVITIES
Clydesdale Wagon Tours with Colonial Horse Treks.
Bookings: 025 227 6120

OTHER PRODUCTS
Local Athena olive oil, pottery and paintings

OWNERS
Grant & Moore families

WINEMAKER
Duncan McTavish

DATE ESTABLISHED 1990

CANTERBURY
Canterbury Plains

Rossendale Restaurant & Vineyard

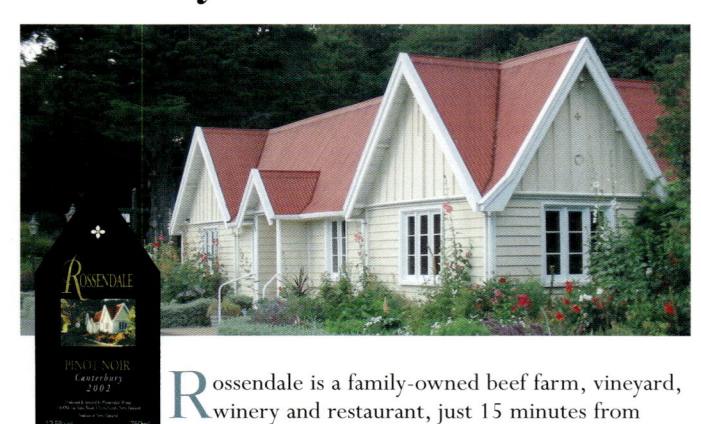

Rossendale is a family-owned beef farm, vineyard, winery and restaurant, just 15 minutes from the centre of Christchurch. The restaurant is in the exquisitely restored gatekeeper's lodge of the historic Lansdowne homestead and gardens. Delicious country-style fare can be enjoyed in the beautiful sheltered garden or indoors where you can relax in old-world ambience. The restaurant is also the cellar door and wine-tasting facility for the premium Rossendale wines.

The home 4.5-hectare vineyard is planted with Chardonnay, Pinot Noir and Gewürztraminer, and in Marlborough they have 33 hectares planted in Sauvignon Blanc.

WINES
Rossendale Canterbury Riesling, Pinot Noir, Chardonnay Gewürztraminer; Rossendale Marlborough Sauvignon Blanc; Rossendale Marlborough Merlot

RECENT AWARDS
Since the first vintage in 1993 Rossendale wines have received numerous accolades and awards

OTHER FACILITIES
Lansdowne homestead, set in 2.5 acres of beautiful gardens, is ideal for weddings and functions. Bookings are made through the Rossendale office.
Enquiries: (03) 322 7780

---

168 Old Tai Tapu Rd
Halswell, Christchurch
Tel: (03) 322 9684 or 322 7780
Fax: (03) 322 9272
Email: office@rossendale.co.nz
Website: www.rossendale.co.nz

DIRECTIONS
Clearly signposted, turn left off Halswell Rd (SH75 and the main Akaroa Highway) into Old Tai Tapu Rd, just south of Halswell. Rossendale is 1.5km on the right.

OPENING HOURS
Lunch & dinner: 7 days, 10am–10pm (closed Christmas Day)

WINERY SALES
Cellar door, retail, mail order, Internet

PRICE RANGE $17–$26

TASTING
Tasting free of charge for diners and casual small groups. For large groups there is a tasting fee of $6 pp for six wines (by appointment).

RESTAURANT
Reservations: (03) 322 9684 or 322 7780

OWNERS
Brent & Shirley Rawstron

WINEMAKER
Alan McCorkindale

DATE ESTABLISHED 1994

CANTERBURY
Canterbury Plains

St Helena Wine Estate

Sitting just north of Christchurch in the Canterbury Plains is St Helena Wine Estate, Canterbury's oldest commercial winery, acknowledged as the pioneer in establishing Pinot Noir in New Zealand. Founded in 1978 by the Mundy family, the vineyard takes advantage of the region's long warm summers and dry autumns to grow some of the best grapes in New Zealand. A stunning collection of wines is produced from their 20-hectare vineyard next to the winery and from another 50-hectare vineyard in Marlborough. Currently over 90 per cent of the winery's production is destined for export markets. Owners Robin and Bernice Mundy and award-winning winemaker Alan McCorkindale are passionate in their dedication to producing exceptional-quality fruit and wine and the development of Canterbury as one of New Zealand's finest wine-producing regions.

WINES
St Helena Pinot Noir, Riesling, Pinot Gris, Sauvignon Blanc, Chardonnay, Pinot Blanc, Gewürztraminer, Late Harvest, Merlot, Fortified Pinot Noir.

RECENT AWARDS
Reserve Pinot Gris 2004 – Gold: Red Hill Cool Climate Wine Show; Sauvignon Blanc 2004 – Gold: Royal Hobart Wine Show; Bernice (Pinot Blanc) 2002 – Bronze: Air NZ Wine Awards 2003, Liquorland Top 100 2004, 4 stars: *Michael Cooper's Buyer's Guide to NZ Wines 2004*

---

259 Coutts Island Rd, Belfast
Tel: (03) 323 8202
Fax: (03) 323 8252
Email: sthelena@xtra.co.nz

DIRECTIONS
A 20-minute drive north of Christchurch, Coutts Island Rd is just north of Belfast off the main road (SH1) to Waipara.

OPENING HOURS
7 days, 10am–4.30pm

WINERY SALES
Cellar door, retail, mail order

PRICE RANGE
$12–$28 (cellar door)

TASTING & TOURS
Tasting is free of charge. Tours by appointment.

OWNERS
Robin & Bernice Mundy

WINEMAKER
Alan McCorkindale

DATE ESTABLISHED 1978

CANTERBURY

Open By Appointment

Cracroft Chase

The vineyard is in a picturesque cul-de-sac valley nestled at the foot of the Christchurch Port Hills. Between 1998 and 1999, five hectares were planted with Pinot Gris, on grafted rootstock. Sheltered on three sides by hills clad in forestry, and fully opened to the nor'west, the valley enjoys a special microclimate. The 'U' trellising system allows air and sun through the canopy, making spraying against botrytis unnecessary. Summer plucking and harvesting are done by hand.

The grapes are processed in the on-site winery, with state-of-the-art Italian machinery. Winemaker Alistair Gardner uses a combination of lees stirring and malolactic fermentation to add complexity to the wine. Alessandro and Wilma Laryn, who immigrated from Italy in 1996, manage the property.

Wines: Cracroft Chase Vineyard – Wood's Edge Pinot Gris
Winery sales: Cellar door, mail order
Price range: $18–$24

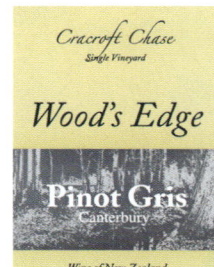

Contact:
110 Shalamar Drive, Cashmere,
Christchurch 8002
Tel: (03) 337 9339 – 027 2288 682
Fax: (03) 337 9577
E-mail: bluesun@xtra.co.nz
Owners: Blue Sun Limited – Alessandro & Wilma Laryn

Muddy Water

Located on the sunny slopes over the Waipara Valley producing hand-crafted Pinot Noir, Chardonnay, Riesling, Pinotage and Syrah from 12 hectares of vines. Open weekends 11am–4pm or by appointment.

Contact: 424 Omihi Rd, Waipara. Tel: (03) 314 6966. Fax: (03) 314 6965.
Email: wine@muddywater.co.nz. Website: www.muddywater.co.nz
Owners: Jane & Michael East

CANTERBURY

Pegasus Bay

Canterbury House

Cracroft Chase (Lyn McKinnon)

Central Otago

CENTRAL OTAGO, comprising the South Island area around the glacial lakes of **Wakatipu**, **Wanaka** and **Dunstan**, is New Zealand's fourth largest wine region, producing some 1 per cent of the national crop. This is New Zealand's highest (200–450 metres above sea level) and the world's most southerly (45°S) wine region. It enjoys a magical setting, with vines planted among spectacular alpine scenery. Mountains and gorges separate its four distinct sub-regions. Cromwell Basin has the bulk of the region's vineyards around the towns of **Bannockburn** and **Cromwell**, and north alongside Lake Dunstan to **Lowburn** and **Bendigo**. The next largest sub-region is the Gibbston area, between **Cromwell** and **Queenstown**, where most vineyards sit on steep sites above the dramatic **Kawarau River** gorge. In the south-west, vineyards occupy a dry basin around the towns of **Clyde** and **Alexandra**. There is also a small, high-altitude area around the town of Wanaka overlooking **Lake Wanaka**. Apart from sheep farming, Central Otago is at the heart of the South Island's tourism industry, centred on Queenstown, and offers innumerable adventure and adrenalin activities.

For more information visit:
www.queenstown-vacation.com, www.centralotago.net.nz, www.lakewanaka.co.nz, www.cromwell.org.nz, www.tco.org.nz
or contact

Queenstown i-SITE Visitor Information Centre
Cnr Camp & Shotover Streets, Queenstown
Tel: (03) 422 4100, Email: info@qvc.co.nz

Cromwell & Districts Information Centre
47 The Mall, Cromwell
Tel: (03) 445 0212, Email: Cromwell@centralotagonz.com

Lake Wanaka i-SITE Visitor Information Centre
100 Ardmore St, Wanaka
Tel: (03) 443 1223, Email: info@lakewanaka.co.nz

Central Otago Visitor Information Centre
22 Centennial Ave, Alexandra
Tel: (03) 448 9515, Email: info@alexandra.co.nz

Amisfield Vineyard

HISTORY
Frenchman John Desiré Feraud, attracted by the Dunstan gold rush of 1862, is said to have planted the region's first vines near Clyde in 1864, and won a prize for his Burgundy-style wine in Sydney in 1881. Trial plantings in the 1950s were followed by the first commercial ventures in the modern winemaking era in the 1970s and 1980s. Bill Grant, of William Hill Vineyard, planted vines at Alexandra in 1973, and in 1976 Rolfe Mills planted the Rippon Vineyard at Wanaka. The first commercial wines flowed after 1987, under the Rippon, Taramea and Gibbston Valley labels.

SOILS
Soils in the region vary dramatically, ranging from wind-blown sands to silt loams and broken schist and mica rock. Most soils are derived from loess or alluvial deposits, often with gravel subsoils that allow free drainage. In the west around Wanaka some soils are based on glacial moraine. Each soil type has a distinct effect on plant growth and grape flavours.

CLIMATE
The region has New Zealand's most continental climate, with marked seasonal extremes of hot summers and cold winters, and a large day/night temperature variation that gives flavour intensity and depth of colour to the grapes. Cold winters mean heavy frosts can occur anytime between March and October. Hot and dry summers are followed by extremely dry, cool autumns, which allow an extended ripening period. A relatively low rainfall, spread evenly throughout the year, results in low risk of fungal diseases.

GRAPE VARIETIES AND WINE STYLES
Pinot Noir is the major grape variety, and one that has won it many accolades. Styles range from perfumed and spicy wines to more fruity, plummier wines grown on warmer sites. Styles of Pinot Gris, the second most planted variety, range from crisp and spicy to rich and oily. Chardonnay, Riesling and Sauvignon Blanc are the other key wines. The region is picked to excel at sparkling wines in the future.

SUB-REGIONS
Cromwell Basin, around the towns of Bannockburn and Cromwell, and north alongside Lake Dunstan to Lowburn and Bendigo, is the warmest sub-region, producing powerful, concentrated Pinot Noirs, limey Rieslings and fresh Pinot Gris.

Gibbston, between Cromwell and Queenstown, with sites at 350–420 metres altitude is the coolest sub-region, producing concentrated Pinot Noirs, appley Rieslings and crisp Pinot Gris.

Clyde and Alexandra, in the south of the region, can produce elegant, perfumed Pinot Noirs from its hot, north-facing sites as well as aromatic Gewürztraminers.

Wanaka, another high-altitude sub-region, has a slightly more temperate climate due to its proximity to the lake. It produces elegant Pinot Noirs, limey Rieslings and flinty Chardonnays.

Rippon Vineyard & Winery

45th parallel, looking across Lake Dunstan

New plantings, Alexandra

Events

- **Central Otago Wine & Food Festival.** Held in the picturesque Queenstown Gardens with the best of the region's wine, food, art and entertainment. Held annually in late January/early February.

- **Clyde Harvest Festival.** A wine and food festival held in Clyde township every Easter.

- **Central Otago Pinot Noir Celebration.** An international gathering of wine writers, winemakers and Pinot Noir enthusiasts which includes two days of seminars, tastings and fine food. Held at the end of January/early February annually. www.pinotcelebration.co.nz

- **Wanakafest, Wanaka.** Five days of food, wine and entertainment. Held in September. www.wanakafest.co.nz

- **Rippon Music Festival.** Open-air music festival held at Rippon Vineyard every two years. Next festival February 2006. www.ripponfestival.co.nz

For more information on events visit:
www.queenstown-vacation.com

Waitiri Creek

45th Parallel Vineyard, Aurum Wines

William Moffitt at Dry Gully

Gibbston area (Arrowtown / Queenstown)

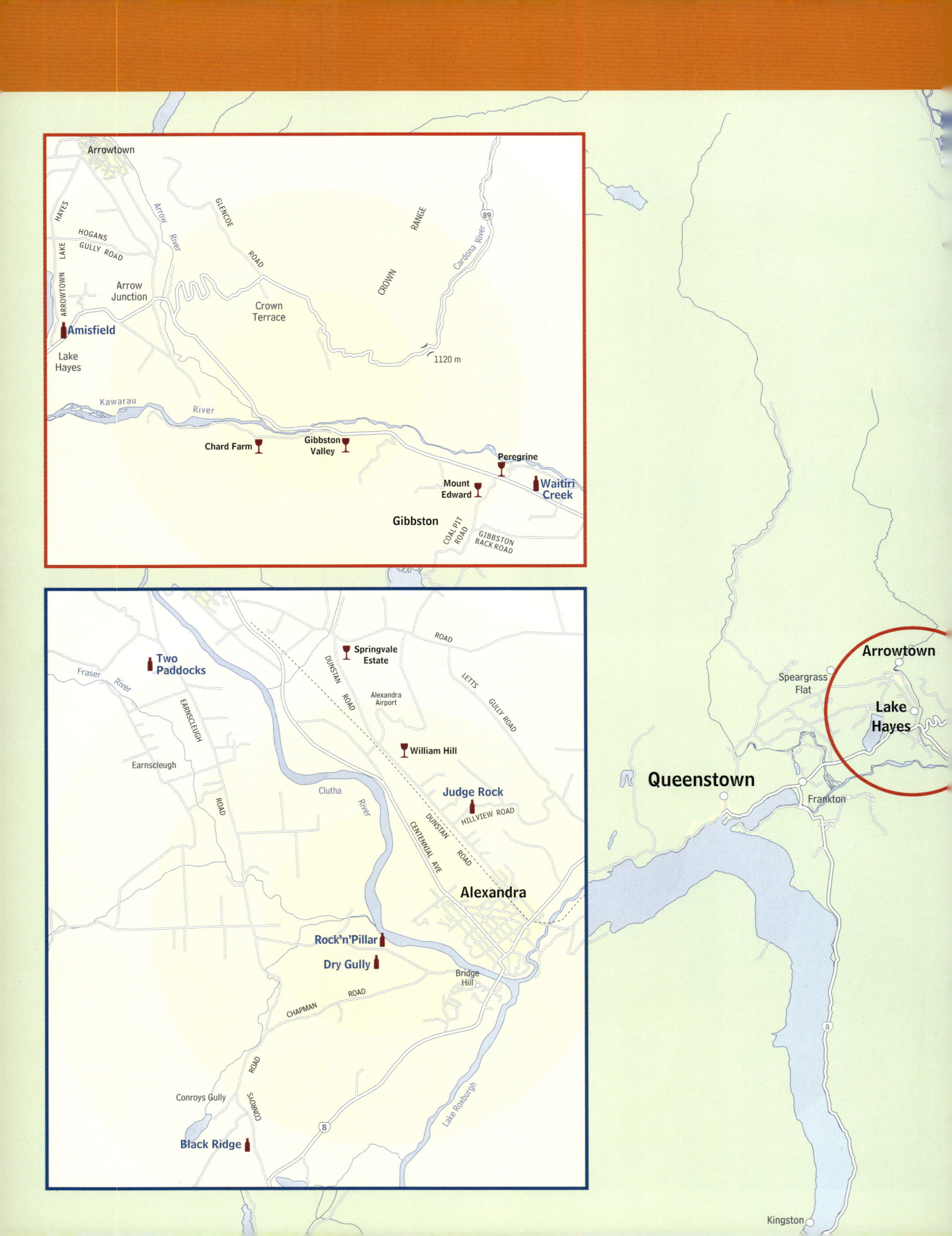

- Arrowtown
- Amisfield
- Lake Hayes
- Arrow Junction
- Crown Terrace
- CROWN RANGE — 1120 m
- Arrow River
- Cardona River
- Kawarau River
- HAYES
- HOGANS GULLY ROAD
- ARROWTOWN LAKE
- GLENCOE ROAD
- 89
- Chard Farm
- Gibbston Valley
- Mount Edward
- Peregrine
- Waitiri Creek
- Gibbston
- COALPIT ROAD
- GIBBSTON BACK ROAD

Alexandra area

- Two Paddocks
- Springvale Estate
- Fraser River
- Clutha River
- EARNSCLEUGH ROAD
- Earnscleugh
- Alexandra Airport
- DUNSTAN ROAD
- LETTS GULLY ROAD
- William Hill
- Judge Rock
- HILLVIEW ROAD
- CENTENNIAL AVE
- Alexandra
- Rock'n'Pillar
- Dry Gully
- Bridge Hill
- CHAPMAN ROAD
- Lake Roxburgh
- Conroys Gully
- CONROYS ROAD
- 8
- Black Ridge

Regional overview

- Arrowtown
- Speargrass Flat
- Lake Hayes
- Queenstown
- Frankton
- 8
- Kingston

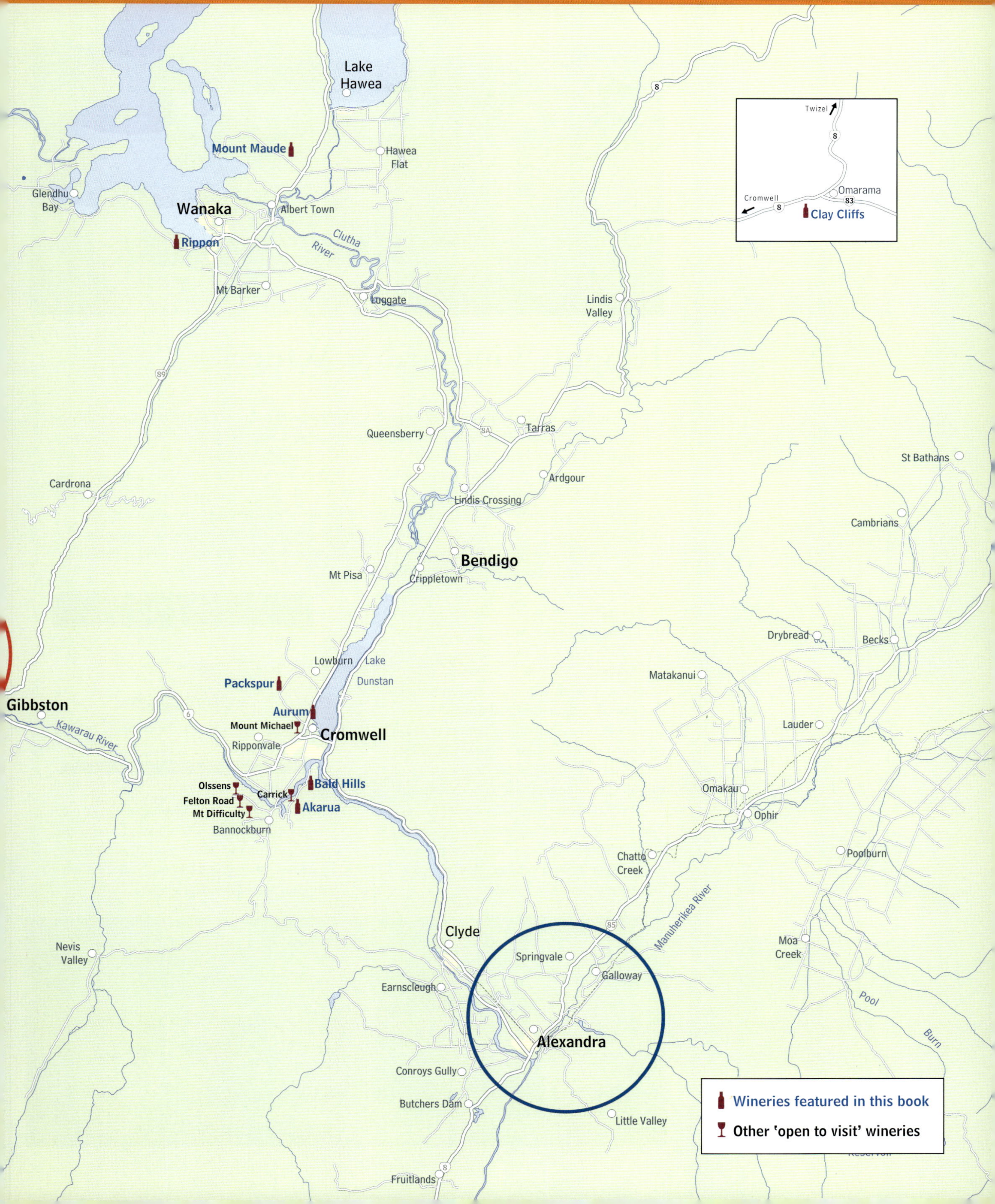

Lake Hawea
Hawea Flat
Mount Maude
Glendhu Bay
Wanaka
Albert Town
Rippon
Clutha River
Mt Barker
Luggate
Lindis Valley
Twizel
Omarama
Cromwell
Clay Cliffs
Queensberry
Tarras
Ardgour
St Bathans
Cardrona
Lindis Crossing
Cambrians
Bendigo
Mt Pisa
Crippletown
Drybread
Becks
Lowburn
Lake Dunstan
Packspur
Matakanui
Gibbston
Aurum
Kawarau River
Mount Michael
Cromwell
Lauder
Ripponvale
Bald Hills
Olssens
Carrick
Felton Road
Akarua
Mt Difficulty
Bannockburn
Omakau
Ophir
Chatto Creek
Poolburn
Manuherikea River
Clyde
Nevis Valley
Moa Creek
Springvale
Galloway
Earnscleugh
Pool Burn
Alexandra
Conroys Gully
Butchers Dam
Little Valley
Fruitlands
Wineries featured in this book
Other 'open to visit' wineries

CENTRAL OTAGO
Wanaka

Rippon Vineyard & Winery
Mount Aspiring Rd (Rural no. 246)
Lake Wanaka
Tel: (03) 443 8084
Fax: (03) 443 8034
Email: info@rippon.co.nz
Website: www.rippon.co.nz

DIRECTIONS
4km from the township on Mount Aspiring Rd towards Glendhu Bay.

OPENING HOURS
Dec–Apr: 7 days, 11am–5pm
May–Jun: closed (appointment only)
Jul–Nov: 7 days, 1.30pm–4.30pm

WINERY SALES
Cellar door, retail, mail order, Internet

PRICE RANGE $15–$50

TASTING
Tasting is free of charge.

OTHER PRODUCTS
Verjus (available in Pinot Noir or Riesling); Sirop de vin (a slightly sweetened wine syrup for vinaigrettes and dessert sauces). Only available from the tasting room.

PICNIC AREA
BYO picnic and enjoy the marvellous scenery on the lawn outside the cellar door; tables provided.

OWNER
Lois Mills

WINEMAKER
Nick Mills

DATE ESTABLISHED 1988

Rippon Vineyard & Winery

The stunningly beautiful Rippon Vineyard is situated on the shores of Lake Wanaka, with views across the lake to Ruby Island and the magnificent snow-capped peaks of the Buchannan Mountains. One of Central Otago's oldest vineyards, it is also one of the highest at 330 metres above sea level with an 1800-metre mountain as a backdrop. The 15-hectare vineyard runs down north-facing schist slopes to the shores of Lake Wanaka. The family-run property is cared for as a diverse and bio-dynamic whole, fostering wines that mirror their dreamscape surrounds.

Pinot Noir makes up 40 per cent of the vineyard plantings; other varietals are Sauvignon Blanc, Gewürztraminer, Riesling, Osteiner and Gamay. The cellar door lies by the lakeshore, providing picnic spots on the lawn for a relaxing afternoon. Or you can test your golfing skills with a game of GolfCross® — Rippon has the distinction of being the birthplace of this game.

ACTIVITIES & EVENTS
GolfCross®: golf with goals instead of holes and played with an oval ball instead of a round one. The challenging course is a rare combination of the best elements of links, woodland and parkland all set against a magnificent mountain and lake backdrop.

Rippon Music Festival is one of New Zealand's best contemporary music events. Held at Rippon Vineyard in February every second year, it is an eclectic mix of well-known and new Kiwi music.

WINES
Rippon Riesling, Sauvignon Blanc, Hotere White (Unoaked Chardonnay), Osteiner, Gewürztraminer, Pinot Noir, Gamay Rosé, Jeunesse (young vines Pinot Noir), Emma Rippon Methode Champenoise.

CENTRAL OTAGO
Gibbston

Amisfield Winery & Bistro

Located 10 minutes from Queenstown with spectacular views over Lake Hayes the Amisfield Cellar Door and Winery Bistro celebrates excellence not only in its wine and food but also its impressive architectural style. Grapes are sourced from the vineyard at Amisfield Farm in Lowburn. Originally a high-country merino stud, it now consists of 60 hectares of vines close-planted on alluvial and glacial schist soils. Yields are kept low to provide concentrated fruit flavour with complexity derived from the range of sites — lakeside to high altitude — within the vineyard.

Amisfield offers a full treat for the palate with their Winery Bistro for daytime dining. This country-style bistro provides a daily changing menu comprising locally sourced and organic produce, paired with their estate-grown wines. The best of Central Otago in a style that is truly unique.

WINES
Amisfield Pinot Noir, Pinot Gris, Sauvignon Blanc, Dry Riesling, Noble Riesling, Rocky Knoll Riesling, Rosé
Arcadia Blanc de Blancs, Non-Vintage Brut

10 Lake Hayes Rd
Queenstown
Tel: (03) 442 0556
Fax: (03) 442 0553
Email: admin@amisfield.co.nz
Website: www.amisfield.co.nz

DIRECTIONS
Leaving Queenstown via Frankton continue on SH6 until you reach the Arrowtown turn-off; Amisfield Winery is located at this junction.

OPENING HOURS
Cellar door & Bistro: 7 days, 10am–8pm. Bistro closed Mon.

WINERY SALES
Cellar door, retail, mail order, Internet

PRICE RANGE $19–$40

TASTING & TOURS
Tastings available.
Tours by appointment.

RESTAURANT
The country-style Bistro provides a daily changing menu comprising locally sourced and organic produce.

WINEMAKER
Jeff Sinnott

DATE ESTABLISHED
Vineyard: 1999
Winery: 2002

CENTRAL OTAGO

Black Ridge Winery & Vineyard

Amisfield Vineyard

Rippon Vineyard & Winery

Amisfield Vineyard

CENTRAL OTAGO
Gibbston

Church Lane, Gibbston Valley
Queenstown
Tel: (03) 441 3315
Fax: (03) 441 3316
Email: info@waitiricreek.co.nz
Website: www.waitiricreek.co.nz

DIRECTIONS
30km from Queenstown on SH6 towards Cromwell, turn left into Church Lane. Winery is well signposted.

OPENING HOURS
Oct–Apr: 7days, 10am–5pm
May–Sep: Open, phone for hours

WINERY SALES
Cellar door, retail, mail order, Internet, export

PRICE RANGE $20–$42

TASTING & TOURS
Tasting fee: $1 per wine (refundable on purchase). Tours by appointment.

OTHER FACILITIES
The winery provides a serene venue for special occasions from private dinner parties to intimate corporate events. Packages can be tailored to suit requirements.

OWNERS
Alistair Ward & Paula Ramage

WINEMAKER
Matt Connell

DATE ESTABLISHED 1994

Waitiri Creek

The magnificent scenery of the Gibbston Valley provides a stunning backdrop to Waitiri Creek, a family-owned vineyard producing Pinot Noir, Chardonnay, Rosé, Pinot Gris and Gewürztraminer. The picturesque tasting facility and café was originally the Wangaloa Presbyterian Church, built in 1893, and moved to the Waitiri Creek vineyard in 2000. Now beautifully restored, it is a tranquil venue in which to taste the much-awarded Waitiri Creek wines and to enjoy a relaxing dining experience whether alfresco or inside. The seasonally changing menu showcases the best regional produce and is matched to complement the Waitiri Creek wines.

WINES
Waitiri Creek estate-grown Pinot Noir, Chardonnay, Harriet Rosé, Pinot Gris, Gewürztraminer

RECENT AWARDS
Waitiri Creek Pinot Noir has consistently achieved silver medal status in New Zealand, Australia and the USA. The entire portfolio has won numerous medals.

CENTRAL OTAGO
Bannockburn

Cairnmuir Rd
Rapid Number 210, Bannockburn
Tel: (03) 445 0897
Fax: (03) 445 0898
Email: warren@akarua.co.nz
Website: www.akarua.com

DIRECTIONS
Travelling from Cromwell towards Bannockburn, turn left at the Bannockburn Bridge onto Cairnmuir Rd; continue for 2km and Akarua is on the right.

OPENING HOURS
Cellar door: 7 days, 10am–5pm
Restaurant: 7 days, all-day menu: 11am–5pm, open late Thurs–Sun

WINERY SALES
Cellar door, retail, Internet

PRICE RANGE
$19.95–$39.95

TASTING & TOURS
Tasting is free of charge. Tours by appointment only.

RESTAURANT
Lazy Dog Café & Wine Bar,
Reservations: (03) 445 3211

OTHER PRODUCTS
Wines can be purchased in wooden gift boxes containing Akarua glasses.

PICNIC AREA
The Bannockburn Bay reserve, a popular picnic spot, is nearby.

OWNER
Sir Clifford Skeggs

WINEMAKER
Jacqueline Kemp

DATE ESTABLISHED 1996

Akarua

Located amongst the dramatic scenery of the Bannockburn area — also known as 'the heart of the desert' — and with its great reputation for warm and friendly hospitality, the Akarua winery and cellar door is a must to visit. Committed to a philosophy of perfection since their first vintage in 1999, they have rapidly developed a reputation for producing quality wines. The 2000 Pinot Noir received an outstanding accolade as the only gold medal awarded at the 2001 International Wine and Spirit Competition in London, while the Akarua Pinot Noir 2002 won the Pinot Noir Trophy and was judged Wine of the Show at the 2003 Air New Zealand Wine Awards. To complement this success, Akarua Pinot Noir 2003 won gold for the third consecutive year at the same event.

The cellar door is surrounded by a 50-hectare vineyard planted with 70 per cent Pinot Noir, the remainder split evenly between Pinot Gris and Chardonnay. Here you can taste and buy the full range of Akarua Wines. Next door is the Lazy Dog Café and Wine Bar. Offering indoor and outdoor dining in a sheltered courtyard, the cuisine boasts a local and eclectic style.

OTHER FACILITIES
The winery complex includes a microbrewery — BannockBrew — producing a range of craft beers branded 'Wild Spaniard' available for tasting and purchase at the cellar door.

WINES
Akarua Pinot Noir, 'The Gullies' Pinot Noir, Chardonnay, Unoaked Chardonnay, Pinot Gris, Pinot Rosé

RECENT AWARDS
Akarua Pinot Noir 2002 – Champion Wine of Show and Pinot Trophy: 2003 Air New Zealand Wine Awards, Gold: 2004 Royal Easter Show, Gold: 2003 Liquorland Top 100; both Pinot Noirs were rated 1st and 2nd by *Cuisine* magazine in 2003; Akarua Chardonnay 2003 – Gold: 2004 Royal Easter Show

CENTRAL OTAGO
Cromwell

Aurum Wines

Aurum Wines is named after gold from the gold-mining days and golden hills of Central Otago. In 1997 Joan and Tony Lawrence planted their first vineyard, 45th Parallel Vineyard, in the prestigious Lowburn area of Central Otago. A second nearby vineyard, Te Wairere, was planted in 2001. Pinot Noir, Chardonnay, Pinot Gris and Riesling bask in the hot gravels deposited 10,000 years ago by glacial outwash and alluvial deposits to produce wines of intense flavour and fine structure. Brook Lawrence and his French wife Lucie will produce Aurum wines from a new winery to be located next to the Tasting Room on Te Wairere Vineyard from 2006.

WINES
Aurum Pinot Noir, Pinot Gris, Riesling, Chardonnay

OTHER PRODUCTS FOR SALE
Extra virgin olive oil from Aurum's 45th Parallel Olive Grove, along with other Central Otago olive oils. The painting *Lindis Pass* on Aurum wine labels is by the well-known Central Otago artist Neil Driver. Neil's paintings are exhibited at the Tasting Room.

140 SH6, Cromwell
Tel: (03) 445 3620
Fax: (03) 445 3640
Email: lawrence@aurumwines.com
Website: www.aurumwines.com

DIRECTIONS
1.5km north of Cromwell on SH6 towards Wanaka.

OPENING HOURS
7 days, 10am–6pm

WINERY SALES
Cellar Door, mail order, retail, Internet

PRICE RANGE
$22–$36

TASTING
Tastings are free of charge.

OWNER
Lawrence family

WINEMAKERS
Brook & Lucie Lawrence

DATE ESTABLISHED 1997

CENTRAL OTAGO
Cromwell

Packspur Vineyard

Packspur vineyard and winery is a small family owned and operated vineyard. Located in the secluded Lowburn Valley it has magnificent views of the Pisa Range, the Dunstans and the St Bathans. It takes its name from the track that was used to pack supplies over the Pisa Range from the Lowburn Valley to the goldfields of Cardrona. Their water right for irrigation is a miners' right dating from 1863 and they are continuing on the tradition of independence and enterprise that characterised those who worked the land before.

Packspur's philosophy as members of Sustainable Winegrowers of New Zealand is to use viticulture techniques that enhance the soil and minimise chemical use. They believe that healthy vines produce bright individual wines that reflect the potential of the terroir. All wines are made from their four hectares of vines planted on the hillside surrounding the winery.

WINES
Packspur Pinot Noir, Pinot Gris, Riesling, Sauvignon Blanc (barrel-fermented)

RECENT AWARDS
Packspur wines regularly receive star ratings from magazines including *Winestate*, *Cuisine*, and *Home & Entertaining*

Heaney Rd, Cromwell
Tel: (03) 445 1638
Fax: (03) 445 1639
Email: annelaurie@packspur.co.nz
Website: www.packspur.co.nz

DIRECTIONS
Turn off at Burn Cottage Rd on the Queenstown–Wanaka Highway (SH6) 1km north of the Cromwell intersection. Continue until you see Packspur on the left. The sign is on top of the mailbox.

OPENING HOURS
By appointment only.

WINERY SALES Cellar door, retail, mail order, Internet

PRICE RANGE $16.95–$30.95

TASTING & TOURS
Tasting fee: $5 pp, refundable on the purchase of three or more bottles of wine. Tours by appointment only.

OWNERS
Anne & Laurie McAuley

WINEMAKERS
Anne & Laurie McAuley

DATE ESTABLISHED 1992

CENTRAL OTAGO
Alexandra

Black Ridge Winery & Vineyard

One of the southernmost vineyards in the world, Black Ridge was established on the outskirts of Alexandra in 1981 through the pioneering vision and determination of Verdun Burgess and Sue Edwards. The vineyard setting is dramatic, carved out of steep rugged outcrops of schist that rise starkly above the vines creating many different microclimates. Pockets of vines cling to the hillside in between, in vivid green contrast to the barren rock.

All wines, made exclusively from their own hand-picked grapes, reflect this unique terroir. Pinot Noir is the flagship wine with eight different clones planted to provide complexity and greater depth. The winery, built out of schist rock in the style of an early Central Otago barn, has an attractive tasting room leading to an outdoor picnic area.

WINES
Black Ridge Pinot Noir, Chardonnay, Gewürztraminer, Riesling, Cabernet Sauvignon, Otago Gold (blended white)

RECENT AWARDS
Blackridge Pinot Noir 2003 – 4 stars: *Cuisine* magazine Oct 04; Chardonnay 2003 – 4 stars: *Winestate* magazine Aug 04

Conroys Rd, Alexandra
Tel: (03) 449 2059
Fax: (03) 449 2597
Email: blackridge@clear.net.nz
Website: www.blackridge.co.nz

DIRECTIONS
Turn into Earnscleugh Rd from SH8 near the Alexandra Bridge. Continue for 4km and turn left onto Conroys Rd. The vineyard is 700m on the right.

OPENING HOURS
Sept–Apr, 10am–5pm; May–Aug, 12pm–4pm

WINERY SALES Cellar door, retail, mail order, Internet

PRICE RANGE
$12.50–$35

TASTING Tasting fee: $1 per wine, refundable in proportion to wine purchased.

FOOD OPTIONS
Gourmet barbecues available for lunch over the Christmas/New Year period.

PICNIC AREA
Just outside the tasting room with tables with umbrellas and a pétanque court.

OTHER PRODUCTS
Paintings of the vineyard by local artist, Janet de Waght

OWNERS
Sue Edwards & Verdun Burgess

WINEMAKER
Kevin Clark

DATE ESTABLISHED 1981

CENTRAL OTAGO
Alexandra

Dry Gully

Dry Gully is a small family-run vineyard and specialist Pinot Noir producer situated in the heart of the Alexandra grape-growing region of Central Otago. In the late 1970s, Bill and Sibylla Moffitt bought a small, 100-year-old apricot orchard and in 1992 — encouraged by their sons, Stephen and James, both viticulturists and who also own vineyards nearby — they planted 1.5 hectares of Pinot Noir grapes. Situated on river silt over alluvial gravels, the vines are surrounded by old thyme-covered gold-dredging tailings. The single wine Pinot Noir that Dry Gully produces has enjoyed remarkable success in competitions and is in high demand with a large portion of production exported to the UK and USA.

WINES
Dry Gully Pinot Noir

RECENT AWARDS
Five Stars: *Cuisine* magazine 2003

Rapid No. 113
Earnscleugh Rd, Alexandra
Tel: (03) 449 2030
Mob: 027 276 9550
Fax: (03) 449 2030
Email: dry.gully@xtra.co.nz

DIRECTIONS
Turn into Earnscleugh Rd from SH8 near the Alexandra Bridge. Continue for 1km and the vineyard is on the right opposite Chapman Rd.

OPENING HOURS
By appointment only.

WINERY SALES
Cellar door (by appointment), retail, mail order

PRICE $29

TASTING
By appointment only. Rock 'n' Pillar wines also available for tasting.

OWNERS
William & Sybilla Moffitt

WINEMAKER
Dean Shaw
(Central Otago Wine Company)

DATE ESTABLISHED 1992

CENTRAL OTAGO
Alexandra

Address: 315 Strode Rd, Earnscleugh
RD1 Alexandra
Phone: 027 289 9220
Fax: (03) 441 2327
Email: sales@twopaddocks.com
Website: www.twopaddocks.com

DIRECTIONS
From Alexandra follow Earnscleugh Rd for 15km, turn left into Fraser Rd and then right onto Strode Rd.

OPENING HOURS
Cellar Door strictly by appointment only.

WINERY SALES
Cellar door, retail, mail order

PRICE RANGE
$16–$40

TASTING & TOURS
Tasting and tours by appointment.

OWNER
Sam Neill

WINEMAKER
Dean Shaw, Central Otago Wine Company

DATE ESTABLISHED 1993

Two Paddocks

Two Paddocks is a small family wine-producing business that is entirely dedicated to making great wine. Starting with modest ambitions, five acres of Pinot Noir were planted in 1993 at the original little vineyard at Gibbston where the owner wanted to produce a good Pinot Noir that would, at the very least, be enjoyed by family and friends. To his great surprise, the first vintage in 1997 was much better than hoped, in spite of a difficult growing season; 1998 was a more distinguished vintage, and in 1999 they were astounded to produce a Pinot that was, they thought, world class — a wine of considerable complexity with an amazing nose, delicious fruit and a good lengthy finish.

Since that time, with each successive vintage they have produced a Pinot Noir that has done them proud, and as they say, 'to be frank, too good to be wasted on their friends though they still somehow manage to bludge a lot off us'. That, combined with the proprietor's generous thirst, accounts for the occasional scarcity of more Two Paddocks Pinot.

WINES
Two Paddocks (premium single vineyard) 'First Paddock' Pinot Noir, 'The Last Chance' Pinot Noir; **Picnic by Two Paddocks** (approachable, affordable, unpretentious and easy-drinking wines) Riesling, Sauvignon Blanc, Socialist Chardonnay, The Sociable Red (Merlot blend), Pinot Noir

OTHER PRODUCTS
Two Paddocks Redbank Lavender Oil. Distilled on site at Redbank Paddocks from French and English lavender grown on this property. Redbank Saffron.

CENTRAL OTAGO
Omarama

CENTRAL OTAGO

Clay Cliffs Estate

At 440 metres above sea level Clay Cliffs is New Zealand's highest-altitude vineyard. Named after the nearby Clay Cliffs with their dramatic sharp pinnacles and deep, narrow ravines the four-hectare vineyard has some of Otago's earliest plantings of Pinot Gris, Muscat and Pinot Blanc. The winery features a Tuscan-style restaurant offering an extensive range of local fare. You can choose to dine inside or outside where you can relax by tranquil ponds, soaking up the sun or under the shade of willows enjoying a wine from their extensive cellar. A trip to Clay Cliffs is an opportunity not only to taste and buy their wines (that are only sold through their restaurant) but also to experience the spectacular Mackenzie Country scenery.

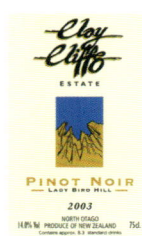

WINES
Clay Cliffs Pinot Noir, Pinot Gris, Muscat, Pinot Blanc;

Mount Cook Chardonnay, Riesling, Pinot Noir, Sauvignon Blanc.

Clay Cliffs Estate
SH8, Omarama
Tel: (03) 438 9654
Fax: (03) 438 9656
Email: claycliffs@xtra.co.nz
Website: www.claycliffs.co.nz

DIRECTIONS
Clay Cliffs is on SH8 at the southern end of Omarama township, 150km from Queenstown and 20km south of Twizel.

OPENING HOURS
Restaurant and cellar door: 7 days, 11am–midnight. Winter hours: June (Queen's Birthday Monday) to end July, 11am–4pm, unless bookings are made for evening dining.

RESTAURANT
From à la carte dining to snacks.

WINERY SALES
Cellar door and mail order

PRICE RANGE $16.50–$31.50

TASTING
Tasting fee: $5, refundable on purchase.

OTHER FACILITIES
Available for weddings and functions.

OWNERS
Brian (The Sheriff) & Judy Gilbert

WINEMAKER
Dean Shaw (Central Otago Wine Company)

DATE ESTABLISHED 1999

45th Parallel Vineyard, Aurum Wines

Bald Hills Vineyard

Packspur Vineyard

145

CENTRAL OTAGO

Open By Appointment

Bald Hills Vineyard
Visitors to Bald Hills Vineyard will enjoy the friendly and casual atmosphere of the private homestead of owners Blair and Estelle Hunt. Award-winning winemaker Grant Taylor of Gibbston Valley fame has crafted distinctive wines for you to taste — Pinot Noir from three vintages and the popular whites Pinot Gris and Dry Riesling. The Hunts obviously enjoy sharing their passion and vision with you while pouring the wines. They do indeed 'live the dream'.

Wines: Bald Hills Pinot Noir, Pinot Gris, Riesling
Winery sales: Cellar door, mail order, retail
Price range: $25.50–$34

Contact:
Rapid 46
Cornish Point Rd
Cromwell
Tel (03) 445 3161
Fax: (03) 445 3160
Email: info@baldhills.co.nz
Website: www.baldhills.co.nz
Owners: Estelle & Blair Hunt

Mount Maude
Mount Maude is a small vineyard owned by Dawn and Terry Wilson in the beautiful Maungawera Valley. It was planted in 1994 on a steep, north-facing terraced slope in Central Otago, providing perfect growing conditions for grapes. All wines are produced exclusively from their four-hectare Maungawera vineyard.
Wines: Mount Maude Pinot Noir, Riesling, Chardonnay and Gewürztraminer
Winery sales: Cellar door – by appointment, mail order, retail, Internet
Price range: $17–$36
Accommodation: Homestays at vineyard homestead
Other Products: Pottery made by Dawn Wilson
Contact details: Maungawera Valley, RD2, Wanaka
Tel: (03) 443 8398 Fax: (03) 443 1908
Email: mountmaude@xtra.co.nz
Website: www.mountmaude.co.nz
Owners: Dawn & Terry Wilson

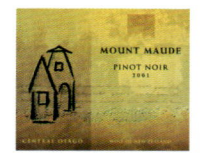

CENTRAL OTAGO

Open By Appointment

Judge Rock, Pinot Wines
Paul and Angela Jacobson's family vineyard is on a westerly-sloping alluvial fan near Alexandra. Their five hectares is planted in Pinot Noir, Dijon and Pommard clones along with 0.5 hectares of Pinot St Laurent. Judge Rock is the first vineyard in NZ to plant St Laurent which produces excellent-quality wines suited to Central Otago conditions. They specialise in Pinot Noir and Pinot Noir Rosé. Their first vintage of Judge Rock Pinot Noir was in 2002.
Wines: Judge Rock Pinot Noir, Venus Rosé
Winery sales: Mail order, retail, Internet
Tasting: By appointment
Price range: $20–$30
Contact details: 36 Hillview Rd, Alexandra
Tel/Fax: (03) 448 5059
Email: wines@judgerock.co.nz
Website: www.judgerock.co.nz
Owners: Paul Jacobson & Angela Chiaroni

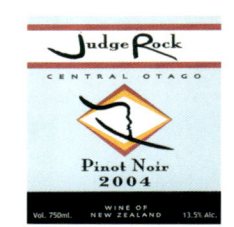

Rock 'n' Pillar
Rock 'n' Pillar produces Pinot Noir from its two-hectare, rocky hillside vineyard. The majority is sold to Dry Gully, with the balance receiving extra treatments for its own premium Pinot Noir.

Sales: Cellar door, mail order, retail
Contact: Tel: 027 276 9550. Email rocknpillar@xtra.co.nz

Mount Maude